1977

THE PLAY MOVEMENT IN THE UNITED STATES

NRPA Recreation and Park Perspective Collection

edited by Dr. Diana R. Dunn
Director of Research
National Recreation and Park Association

Education through Play	Curtis, H.	$19.00
Education through Recreation	Jacks, L.	$13.00
Education by Plays and Games	Johnson, G.	$15.00
The New Leisure Challenges for the Schools	Lies, E.	$17.00
Play in Education	Lee, J.	$25.00
Play and Mental Health	Davis, J.	$15.00
Education through Recreation	Johnson, G.	$10.00
The Practical Conduct of Play	Curtis, H.	$19.00
The Play Movement	Rainwater, C.	$21.00
The Play Movement and its Significance	Curtis, H.	$19.00
Playground Technique and Playcraft	Leland, A. & L.	$17.00
American Playgrounds	Mero, E.	$17.00
Leisure in the Modern World	Burns, C.	$15.00
The Threat of Leisure	Cutten, G.	$12.00
The Normal Course of Play	NRA	$16.00
The Education of the Whole Man	Jacks, L.	$12.00
The Challenge of Leisure	Pack, A.	$14.00
Off the Job Living	Romney, G.	$15.00
A Philosophy of Play	Gulick, L.	$16.00
Europe at Play	Weir, L.	$45.00
Music in American Life	Zanzig, A.	$28.00
Music in Institutions	Van de Wall, W.	$35.00
The First County Park System	Kelsey, F.	$15.00
County Parks	NRA	$14.00
Central Park—First Annual Report	New York	$14.00
The Spirit of Youth and the City Streets	Addams, J.	$12.00
Annals March 1910	AAP&SS	$16.00
Municipalization of Play and Recreation	Fulk, J.	$10.00
Luther Halsey Gulick	Dorgan, E.	$14.00
Constructive and Preventive Philanthropy	Lee, J.	$15.00

order from:

MC GRATH PUBLISHING COMPANY
821 Fifteenth Street N.W.
Washington, D.C.

THE PLAY MOVEMENT IN THE UNITED STATES

A STUDY OF COMMUNITY RECREATION

BY

CLARENCE E. RAINWATER, Ph.D.

Assistant Professor of Sociology, University of Southern California; formerly Instructor in Playground Administration, University of Chicago, and Director of Hamilton Park Playground and Recreation Center, South Park System, Chicago.

McGrath Publishing Company

&

NATIONAL RECREATION AND PARK ASSOCIATION

WASHINGTON, D.C.

LC#76-143068
ISBN 0-8434-0430-2

PREFACE

Every period of social advance has been accompanied by the spirit of play. The contemporary generation in our own country is no exception to that rule. Industrial developments, immigration, the growth of the democratic spirit in education and in economics as well as in government have not characterized the present age more than have amateur sports, commercialized amusements, and socialized art. Eighty thousand people have witnessed a single football contest, ninety thousand a prize fight, while baseball has become "the American game" and athletics a recognized feature of both high school and college life. Few cities are now without municipal bands, orchestras, or auditoriums, as well as swimming pools and public golf links. The municipal pier of Chicago extends into the lake three-quarters of a mile and terminates in a magnificent auditorium seating five thousand and dedicated to amateur dramatic and musical expression. Transcontinental automobile routes outnumber the railroads, the motion picture industry is fifth in the United States, while it is estimated that the population of our second largest city alone expends two hundred fifty million dollars annually in leisure-time pursuits. Festivals, pageants, tournaments, fairs, and expositions

v

have also engaged their thousands of participants as well as hundreds of thousands of spectators. The pageant and masque of St. Louis,
given in 1914, involved seven thousand actors
and one hundred twenty-five thousand spectators at each performance. These events suggest
many more, among which, and involving in some
instances either their creation or incorporation,
may be mentioned "the play movement," also
known as the playground and recreation movement.

This volume is an analysis of the play movement in the United States. It is the first attempt
to produce a complete and authentic report of
the structure and concept of function of that
movement. It comprises more than a description
of sand gardens or playgrounds for children,
since the term "play" is used to embrace most
of the activities occurring in social and community centers, in community music, drama, and
pageantry, and in community service and organization. This study, moreover, is not merely a
composite of the statements of previous writers
on the play movement, but an attempt to recon-
struct a view of the events in question based
upon primary rather than secondary sources,
such as pictures, programs, published reports,
and personal experiences and observations of the
present writer. The sections containing the
greatest contribution to a knowledge of the subject, as well as being of the most significance to

both the practical administrator and the general reader, are doubtless those on the "stages" and the "transitions." Those chapters define the present structure and concept of function by the aid of a comparison of contemporary methods with those pursued in previous periods of its development. It will be seen, upon examination of those portions of the text, that an elaborate technique containing many interesting mechanisms has evolved. This technique *is* the structure and the concept of the function of the play movement in the United States today. It may be fully understood only by a knowledge of how it came to be.

Among those who have helped materially to gain access to the sources of information, especially concerning the origin and earlier stages of the movement, are Miss Ellen M. Tower, of Lexington, Mass., who loaned me pictures and other valuable material, and the Library of the City of Boston which loaned rare copies of annual reports of societies conducting playgrounds.

For a decade the present writer was actively engaged in the work of administering play, being director of Hamilton Park Recreation Center, South Park System, Chicago, from 1910 to 1917, and in teaching normal classes in play and recreational administration since 1913, in the University of Chicago, the American College of Physical Education, the University of Southern California, and others. In these associations he has been permitted to make many observations and test many suggestions in the laboratory of practical experience on the field and in the class room. It is hoped that this volume may serve as a text-book in normal classes, a book of reference to the general reader, and a guide to the practical director of play. It has been ten years in the making, and is the first of a series now in preparation which includes further studies in the "theory," the "history," the "direction," and the "administration" of play and recreation.

While I am indebted to many for the ideas incorporated in this study, and wish to convey in this manner my gratitude to all with whom I have been associated in the past, for the assistance that contact with them afforded me, I wish especially to thank Professors E. W. Burgess and R. E. Park of the University of Chicago, for their constructive criticisms of the manuscript which has been accepted in partial fulfilment of the requirements for the degree of doctor of philosophy in the Department of Sociology of that institution; and to express my indebtedness to my wife who was associated with me throughout my practical and teaching experiences and who gave invaluable aid in gathering the materials, reading the proofs, making the index, and without whose encouragement this book would doubtless remain as yet unfinished.

CLARENCE E. RAINWATER

CHICAGO, ILLINOIS,
September 1, 1921

TABLE OF CONTENTS

LIST OF ILLUSTRATIONS

xi

I. INTRODUCTION

A. *The concept of a movement.* A discussion of the subject of this investigation is incomplete if the use of the concept "movement" is not made clear. An explanation, then, of the sense in which it is here employed is in place at the outset of this report. The word itself is a popular equivalent to certain types of social change that are unilateral and progressive and eventuate in institutions when not disapproved by the group. A "movement" is a mode of collective behavior occasioned by social disorganization or contacts, involving intercommunication of desires, and manifested by an organization of social activities intended to accomplish a common object. These activities consist of adjustments to the given social situation.[1]

There are four characteristics common to movements: (1) a series of events involving adjustments to a social situation; (2) an extension of this series in time and space; (3) an object to be realized by means of the adjustments involved; and (4) a tendency toward the attainment of that object, disclosed by stages in its development and transitions in its policy and activities.

A series of events in the sense peculiar to a movement, however, comprises more than a num-

[1]Cf. Robert E. Park and Ernest W. Burgess, *Introduction to the Science of Sociology*, University of Chicago Press, 1921, pp. 54–55.

ber of incidents of similar or identical content and motive, occurring at different times and in various places, having a common object and involving adjustments to a social situation. A cause and effect relation between the incidents of the series is an essential element of a movement. Later events are incited by motives received from earlier ones as in a mathematical series in which each of the terms is derived from one or more of the preceding ones or an electrical series by which the parts of a circuit are connected successively from end to end to form a single path for the current. Incidents that are unaffected by this relation are not components of a movement. They are sporadic and usually antedate it. A consideration of this fact is paramount in determining the inception of a given movement.[2]

The events of a series, however, are not always identical in structure. The concept of the function of a movement does not remain changeless throughout its history. Modifications occur with extension in time and space. Differences in structure result from changes in the concept of its function, and these, in turn, are occasioned by new adjustments to the social situation. These adjustments indicate the evolution of a movement and are disclosed by stages, transitions, and tendencies in its history.

[2]This is true of the inception of the play movement in the United States, as will be shown in Part I of this report. No less than seven dates have been assigned, ranging from 1634 to 1898.

A movement, furthermore, is transitory, becoming in time transformed into an institution when its program of adjustment to a social situation is established, or disintegrating with the passing of the social situation or the illusion concerning the same that incited it. Movements, then, differ comparatively in both the efficacy and the ethics of their programs. Some are negative, seeking the destruction of an institution; others are positive, making new adjustments by the organization of social activities. Movements are incidental to social interaction. They are essential in certain phases of social evolution, as when they incite a group consciousness of maladjustments within the existing social situation and arouse popular interest in some scheme of readjustment, while at other times, as in certain forms of fashion imitation, they may result in merely a transitory diversion of public attention.

A movement, then, as the concept is employed in this report, is a series of events involving adjustments to a social situation; connected by a cause and effect relation; possessing an extension in time and space; and disclosing stages, transitions, tendencies, that are correlative with a changing concept of its function and indicative of its evolution.

Many movements have arisen in the United States during the last forty years. They have attempted to make adjustments to a social situation which in most instances developed from conditions produced by urbanization, immigration, and specialization in industry, and of whose existence, philanthropists and others did not become aware until during or since the last quarter of the nineteenth century. The first of the recent movements, and one that came with the awakening of a new social spirit following the Civil War, was a sanitary one.[3] It sought to enforce cleanliness, and secure better light and purer air in the homes of immigrants who formed a large percentage of the wage earners in urban communities. As urbanization and immigration continued, attempts to make adjustments to other social situations gave rise to additional movements. One of these was the "play movement." An explanation of the sense in which the terms "play" and "play movement" are used in this investigation will now be made.[4]

B. *The use of the term "play."* In the language of Dewey, "play" describes "those activities which are not consciously performed for the sake of any reward beyond themselves."[5] According to Patrick, it involves "not merely children's play and grown-ups' sports . . . . but

[3]It is significant in this connection that a hygiene society, the Massachusetts Emergency and Hygiene Association of Boston, was involved in the inception of the play movement.

[4]For an analysis of the scientific attempts to define the nature and function of play, consult *The Meaning of Play* by C. E. Rainwater, University of Chicago Press, 1915.

[5]John Dewey, "play," in *Cyclopedia of Education*, Paul Monroe, 1914.

many forms of so-called work.''[6] While according to Blackmar and Gillin, ''only in groups does it get its compelling and socially useful intensity,''[7] thus confirming another point made by Dewey, that ''the stimuli become more social as intelligence develops.''

''Play'' is generic to maturity as well as to immaturity, to some forms of ''work'' as well as to ''leisure pursuits.'' Its origin lies in the active processes in which life manifests itself. Its varieties of organization arise from the interaction of agent and stimuli as the responsive activity returns upon the stimulus, maintaining it, varying it, awakening a sense of satisfaction in the consciousness of the subject performing it, and supplying the stimuli for keeping up more action which becomes more social as intelligence develops, evolving in many instances ''an attitude of mind''[8] by which much that is called ''work,'' such as scientific inquiry for its own sake, is insensibly transformed into ''play.''

In any case the starting point is the active processes in which life manifests itself. The moving spool draws the organic response of the kitten to itself; this response continues to gives the spool the kind of movements which continue to excite organic reactions. . . . . The stimuli become more social as intelligence develops. The interests and occupations of adults are the points of departure and the directing clues of children's actions. . . . .

[6]G. T. W. Patrick, "The Psychology of Relaxation," *Atlantic Monthly*, June, 1914.
[7]F. W. Blackmar and J. L. Gillin, *Outlines of Sociology*, p. 296.
[8]Dewey, *supra*.

It is also desirable to distinguish an attitude of mind
. . . . distinguishable from inability to enjoy intellectual
activity upon a subject except in the interest of some pre-
conceived theory or some practical utility. . . . . Unless
play takes this intellectual form, the full spirit of scientific
inquiry is never realized; much, if not all, of what is termed
the love of truth for truth's sake in scientific inquiry represents the attitude of play carried over into enjoyment of the
activities of inquiry for its own sake.[9]

"Play," furthermore, is not a given type of
activity, such as, "sports," "games," "recreations," or "relaxations"; nor is it the "motor
habits and spirits of the past of the race, persist-
ing in the present" (Hall),[10] although it frequently does exercise "those nerve centers that
are old in the race" (Patrick).[11] It does not consume merely the "surplus energy" of the "individual" by "superfluous and useless exercises of
faculties that have been quiescent" for a time
(Spencer),[12] but on the contrary, since "a person
is a center of conscious impulses which realize
themselves in full only in realizing a society"
(Small),[13] it frequently happens that "all the
energy is expended in play" (Patrick) in response
to group stimulation. "Play is the most important method," most likely "of realization of
the social instincts" (Baldwin).[14] It does not
simply "prepare for the necessary duties of ma-

[9]Dewey, *supra.*
[10]G. Stanley Hall, *Adolescence*, Vol. II, 206–36.
[11]G. T. W. Patrick, *supra.*
[12]Herbert Spencer, *Principles of Psychology*, p. 628.
[13]A. W. Small, *General Sociology*, p. 476.
[14]J. M. Baldwin, *Social and Ethical Interpretations*, pp.
148–56.

ture life'' (Groos),[15] for it is common to maturity
as well as immaturity, involving ''those activities
which are not consciously performed for the sake
of any reward beyond themselves'' (Dewey)[16] during any age period of personal experience and in
any portion of a given day, in working hours as
well as in leisure time, since play is ''an attitude
of mind'' (Dewey)[17] that anyone may attain in
any situation ''in which interest is self-develop-
ing'' (Patrick).[18] It is pleasurable, relatively
spontaneous, a motive force which finds expression in art and in certain types of work, as in the
''instinct of workmanship,'' but when balked may
take the form of anti-social behavior.[19]

The variety of playful activities that may take
place in a given community is virtually unlimited
because ''play'' is generic to all periods of personal experience, is determined by the response of
inherited and acquired capacities of persons to
the social situation, and is intrinsically related to
what ethnologists describe as the culture of the
group. Dewey implied it with respect to childhood by noting that ''the interests and occupations of adults are the points of departure and the
directing clues of children's actions,''[20] while

[15]K. Groos, *The Play of Man.*

[16]J. Dewey, *supra.*

[17]*Ibid.*

[18]G. T. W. Patrick, *supra.*

[19]Luther H. Gulick, "Play and Democracy," *Charities and the Commons*, Aug. 3, 1907.

[20]John Dewey, *supra.*

Patrick stated it concretely with respect to adults as well as children as follows:[21]

Play will thus include practically all the activities of children and the larger share of those of adults, such for instance, as baseball, football, tennis, golf, polo, billiards, and countless other games and sports; diversions such as traveling, hunting, fishing, yachting, motoring, flying, dancing, vacation outings, games, races, spectacles, fairs, tournaments, and expositions; the theatre, opera, moving pictures, lectures, and entertainments; the enjoyment of music, painting, poetry, and other arts; the daily paper, the magazine, the short story, and the novel.

"Play," then, as the concept is used in this report, is a mode of human behavior, either individual or collective, involving pleasurable activity of any kind not undertaken for the sake of a reward beyond itself and performed during any age period of the individual, the particular action being determined at a given time by the somatic structure and social attitudes of the agent in conjunction with the life of the group or groups of which he is a member. Thus the child does not behave as the adult at play; nor the savage as the civilized.

C. *The use of the term "play movement."* Until the latter half of the nineteenth century, as pointed out by Newell,[22] the children of the United States possessed a richer play tradition than those of any other civilized nation. This fact was due first, to our inheritance of play from Elizabethan

[21]G. T. W. Patrick, *The Psychology of Relaxation*, Houghton Mifflin & Co., 1916, p. 47.
[22]William Wells Newell, *Games and Songs of American Children*, Harper and Brothers, N. Y., 1911, pp. 3 ff.

England, and second, to two centuries of comparative isolation from events that might have impaired its traditional forms of expression. And play traditions were as strong, says Lee,[23] in Puritan New England as in the South or the Middle States. But the *laissez faire* attitude of the public toward child play, the restrictions placed upon space in which to play as urbanization increased, and the differences between the languages and the games of the children of many nationalities mingled in the cities, resulted in a rapid disorganization of child play in urban communities, while isolation in rural districts wrought a similar effect upon the play of the children of that element of the population.[24]

The same forces that caused disintegration of the play traditions of children were largely instrumental in disorganizing many recreational activities of adults. The creation of American folk music, folk dances,[25] and folk games ceased with the decline of village social life. The gathering of May baskets, the singing of Christmas carols, the husking-bees, spelling-matches, and singing-schools, alike were discontinued with the growth

[23]Joseph Lee, "American Play Traditions and Our Relations to Them," *The Playground*, 1913, pp. 148–59.

[24]*Ibid*, p. 148. "We are at present in imminent danger of losing a large part of the precious tradition. The danger, like so many others that threaten our social life, arises largely from the crowding of our cities and the increasing loneliness of our country districts. . . . . Immigration is the other cause."

[25]E. B. Mero, *American Playgrounds*, Baker & Taylor Co., pp. 108, 119.

of population in urban communities and of isolation in rural districts.[26] In the cities, where a consciousness of the social situation first arose, the behavior of children, youths, and adults during their leisure hours and holidays frequently became delinquent conduct, play became crime,[27] while leisure pursuits became commercialized to an extent without precedent.[28] Whereas formerly both children and adults had participated in play and recreation, now they became spectators. The motion picture accelerated this tendency; but it had begun long before the invention of the cinematograph. With the shifting of population from small communities, in which play and recreational traditions that were centuries old still survived, to newly grown and congested centers of heterogeneous population, the home, the neighborhood, the community, alike lost their former significance in the recreational life of the people. The social situation was fundamentally changed. Adjustments were necessary. The people *did* not participate in recreation because they *could* not under existing conditions since they lacked both the physical facilities and the social organization for doing so. The "first pathetic expression," said Robinson, [29] of a consciousness of this fact, and the

[26]E. J. Ward, *The Social Center*, D. Appleton & Co., N. Y., 1913, p. 306.
[27]John Collier and Edw. M. Barrows, *The City Where Crime Is Play*, Peoples Institute, New York, 1916.
[28]M. M. Davis, *The Exploitation of Pleasure*, Russell Sage Foundation, 1910.
[29]Charles Mulford Robinson, "Improvement of City Life," *Atlantic Monthly*, April 1899, p. 534.

first effort to make an adjustment to the changed social situation, came with the sand gardens for little children. Subsequent adjustments made provision for youths and adults, respectively, while the initial forms of each have been altered by more recent changes, especially in the last decade, in both the structure and the concept of the function of the "play movement." These various attempts to bring about an adjustment of both the play life of children and the recreational activities of youths and adults to the social situation in both urban and rural communities, in so far as they form a series of related events, constitute the "play movement" in the United States as the term is employed in this report.

The "play movement" is a positive movement rather than a negative one. It seeks to bring about adjustments through the organization of social activities. Among these have appeared the sand gardens and the model playgrounds; the recreation center, the social center, and the community center; community music, community drama, and pageantry, municipal theatres, piers, bands and orchestras; community service and community organization.

D. *The problem of this investigation.* A preliminary survey of the evolution of the play movement in the United States raised five questions which will be answered in as many sections: (1) What was the origin of the movement? (2) What have been its stages? (3) What transitions have

occurred in its policy and activities? (4) What is
its trend? And (5) should not all the facts relative to the evolution of the play movement be
brought together in a unified whole with reference
to the changed social situation? The facts derived from a study of (*a*) the origin, (*b*) the
stages, (*c*) the transitions, and (*d*) the trend, will
be summarized and presented in defense of the
proposition that there has been an evolution in
the structure and the concept of the function of
the play movement in the United States in adjustment to the modern social situation.

II. THE ORIGIN OF THE PLAY MOVEMENT[1]

In accordance with the concept of a movement formulated in the preceding section, there are but two tests to be applied to an event to determine whether or not it marks the origin of a movement: First, was it a conscious provision for the object of the movement in question? second, Was it the first of a series of events bearing a cause-and-effect relation toward one another and performed with that purpose in mind which characterized the movement? Notwithstanding the simplicity of this method, there is a difference of opinion concerning the event which marked the beginning of the play movement in the United States. No less than seven incidents are mentioned by various authors as designating that fact. Since the establishment of the date, place, and action marking its origination is essential to a study of its stages, the facts relative to the origin of the play movement will now be analyzed.

A. *Incidents mentioned as the origin of the movement.* The earliest action that has been suggested as the beginning of the play movement in the United States is the provision of the New England town commons which dates from the early part of the seventeenth century,[2] the Boston com-

[1]See Appendix A for list of sources consulted in the study of the origin of the play movement.

[2]Cf. Joseph Lee, *Constructive and Preventive Philanthropy.* The Macmillan Co., 1902, p. 123.

13

mon having been established in 1634. There is
abundant evidence that these commons have been
used for play by each succeeding generation of
boys since colonial times; and seventeen of these
spaces are now incorporated in the metropolitan
park district of Boston alone. They fail, however,
to meet both tests mentioned above, since their
original provision was for pasturage, while their
recent utilization in municipal recreation came
later than other events that meet with the first
requirement.

During 1821-30 outdoor gymnasiums were constructed for the first time in the United States[3]
and in connection with the schools and colleges of
New England and New York City. The Salem
Latin School opened an outdoor gymnasium in
1821, equipped with crude apparatus but without
supervision. The Round Hill School at Northampton, Massachusetts, opened another in 1825,
equipped with German gymnasium apparatus and
supervised by a former pupil of Jahn. A third
was conducted for a year in Washington Garden,
Boston, also under the supervision of a pupil of
Jahn, attendance falling from four hundred the
first season to four the second because ''the nov-
elty had ceased, and some of the gymnasts had
been caricatured in the print shops.'' Similar
gymnasiums were established at Harvard, and
Yale in 1826, at Williams, Brown, and Amherst

[3]Cf. F. E. Leonard, *Pioneers of Modern Physical Training;*
E. B. Mero, *American Playgrounds*, Baker & Taylor Co., 1908,
pp. 244-45; Phillips, *A Short History of Amherst College.*

in 1827, and at the New York High School the following year. By 1830, however, interest had subsided, owing chiefly to the return to Germany of those political exiles whose presence in America had led to a temporary enthusiasm for play and organized physical exercise. Subsequent developments in college athletics did not appear until thirty years later and were due to impulses from another source: namely, the sanitary movement following the Civil War. Thus these early college and school gymnasiums were not the first of a series of events now understood as the play movement in the United States.

In 1868 an outdoor children's playground was established under the auspices of the old First Church of Boston[4] in the yard of a public school near Copley Square and in connection with a vacation school maintained at that place. While this event was a definite provision for play, it received little, if any, attention at the time and was conducted for only one reason. There is no evidence that it was related to subsequent developments in that city or elsewhere. It was, at most, but a sporadic expression of the consciousness of a need that did not gain lasting recognition until fully twenty years later.

The fourth incident that has been mentioned as the beginning of the play movement was the purchase of two tracts of land to be used for play

[4]Cf. *The Playground*, "A Brief History of the Playground Movement in America," April, 1915, pp. 1 ff.; *Charities and the Commons*, "Vacation Schools," Sept. 6, 1902.

activities by vote of a town meeting of Brookline,[5] Massachusetts, on April 10, 1872. Concerning this act the following statement is made in the Town Records of Brookline, published in 1887:

Twenty-first Article taken up:

To see if the town will approve and confirm the deeds taken of the lands bought for commons or playgrounds, and the action of the Selectmen thereon.

The following preamble and vote were passed; viz.:

WHEREAS, at a legal meeting of the inhabitants of Brookline, holden May 2, 1871, for the purpose of acting, among other matters, upon the report of the committee appointed at the last annual meeting, upon the subject of procuring land for public commons or playgrounds, the town, pursuant to said report, voted to buy for said purpose two lots of lands described in said vote; and whereas the Selectmen, upon the seventeenth day of May, in the year 1871, in behalf of the town, and in pursuance of its votes, accepted a deed to the town from Col. Thomas Aspinwall of the lot of land on Brookline Avenue, bought as aforesaid, and upon the twenty-second day of May accepted a deed to the town from William B. Craft, James Murray Howe, and Samuel Clark of the lots of land on Cyprus and other streets, bought as aforesaid, and have paid in behalf of the town to said grantors the consideration named in said deeds according to said votes: now it is hereby

VOTED, to confirm, ratify and approve the said deeds, and to approve, ratify and confirm the doings of the Selectmen in the premises as set forth in their report to the town.

While this act by the town of Brookline was a conscious provision for play, as were the events of 1868 and 1821-30 discussed above, there were no immediate acts, either in that village or elsewhere, that are known to have resulted from it.

[5]Cf. Joseph Lee, *op. cit.*, p. 163; E. B. Mero, *op. cit.*, p. 242.

The next city to acquire land for play uses was Boston in 1894, more than twenty years later; and there was no causal relation between these municipal acts, the latter being only an incident in the general development of provision for play in Boston which began in 1885. The action of Brookline is noteworthy simply as being the first instance of public provision of space for play in the United States. It was sporadic, however, local interest quickly subsiding, while apparatus and supervision were never provided. A motion for their provision was "laid on the table, indefinitely" on December 15, 1874.

The opening of the "meadow" in Washington Park, Chicago, for team games, in 1876, has been mentioned by various writers[6] as a possible date for the origin of the play movement. An examination of the annual reports of the South Park Commissioners, however, disclosed the fact that no games were played in Washington Park until 1886, when two tennis courts were first provided at the north end of this tract. That year two other courts were placed in Jackson Park, where permission was also given to play baseball. In 1887, four additional tennis courts were added in Jackson Park and two baseball diamonds laid out and clayed; while the following year the number of courts and diamonds remained unchanged, with 165 acres turfed in Jackson Park and 15 acres in Washington Park, the latter containing two

[6]Cf. Joseph Lee, *op. cit.*, p. 159; E. B. Mero, *op. cit.*, p. 242.

tennis courts but no baseball diamonds, although
the privilege of playing ball was granted. Fifteen
years were required to drain the ground and build
up the soil so as to permit its being turfed. Two
hay crops were harvested annually from the drier
portions in these parks, hence the significance of
the term "meadow." Originally great swails and
marshes covered the central areas of Washington and Jackson Parks and the Midway which
now connects them, and during stormy weather
the waters of Lake Michigan were driven into
these lowlands. Hence the great expense and
time required to provide a playing surface.

Aside from the error in date and the fact that
the event in question was a conscious provision
for play, the opening of the "meadow" in both
Washington and Jackson Parks was not dynamically related to subsequent developments in
provision for play in Chicago or elsewhere. In
Chicago, for instance, the initiative of the recrea-
tion-center development that later made famous
the South Park System came from sources outside
the park commission and contemporary with the
work of the special park commission formed in
1899. These sources may be designated as the
early efforts by settlements and the associated
charities of the west side of the city to provide
play facilities for children during 1894 and 1897,
where it was pointed out that children in the congested sections had no suitable space in which to
play and did not make long trips to the large

parks or the lake. The slogan of the small parks movement, therefore, came to be, "Take the parks to the people, if they can not come to the parks"; hence the "small parks" constructed in 1903-5. The Washington Park playfield of 1886 also fails to meet the second criteria of the origin of the play movement.

Another date for the beginning of the movement mentioned by a well-known writer on playground activities is "1898, when New York City opened some 31 playgrounds under the Board of Education."[7] The reasons given in the context in support of the statement are two: (1) that it "received abundant notice in the New York dailies"; and, (2) that "a number of cities took up the movement immediately afterwards." While fulfilling the first criteria that it was a conscious provision for play, this event fails of the second if it cannot be proven that it was the first of a series of related events that are now recognized as the play movement, the developments in other cities beginning subsequently if not "immediately afterwards" as asserted. In order either to establish or refute the claim, two questions must be answered: (1) What are the dates of the beginning of provision for play in the respective cities of the United States? (2) Do they indicate that many began "immediately" after 1898?

[7] H. S. Curtis, *The Play Movement and Its Significance*, The Macmillan Co., 1917. The correct date, however, for the opening of the thirty-one schoolyard playgrounds was 1899, not 1898. Cf. Lee, Zueblin *et alia*. Twenty playgrounds were opened in 1898.

Inasmuch as the advocate of the New York experiment as the beginning of the play movement did not support his assertion by a statement of the facts relative to provision by cities both before and after the year 1898, the writer has arranged Table I after a careful analysis of the whole period of playground history.[8]

TABLE I

NUMBER OF CITIES IN THE UNITED STATES, REPORTING SUPERVISED PLAYGROUNDS ESTABLISHED FOR THE FIRST TIME, BY YEARS

Date	No.	Date	No.	Date	No.	Date	No.	Date	No.
1885	1	1897	2	1902	2	1907	6	1912	43
1889	2	1898	4	1903	2	1908	13	1913	70
1893	1	1899	1	1904	5	1909	35	1915	116
1894	2	1900	7	1905	4	1910	35	1916	43
1896	1	1901	5	1906	9	1911	43	1917	52

Grand Total for the Period............504

An analysis of Table I discloses three facts that have an important relation to the origin of the play movement: (1) There were thirteen cities[9] that had provided supervised play facilities prior to 1899, the correct date for the opening of the thirty-one schoolyard playgrounds in New

[8]The Playground and Recreation Association of America, upon whose published statistics the writer relied for the data contained relative to developments since its organization, did not furnish a report for 1914; that for 1915 represents two years of progress.

[9]The names of these cities with their respective dates of beginning the play movement are as follows: Boston, 1885; New York, and Brooklyn, 1889 (these playgrounds were sporadic and of short duration, the permanent establishment coming in Brooklyn in 1897, and in New York in 1899); Chicago, 1894 (sporadic in 1894, permanent in 1898-1899); Philadelphia, 1893; Providence, 1894; Pittsburgh, 1896; Baltimore and Milwaukee, 1897; San Francisco (sporadic), Cleveland, Minneapolis and Denver, 1898. The first playground in Louisville, 1899, was planned by the same landscape architect who designed the Charlesbank outdoor gymnasium in Boston, in 1889.

York City. (2) Between 1899 and 1906, the date
of the organization of the Playground Association
of America, there were twenty five cities that provided for play, while between 1906 and 1910 there
were fifty-five, the first great increase coming
after the organization of the playground association rather than "immediately after" the opening
of schoolyard playgrounds in New York City. (3)
During 1910, the first year that field secretaries
were sent out by the playground association, and
during each year since that time, the number of
cities providing playgrounds for the first time
was greater than that for the whole period between 1899 and 1906. In so far as these three facts
are related to the origin of the play movement they
indicate that the number of cities making provision for the first time slowly but steadily increased between 1885 and 1899, and that the
greatest period of increase came after the organization of the national playground association, and
not as the result of any publicity that certain
newspapers of New York City may have given to
the movement during the summer of 1899.

Since Boston is the city referred to by the
earliest date of the table, 1885, the facts relative
to events there and their influence upon the play
movement will now be analyzed in connection with
the study of the last date that has been frequently
mentioned as marking the origin of the movement, the provision of sand gardens in Boston in
1885.

The one provision for play which has been
most frequently designated as the origin of the
movement is the establishment of sand gardens
in Boston.[10] Dr. Marie E. Zakrsewska, while visiting in Berlin during the summer in 1885, observed heaps of sand in the public parks in which
the children of both the rich and the poor were
permitted to play under supervision of the police.
As a result of her report by letter to Mrs. Kate
Gannet Wells, chairman of the executive committee of the Massachusetts Emergency and Hygiene
Association, a large heap of sand was placed in
the yards of the Parmenter Street Chapel and the
West End Nursery. The latter experiment was
unsuccessful since "the children there were
hardly two years old and cared little for it,"[11] but
at the former an average of fifteen children connected with the chapel attended three days in the
week during July and August, 1885, and, under
the guidance of a lady living in the neighborhood,
dug in the sand with their little wooden shovels and made
countless sand pies, which were re-made the next day with
undismayed alacrity. They sang their songs and marched
in their small processions, and when weary, were gathered
in the motherly arms of the matron.[12]

[10]Cf. Joseph Lee, *op. cit.*, p. 125; E. B. Mero, *op. cit.*, p. 240;
S. V. Tsanoff, "Children's Playgrounds," *Municipal Affairs*,
1898, p. 293; C. M. Robinson, "Improvement of City Life,"
Atlantic Monthly, April, 1899, pp. 533–36; Sadie American,
"The Movement for Small Playgrounds," *American Journal of
Sociology*, Sept., 1898, pp. 159–76.

[11]*Annual Report Massachusetts Emergency and Hygiene
Association*, 1885.

[12]*Ibid.*

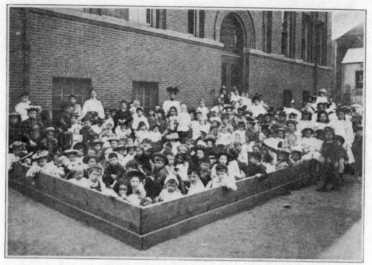

EARLY SAND GARDEN IN BOSTON
[COURTESY MISS ELLEN M. TOWER]

EARLY SCHOOLYARD PLAYGROUND, BOSTON
[COURTESY MISS ELLEN M. TOWER]

During the summer of 1886 "three piles of yellow sand were placed in the yards of the Children's Mission, Parmenter Street Chapel and Warrenton Street Chapel," as a result of the success of the preceding season. These sand piles were provided for children under twelve years of age. During the first years there was no supervision except that given voluntarily by interested mothers or other women living in the respective neighborhoods. Matrons were employed, however, during the summer of 1887, when the number of sand gardens was increased to ten, of which one was in a school yard, while most of the others were located in the courts of tenement houses. The method of supervision by matrons was followed until 1893, when a superintendent of all sand gardens with assistants, kindergartners, located at each, were employed. Digging instruments and building blocks were furnished, games played, and "occupation work" encouraged. By 1899 the number of playgrounds of this type, conducted by the Association in Boston, had increased to twenty-one, of which all but one were on schoolyards. During this year, the city council appropriated $3,000 toward their support.

Table II summarizes the first sixteen years of history of the playground activities of the Association by years, showing the number of sand gardens maintained, the cost of their support, the number of hours per day and the number of days per week during which they were

TABLE

The Development of Playgrounds by Massachusetts

Year	No,	Cost of Maintenance*	Operation per Week	Period	Location
1885.....	2	Service donated	3 hours on 3 days	6 weeks, July and August	Mission yard and nursery
1886.....	3	Service donated	3 hours on 3 days	6 weeks, July and August	Mission yards
1887.....	10	Toys $9.00; matrons employed	3 hours on 3 days	6 weeks, July and August	Mission yards
1888.....	10†	Matrons employed	3 hours on 4 days	6 weeks, July and August	7 schoolyards; 2 courts; 1 vacant lot
1889.....	11‡	$928.04	3 hours on 4 days	6 weeks, July and August	One lot added to above
1890.....	17§	Expenses ?	3 hours on 4 days	6 weeks, July and August	Mostly school-yards
1891.....	10	Expenses ?	3 hours on 4 days	6 weeks, July and August	Mostly school-yards
1892.....	10	Expenses ?	3 hours on 4 days	36 days in July and August	Mostly school-yards
1893.....	10	$1,407.71	3 hrs. every day ex.Sun.	36 days in July and August	9 school-yards; 1 on lot
1894.....	10	$1,395.00	3 hrs. every day ex.Sun.	50 days in July and August	All on schoolyards
1895.....	10	$1,526.38	3 hrs. every day ex.Sun.	10 weeks	All on schoolyards
1896.....	10	$1,688.00	3 hrs. every day ex.Sun.	10 weeks	All on schoolyards
1897.....	10	$1,480.32	3 hrs. every day ex.Sun.	10 weeks	All on schoolyards
1898.....	12	$1,849.00	3 hrs. every day ex.Sun.	10 weeks	All on schoolyards
1899.....	21	$4,313.77	3 hrs. every day ex.Sun.	10 weeks	All on schoolyards
1900.....	21	$4,200.00	3 hrs. every day ex.Sun.	10 weeks	All on schoolyards

*Sand was donated in every case.
†Sand pails and shovels were sent to eight different localities in addition to these ten playgrounds.

II.
EMERGENCY AND HYGIENE ASSOCIATION, FROM 1885 TO 1900

Public Subsidy	Supervision	Average Daily Attendance	Play Room Experiment
None	Voluntary by mothers in vicinity	Average of 15 daily	....
None	Voluntary by mothers in vicinity	Not given	....
None	Employed ma-trons	Not given	....
None	Employed ma-trons	400, all play-grounds	....
$1,000 and Charlesbank opened for men	Employed ma-trons	1,000 for all	First opened 16 weeks 12-9 p. m. after Jan.1
Charlesbank Outdoor Gym. for men.	Employed ma-trons	Not given	16 weeks 12-9 p. m. after Jan. 1
Charlesbank Out-door Gym. for men and women.	Employed ma-trons	Not given	16 weeks 12-9 p. m. after Jan. 1
Charlesbank Out-door Gym. for men and women.	Employed ma-trons	1,210 daily; seasonal 43,560	Playroom taken over by Nat. Ed. Union
Charlesbank Out-door Gym. for men and women.	Supt. with kindergarten assistants	1,400 daily	....
Charlesbank Out-door Gym. for men and women.	Supt. with kindergarten assistants	1,588 daily; seasonal 79,400	....
Franklin Field added	Supt. with 22 assistants	1,804 daily; seasonal 128,240	....
Brighton play-ground pur-chased	Supt. with 22 assistants	1,802 daily	....
Charlesbank, Franklin Field, Brighton	Supt. with 22 assistants	1,827 daily	....
20 playgrounds added	Supt. with 22 assistants	2,080 daily	....
$3,000 by city council‖	Supt. with 66 supervisors	4,000 daily	....
$3,000 by city council‖	Supt. with 64 supervisors	4,300 daily	....

‡One of these was in Brookline, Mass., outside city limits.
§Two in Brookline, one in Charlestown, two in South Boston, two in Roxbury, while the remaining ten were in Boston.
‖Added for sand gardens.

open, the months of the year and the total number of days of operation, the nature of their respective sites, the dates and extent of public subsidy, the method of supervision and number and type of supervisors, the record of attendance giving the average per day for each season and the total for the respective summers, and the history of the play room experiment, that is, the conduct of indoor play for a given, brief period during the winter. This table is compiled from the statements published in the annual reports of the Massachusetts Emergency and Hygiene Association from 1885 to 1901 inclusive.

Analysis of this table discloses, (1) an increase from two to twenty-one playgrounds; (2) a transition from support and service through donations of materials or time to an annual budget of $4,200 with a maximum of $4,313.77 in one of the later years; (3) from three days to six days per week; (4) from 18 to 60 days per season, during July and August; (5) from mission yards and tenement courts to schoolyards and parks; (6) from support entirely by philanthropic subscriptions to public subsidy of $3,000 annually; (7) from volunteer and untrained supervision to paid and trained supervisors under the direction of a superintendent; (8) from an average attendance of 15 per day at one playground to 4,300 per day on twenty-one playgrounds; (9) the development of indoor play provision which after three years of experimentation was taken over by another

association in the city; and (10) the actual conduct of sand gardens in three cities other than
Boston.

Two questions arise which, if answered in the
affirmative, will establish the beginning of the
play movement in the United States with the
sand piles of Boston in 1885. First, Did the development of similar facilities in other cities come
subsequently and through impulses received from
them? and second, Did the incorporation in the
play movement of facilities for adolescents and
adults result from the sand gardens which were
designed in Boston for the play of children? That
each of these questions must be answered in the
affirmative is established by the following two
groups of facts: (1) those relative to developments within Boston, and (2) the influence of
these events upon developments in other cities.

B. *Influence of the "sand gardens" within
Boston.* Relative to early developments in provision for play in Boston, there is conclusive evidence that pioneer work in both the parks and the
schoolyards, leading from philanthropic to public support, resulted from the sand pile experiment of 1885 and the unbroken series of subsequent summer provisions made by the Massachusetts Emergency and Hygiene Association
from that date until 1899, when their playgrounds, which at that time had increased in number to twenty-one, were supported in part by an
appropriation made by the School Committee of

the City of Boston. Table II calls attention to
eight events which indicate a relationship between
contemporaneous developments in providing for
playgrounds in Boston and the work of the Association.

The first of these events growing immediately
out of the influence of the sand gardens was the
appropriation by the park department in 1889 of
$1,000 to grade and grass a vacant plot for play-
ground uses, the management being left to the
Association.[13] The second and third events pertained to the construction and operation respectively of the Charlesbank Outdoor Gymnasium in
1889-91. The construction of this playground was
undertaken by the Park Department, in response
to an appeal by the "playground committee,"
appointed by the Association in 1887, for aid in
providing playgrounds. They converted a ten-
acre tract along the Charles River in a congested
section of the city into an open-air gymnasium
for boys and men in 1889, and for girls and
women in 1891. This playground, known as the
Charlesbank Outdoor Gymnasium, was fenced,
parked, equipped with swings, ladders, see-saws,
a one-fifth mile running track, a sand garden, and
provided with wading, rowing, and bathing facilities, all free to the public. Land and equipment
were contributed by the park department, operation by private associations, that of the children's
and women's division being entrusted to the

[13]Cf. *Annual Report of Massachusetts Emergency and Hygiene Association* for 1890.

Massachusetts Emergency and Hygiene Association. In confirmation of the foregoing are the following three statements:

The sand pile work having been started so successfully, the park commissioners of Boston investigated the matter and decided to use some of the city parks for similar purposes. They also fitted up the Charlesbank open air gymnasium.[14]

The success of the sand heaps led the park commissioners to place the women's division of Charlesbank under the control of the Massachusetts Emergency and Hygiene Association.[15]

The new work of the Association this past year has been the management of the Women's Division of Charlesbank, the name by which that portion of the Park System of Boston is designated that lies along the Charles River between Cambridge and Craigie Street Bridges.[16]

The fourth, fifth, and sixth events indicative of the influence of the experience and activity of the Association were related to other park developments of Boston and the surrounding environment. These were, respectively, (1) the incorporation of the plan of providing "numerous small squares, playgrounds, and parks in the midst of the dense populations" in the program of the Metropolitan Park Commission of Boston organized in 1892; (2) the purchase of Franklin Field by the park department of the city of Boston in 1894 as an initial step in that direction, a recogni-

[14]H. H. Buxton, in unpublished thesis of 1899, from which sections are quoted in E. B. Mero, *American Playgrounds*, pp. 243–52.

[15]Charles Mulford Robinson, "Improvement of City Life," *Atlantic Monthly*, 1899, pp. 533–36.

[16]*Annual Report Massachusetts Emergency and Hygiene Association*, 1892.

tion of the popular interest in playgrounds that
prevailed in Boston at that time, and a step far
in advance of other cities; and (3) the purchase
of land for the Brighton playground in 1895 at
the cost of $25,000. The incorporation of play-
grounds in the plans of the Metropolitan Park
Commission was made by Mr. Charles Eliot, one
of the most active individuals in the work of
creating the commission and a member of it, on
October 6, 1892, when he outlined the work of the
Commission as follows:[17]

As I conceive it, the scientific "park system" for a district such as ours would include (1) spaces on the ocean
front, (2) as much as possible of the shores and islands of
the bay, (3) the courses of the larger tidal estuaries, ...
(4) two or three larger areas of wild forest on the outer rim
of the inhabited area, (5) numerous small squares, playgrounds, and parks in the midst of the dense populations.

The first annual report of the Metropolitan
Park Commission of Boston,[18] under whose jurisdiction were placed the parking authorities of
eleven cities and twenty-five towns, devotes fourteen pages to a discussion of plans for small
parks or playgrounds, beginning with:

The subject of smaller open spaces for local playgrounds
or "breathing spaces" as they are appropriately called, is
one so different in its nature as to require a special consideration.

Then follow maps of Charlesbank and other
parked playgrounds in Boston and vicinity, some

[17]Zueblin, *American Municipal Progress*, The Macmillan
Co., 1916, p. 285.

[18]*Annual Report Metropolitan Park Commission of Boston*,
1893; pp. 67–81.

of which had already been constructed while others were only proposed, showing that the idea of a small area equipped for play and located near the homes of the people had obtained at that time a definite place in the plans of the park department. Charlesbank had demonstrated the value of these facilities, and the sand gardens had first shown the need for them.

The seventh event indicative of the influence of the sand gardens upon subsequent provisions for play in Boston was the development of public support and control of the schoolyard playgrounds. Since 1888 the Massachusetts Emergency and Hygiene Association had conducted seven or more playgrounds of the sand-garden type on schoolyards, and by the summer of 1898, the number had increased to twelve. During that summer Mayor Quincy of Boston opened twenty schoolyard playgrounds. This experiment was not successful because of lack of leadership, the grounds being placed under the supervision of caretakers. As one boy expressed it, "there was nothin' to do and no discipline." In a fortnight these playgrounds were almost deserted. The following summer, 1899, at the suggestion of the mayor, the school committee appropriated $3,000 toward the support of certain schoolyard playgrounds, the funds to be spent under the direction of the Massachusetts Emergency and Hygiene Association. Twenty-one playgrounds in all were conducted by this arrangement between the school committee and the association, sixty supervisors were employed, $4,313.77 expended for materials and supervision, and 4,000 children attended them daily on the average. During the summer of 1900 the experiment was repeated with the result that sixty-four supervisors were employed, $4,200 expended, while the average daily attendance was 4,300. In the summer of 1901, the transition from philanthropic to public control, as well as support, was effected by the withdrawal from the Association of financial assistance on the part of the school committee, and the establishment, under their own administration, of "four vacation schools and three playgrounds" for which $5,000 were appropriated. During the summer of 1902, $7,500 were appropriated and "seven schools and five playgrounds" were maintained. The Massachusetts Emergency and Hygiene Association, however, continued to conduct playgrounds as they did before public support was added; twelve for the summer of 1901, with an average daily attendance of 3,479, for which $2,462.33 were expended from voluntary contributions.

Admission by the school committee of its dependence upon the Association and confirmation of the statements concerning the beginnings of public support of schoolyard playgrounds is contained in their annual report of 1902, as follows:

In May, 1900, an appropriation of $3,000 was made for the maintenance of vacation schools. . . . . The success of these schools was such that an appropriation of $5,000 was made for their support during the summer of 1901, and four schools and three playgrounds were established for a term of six weeks beginning July 8. . . . . For the further continuance of vacation schools and playgrounds during the summer of 1902, the school committee appropriated $7,500, and seven schools and five playgrounds were conducted . . . . for a term beginning July 7 and closing August 15.

In addition to the school playgrounds maintained by the city, the Massachusetts Emergency and Hygiene Association (which for many years has been interested in and supported playgrounds in various schoolyards), the Massachusetts Civic League, the Brighthelmston Club, the Women's Educational and Industrial Club, and other associations and individuals were allowed to use the various school premises. . . . . To the public spirited and kindly women (the Massachusetts Emergency and Hygiene Association) who have personally interested themselves in this work is due a debt of gratitude for their unselfish concern in the happiness of little children during the long and unoccupied summer months.[19]

In the paper entitled "Play Grounds and Sand Gardens," read before the Montreal Local Council of Women, in April, 1902, by Miss Ellen M. Tower, Chairman of the Playground Committee of the Massachusetts Emergency and Hygiene Association, the following statement of the relation of the work of that association to the development of the first publically administered schoolyard playgrounds in Boston was made:

In 1899 . . . . municipal aid was rendered to the playgrounds when, at the suggestion of Mayor Quincy, the School Committee appropriated $3,000 for expenses connected with

[19]*Annual Report School Committee*, Boston, 1902, pp. 25–28, also Public School Document No. 14, on *Vacation Schools*, 1902.

the opening of certain schoolhouse yards during the summer vacation, to be spent under the direction of the Massachusetts Emergency and Hygiene Association.

. . . .

This experiment was sufficiently successful to warrant continuing in 1900, when the school committee again appropriated $3,000 to be spent by our Association. . . . .

In 1901 the School Committee, thinking that the time draws near when play will be, or should be, considered an integral part of education, and that therefore the playgrounds and vacation schools should be alike under the care of their own Board, declined to bestow money upon the Emergency Association, but established . . . . sand gardens under their own supervision. . . . . They paid the Association the implied compliment of adopting its methods and asking its advice. This seeming reverse is, in fact, our greatest triumph. We have been doing as amateurs, and, as a temporary expedient for helping the children, what the educational branches of our Government should do professionally and systematically. Next season we hope to be driven still further afield, and may conclude that our mission is accomplished.

The eighth event indicative further of the relation of the work of the Massachusetts Emergency and Hygiene Association to that of other philanthropic societies making similar provision for play in Boston was that of the construction of a playground by the Massachusetts Civic League in 1901, after the plan of those previously conducted by the Association. Direct confirmation of this fact is presented in the report of the League for that year.

We have a children's corner modeled upon the work of the Emergency and Hygiene Association. Indeed the location was chosen and the principal apparatus got under the advice of Miss Ellen M. Tower, Chairman of the Playgrounds

Committee of the Association, who has had so large a part in carrying on this branch of the work of that Association.[20]

The direct influence of the sand gardens of Boston, first conducted in 1885 and permanently established in 1887, upon the provision of both philanthropic and public play facilities in that city, is shown by the analysis above. It has been found that, while the earliest efforts on the part of the Emergency Association were in behalf of pre-adolescent children, later activities included the provision of facilities for youth and maturity. The first of these events was the influence which the Association exerted upon the park department which resulted in the building of Charlesbank Outdoor Gymnasium, the section for men being finished in 1889, and that for women in 1891. A second event was the incorporation of the idea of constructing "small squares and playgrounds" in the plan of the Metropolitan Park Commission of Boston in 1893. A third event was the opening of Franklin Field, of which forty acres were devoted to team games and athletics, in 1894. The fourth event was the provision for Brighton Playground in 1895. A fifth connection was made in 1899, when, with the aid of the School Committee, twenty-one playgrounds were maintained that summer, of which three were designed particularly for boys between twelve and fifteen years of age. Concerning this provision, Miss Tower said:

[20]*Annual Report of Massachusetts Civic League*, 1901.

Eighteen sand gardens were devoted to the little children
and to all the larger boys who wished to play with the little
ones, to aid the matrons, or to sit quietly by and sew or read
or play checkers. The other three, as an experiment, were
provided with a limited outfit of gymnastic apparatus, and,
under the care of young men trained in the art of physical
culture, were designed especially for boys from twelve to
fifteen years of age. This experiment was sufficiently successful to warrant continuing in 1900.[21]

In 1901 the School Committee decided to
administer playgrounds on their own account but
"they paid the Association the implied compliment of adopting its methods and asking its
advice." In that year, also; the Massachusetts
Civic League opened its first playground, a
"model playground," containing a "children's
corner" and a "big boy's playground" as well
as a space for the older girls; and in planning it,
the advice of Miss Tower of the Association
was followed. Thus the question whether the
incorporation in the play movement of facilities
for adolescents and adults resulted from the sand
gardens experiment is answered in the affirmative.

C. *Influence of Boston upon other cities.*
The facts relative to the second question raised
above, Did the development of initial play provision in other cities come subsequently and
through impulses derived from the early experience of conducting sand gardens in Boston? will
now be analyzed. There are five types of sources

[21]Ellen M. Tower, "Play Grounds and Sand Gardens,"
World Wide, April 2, 1902.

of information: (1) the opinions of contemporary
writers on play and playgrounds; (2) the asser-
tions by the Massachusetts Emergency and
Hygiene Association that other cities consulted
them before inaugurating playgrounds; (3) the
admissions of these organizers of playgrounds in
other cities than Boston; (4) the visit of Miss
Ellen M. Tower, chairman of the playground
committee of the Association, to Baltimore, to
deliver a lecture upon playgrounds at the request
of a committee in that city, which had the subject
under advisement; and (5) the structure and concept of the function of the early playgrounds in
all cities.

Among the comments made by those who
wrote contemporaneously with the genetic stage
of the movement is that of H. H. Buxton, a grad-
uate student in the International Training School
of the Young Men's Christian Association at
Springfield, Massachusetts, in his Master's
thesis, an unpublished manuscript, in 1899. Concerning the relation of the sand gardens of Boston in 1885 to the development of playgrounds in
other cities up to 1899, he made the sweeping
declaration:

This was the starting point of the present playground
movement in America.

Buxton did not present any facts in support
of his claim other than that Miss Tower, chairman of the playgrounds committee that was in
charge of the sand gardens in Boston, lectured in

Baltimore at the invitation of the committee there that was considering the provision of playgrounds. He wrote so near to the time of the events which he was studying that the relation probably seemed too obvious to necessitate analysis or support.

Another statement of the influence of Boston on the beginnings of provision for play by other cities is the following by Charles Mulford Robinson, later a playground architect and adviser, written also in 1899:

> In Boston, which was the pioneer, the municipal sand piles of 1887 were the first pathetic expression of a need of a playground and of an effort to satisfy it. Their success has led to their adoption in many large cities.

The word municipal is here used in a very loose sense, not meaning public support and control; and the date is slightly erroneous owing to the fact that the permanent establishment of the sand gardens did not occur until 1887, although the initial experiment was made two years prior to that date. The reports of the Massachusetts Emergency and Hygiene Association give 1887 as the date of permanent establishment, a statement that was somewhat arbitrary since there was no change in structure or concept of function at that date except the employment of matrons to supervise the children who used the gardens.

A third declaration made contemporaneously with the early stages of the play movement was that by Joseph Lee who was associated with the development of the movement in Boston, being for several years chairman of the playground committee of the Massachusetts Civic League, and who made a careful study of published reports of societies conducting playgrounds before 1900, in the preparation of his volume entitled *Constructive and Preventive Philanthropy*. After describing the origin of the Boston sand gardens, he sets out to relate the developments in other cities by the following sentence:

The first city, so far as I can ascertain, to follow the example of Boston was Philadelphia, in which, in 1893, two summer playgrounds were started by philanthropic people. In 1895 the City Council, in response to a petition from the Civic Club and a large number of other organizations, opened the available schoolyards, four of which were equipped as sand gardens, and appropriated $1,000 to carry on these latter.

While there is no analysis of the facts pertaining to the influence of Boston upon Philadelphia, his statement represents an opinion based upon a study of the history of the period.

Before 1900, no statement was made, as far as the writer is aware, to the contrary of the opinion expressed by the three authors quoted above. The consensus of view seems to have been in favor of Boston as the pioneer in the play movement.

Contemporary confirmation of the above opinions was made by the Massachusetts Emergency and Hygiene Association in its annual reports for 1892, 1897, and 1898, respectively, as follows:

Boston playground ideas have been carried to New York City, and to Providence, R. I.

The people who have started playgrounds in New York, Philadelphia, and Providence have consulted and in a measure followed the methods of the Massachusetts Emergency and Hygiene Association.

The sand gardens have been much written about in magazines and journals and many inquiries have been made in' regard to their management. New York, Philadelphia, and Providence long since established playgrounds unquestionably better than ours, but in the beginning they came to Boston for suggestions and advice. In 1897, the United Women of Maryland asked that some one might be sent to Baltimore to talk to them on the subject, and the chairman of your committee went. Brooklyn, N. Y., Newark, Providence, and Worcester sent representatives to study our work, and this Spring Chicago, Portland, and Manchester, England, have written for information. The experiment seems hopeful to all interested, if we may judge by the reports that reach us.

The foregoing declarations indicate that the nine cities beside Boston that took initial steps or were contemplating provision prior to 1898 (namely, Philadelphia, New York, Providence, Brooklyn, Baltimore, Newark, Worcester, Chicago, and Portland) came to Boston for suggestions and advice. Ostensibly here was a cause-and-effect relationship characteristic of a series of events common to movements.

Confirmation of the claims expressed by the Massachusetts Emergency and Hygiene Association is made in the annual reports of two societies providing playgrounds before 1900. In that of the Union for Practical Progress which initiated the movement in Providence, for the year 1897, occurs the following frank admission of a conscious effort to copy methods followed in Boston, the particular references being to the sand gardens and the Charlesbank Outdoor Gymnasium:

Their growth (referring to the playgrounds of Providence) has been quite as rapid and encouraging as was that of Boston during the early years of the movement. . . . . One phase of development lies along the lines of the open-air gymnasium, with apparatus and grassy playground. The success of this institution in Boston should be called to the attention of public spirited citizens, that reservations of lawns may be made in needy parts of the city.[22]

Regarding the origin of the movement in Brooklyn, in 1897, two references to Boston as the prototype are made in the annual report of the department of parks for that year. The first was that by the committee which had charge of a small initial playground in City Park during the summer of 1897, while the second was by the secretary of the park department. Both disclose a conscious dependence upon Boston:

So far as we are aware, the City Park playground is the first one to have been established in Brooklyn. Other cities have for several years made similar provision for the children either through private enterprise or through some one of the municipal departments. For ten years playgrounds have been opened during the summer in Boston. Private individuals furnish the funds and the board of education grants the use of the grounds.[23]

The Department was petitioned, in the latter part of the summer, to start open air gymnasiums in the parks. The

[22]*Fourth Annual Report of Joint Committee on Summer Playgrounds*, Providence, 1897.

[23]*Annual Report of Dept. of Parks*, Brooklyn, 1887, p. 45.

subject was taken into consideration, and investigation of the work in Boston was made.[24]

Secondary statements derived from those who had charge of the initial work of providing for play in Baltimore and Providence are made by Buxton.

To the United Women of Maryland is due the credit of starting the playground movement through inspiration that came from Boston, largely through an address given in Baltimore by Miss Ellen M. Tower, chairman of the Comittee on Playgrounds of the Massachusetts Emergency and Hygiene Association.[25]

The Union for Practical Progress started the playground movement in Providence, R. I., in 1893, after investigating what was done in Boston.[26]

Two references have previously been made to the fact that Miss Ellen M. Tower, for many years chairman of the playground committee of the Association conducting the sand gardens in Boston, visited Baltimore in 1897 at the request of the United Women of Maryland, and delivered an address on sand gardens.[27] This address is eloquent evidence of the influence of Boston upon other cities during the early stages of the movement.[28]

Mute evidence of a relationship, were this testimony necessary, is present in the very struc-

[24]*Annual Report of Dept. of Parks*, Brooklyn, 1887, p. 25.

[25]H. H. Buxton, "History of the Playground Movement," in Mero's *American Playgrounds* (written in 1899), p. 248.

[26]*Ibid.*

[27]Ellen M. Tower, *Annual Report Massachusetts Emergency and Hygiene Association*, 1898.

[28]It is also significant in this connection to note that Miss Tower delivered a similar address in Montreal, Canada, in 1902.

ture of the playgrounds themselves; in every city the sand garden type was followed. If they were not modeled after Boston, then the coincidence is phenomenal. In the third part of this investigation the writer has chosen to designate the first stage through which the play movement has passed as the "sand garden" stage in recognition of the nature and uniformity of structure and concept of function that prevailed. The descriptions of these playgrounds will also be presented there.

D. *The conclusions*—The evidence studied is unmistakably in support of the view that the initial action in provision for play in Philadelphia, Providence, Brooklyn, Baltimore, Chicago, Newark, Worcester, Portland, and New York was the result of an impulse derived from the experience of Boston. In the absence of any evidence to the contrary, it is reasonable to infer that these were the "many large cities" referred to by Robinson, and also the explanation of the expression of Lee, "the first city, so far as I can ascertain, to follow the example of Boston." Provision in Boston preceded that in thirteen cities, as shown by Table I, by a lapse of time sufficient to permit information to have reached them before 1899 concerning the action of both philanthropic and public agencies of Boston, while in each of these cities the initial provision was identical in structure and function with that of Boston. In each of the thirteen cities, as in Boston, provision for children under twelve years of age preceded that for older boys and girls and adults, as has been shown by Lee.[29] A universal and distinctive feature of equipment in each of them, as in Boston, was the sand pile; and in every instance, philanthropic maintenance preceded public support and control.

The facts relative to the origin of the play movement have thus been analyzed. The inception of the movement has been traced to the sand piles of Boston, in 1885. It has been disclosed: (1) that the play movement in Boston dated from the sand gardens conducted by the Massachusetts Emergency and Hygiene Association and was aided and directed by both their example and the personnel in charge of them; (2) that the development of similar facilities in other cities came subsequently and through motives received from the Boston sand gardens experiments; and (3) that the incorporation in the movement of facilities for adolescents and adults were logical attempts to make an adjustment to a social situation with respect to which the sand piles of Boston of 1885 were the first of a connected series of provisions for play that passed from philanthropic to public support through action by both park and school boards, and were later repeated in other cities. In the following section, the respective stages through which the play movement has since passed will be analyzed.

[29]Joseph Lee, *Constructive and Preventive Philanthropy*, pp. 123 ff.

III. THE STAGES OF THE PLAY MOVEMENT

A survey of the history of the play movement discloses seven periods in its evolution that are characterized by the incorporation of particular features in its structure correlative with an emphasis upon given changes in the concept of its function. These periods of emphasis upon given features of structure and function may be defined as "stages" in its evolution; the term "stage" signifying a period in a development or a degree of advancement in a process. It is not understood, however, that these "stages" were mutually exclusive, that is, that their essential traits did not retain a permanent place in the movement, neither is it meant that the distinguishing features of a given "stage" were present in all contemporaneous provisions for play, nor that they represented the average provision at a specified time. The "stages," as the term is here used, were more or less clearly defined periods of emphasis by the leaders of the movement upon certain phases of its structure and the concept of its function correlative with their incorporation by a portion, if not all, of the societies and communities making contemporary provision for play.

The titles chosen by the present writer to designate the "stages" of the play movement and the dates that roughly approximate the periods

of their respective manifestations are as follows:
(1) the "sand garden" stage, dominant during
1885-95; (2) the "model playground" stage,
about 1895-1900; (3) the "small park" stage,
about 1900-5; (4) the "recreation center" stage,
1905-12; (5) the "civic art and welfare" stage,
1912-15; (6) the "neighborhood organization"
stage, 1915-18; and (7) the "community service"
stage, since about 1918. The facts relative to the
particular features of structure and concept of
function that received emphasis during these
respective periods or "stages" will now be analyzed from the standpoint of the evidence, if any,
that they contain concerning the evolution of the
play movement in the United States.

A. *The "sand garden" stage, 1885-95.* The
term "sand garden"[1] designates that form of
provision which consisted of a sand heap or
sand box with or without other apparatus such
as swings and see-saws. The sand garden was
located out of doors, in settlement yards, tenement courts, school yards, or in parks, and was
designed for the use of children under twelve
years of age. With the single exception of the
Charlesbank Outdoor Gymnasium of 1889-91,
which also included a sand garden in its equipment, it was the universal provision for play during the first decade of the movement.

As disclosed in the discussion above of the
origin of the play movement, the two earliest sand

[1]Other names for this type of provision are: sand piles,
sand heaps, sand bins, sand boxes, sand courts.

gardens were placed on mission chapel and
nursery yards in Boston in 1885. Ten, in all, were
located in chapel yards, tenement courts, and
schoolyards in 1887; one in a park in 1889; with
a transfer of all but one to schoolyards by 1894,
when ten were maintained by the Massachusetts
Emergency and Hygiene Association in Boston.

A description of these sand gardens, given by
the chairman of the committee of the Association
in charge, is as follows:

The place is the shady side of a school yard. It must be
shaded, as it is impossible to play on hot bricks in summer
with the burning sun overhead. The time, therefore, is regu-
lated by the falling of the shadows.

In the shadow stands a wooden box with a heavy cover,
padlocked tightly at either end. In the box is the sand, and
in the basement of the school building are the toys and materials for work or play. If the kindly shadows fall in the
morning the gate is swung open at nine, and long before the
hour a crowd of little boys and girls has gathered on the
sidewalk, or if in the afternoon, the children do not assemble
until two o'clock. At fifteen minutes before the hour of
opening, the matrons enter the yard and admit some of the
larger children who, under their direction, must sweep and
gather up the litter in the yard, consign it to the waste bar-
rel, bring out from the basement of the building the seats,
pails, and shovels, lift the cover from the sand box, and
arrange the toys in different parts of the yard that the
children may go to the spot, where for instance the blocks
are placed, if they wish to play with blocks. This done,
the key is turned and the waiting crowd let in as the clock
strikes. To open and close punctually lends an air of seri-
ousness and importance, and the children enjoy and respect
a certain amount of discipline.

When once in the yard, the babies flock to the sand box, their elders seek for toys or books, one monitor distributes horse reins, another skipping ropes or toy brooms, and there is a rush for the seats. Nothing adds so much to the comfort of children and mothers as plenty of movable benches. Sometimes there is marching to the sound of a drum, and the waving of numberless flags. On two days in the week sewing cards and bright worsteds are the chief attraction, on two other days brilliantly colored soldiers, animals, rough riders, or hospital nurses are distributed to be "cut out." There are, perhaps, seven or eight pairs of scissors in a yard, each pair hung upon a red string to pass over the head of the urchin using it. This fortunate youngster sits comfortably and prolongs his pleasure, as opposite him against the wall stands a wriggling line of his comrades awaiting their turn.

They are much more excited and interested than they would be if there were scissors enough for all. The express carts run continually, two boys or girls pulling, two babies riding inside. Fifteen minutes is the usual time allowed for a trip.

Kindergarten songs and games form an important part of every day's amusement, and under the guise of play an earnest effort is made to teach the brief creed . . . . "to play fair, keep clean, and speak the truth." As the closing hours approach the children gather the toys together, bring them to the matrons, aid in putting them away, and then form a line or a ring and file out of the gate one by one.

The parents are frequently visitors.[2]

Similar provision was made in New York City in 1889, through the initiative of two philanthropic women, at 50th Street and the North River; and again in 1891, at 99th Street and Second Avenue, under the auspices of the New York Society for Parks and Playgrounds. This play-

[2]Ellen M. Tower, "Play Grounds and Sand Gardens," in *World Wide*, April 26, 1902.

ground covering sixteen city lots, an area equivalent to about an acre, in a tenement district, was
supervised by a caretaker and equipped with
"apparatus for exercise, play, and comfort,"
consisting of "swings, see-saws, small wagons,
wheelbarrows, shovels, footballs, flags, drums,
banners, and a sand pile." Three additional
playgrounds were opened by this society.[3] Two
others were provided by settlements; one "under
a wisteria vine in the back yard of the Nurses'
Settlement on Henry Street in 1895"; the other,
somewhat larger, in the yard of the Union Settlement on South 104th Street, in 1896.

A sand garden type of playground was
opened at Hull-House, Chicago, in 1894, on land
donated by William Kent; in Philadelphia in
1893, when two playgrounds were opened, but
without supervision, by philanthropic people, and
again, through the co-operation of several societies including the Civic Club, the Culture Extension League, the College Settlement, and the City

[3]With the opening of the first playground by this society,
the movement in New York City received much local attention. "On Saturday, November 21, 1891, twenty-seven prominent Jewish Rabbis spoke before their congregations on the
need of playgrounds for children, and the next day one hundred clergymen preached on the same theme." A certain
newspaper cast discredit upon the work of this society, however, by claiming the movement as its own, endeavoring to
make capital of it; and only three additional playgrounds
were opened by it. Progress in New York was consequently
slower than that in Boston, Chicago, and Philadelphia during
the remainder of the last decade of the nineteenth century.
A revival of city-wide interest began in 1897 with the appointment of Mayor Strong's committee. The details of this
awakening of interest will be presented under the discussion
of the "model playground" stage.

Park Association in 1893-94;[4] and in **Providence, R. I.**, in 1894, under the auspices of the Union for Practical Progress and the Provident Free Kindergarten Association, after investigating what was done in Boston.

These five cities (Boston, New York, Chicago, Providence, and Philadelphia) are the only ones in which authentic reports[5] show provision for play to have been made during the period from 1885 to 1895; and in each instance the sand gar-

[4]Concerning the beginnings of permanent provision for play in Philadelphia, H. H. Buxton says: (Cf. E. B. Mero, *American Playgrounds*, p. 248) "The first meeting to consider the advisability of establishing playgrounds for children in the crowded districts was held in the winter of 1893 under the auspices of the City Park Association. The matter was kept before the public through the newspapers preceding a large meeting May 25, 1894. The City Park Association opened a playground that summer.

"June 12, 1894, the Woman's Christian Temperance Union petitioned the board of education to keep open public school playgrounds during the summer months. A similar petition was communicated to the board in February of the following year by the people who had been advocating playgrounds. Further efforts were made to get the board of education to favor the movement. The favor was finally secured and four grounds were opened during July and August, 1895, as an experiment. The result was favorable so that for the year 1897 the appropriation was increased from $1,000 to $3,000, thus insuring the growth and efficiency of the movement. In 1898 twenty-five playgrounds were maintained by the board of education with the aid of the Civic Club."

[5]According to statements published by the Playground and Recreation Association (Cf. *The Playground*, April, 1915, pp. 1 ff.), provision of an unspecified kind was made in Brooklyn in 1889 by the Brooklyn Society for Parks and Playgrounds, "on land donated for the purpose" and entailing for an uncertain time as much as "from $2,000 to $3,000, including the salary of a chief supervisor"; and in Golden Gate Park, San Francisco, in 1898. This latter provision did not include supervision, and the length of time during which it was maintained is not mentioned. After fruitless efforts, the writer is unable to verify either of these stated provisions. If they occurred, they must have been sporadic. The events in Brook-

den type was followed. This form of playground was also constructed in Pittsburgh in 1896; in Brooklyn, Baltimore, and Milwaukee in 1897; and in Cleveland, Minneapolis, and Denver in 1898. In the cities in which the movement began before 1895, it passed during these years into the second stage of its development.

An analysis of the structure and function of the play movement during the first stage of its development, as indicated by Table III, discloses the following characteristics: (1) provision only for children of pre-adolescent age; (2) maintenance during the vacation period, or July and August; (3) operation for only a portion of the day in three of the five cities involved in the movement at that time; (4) equipment for outdoor uses only, thus restricting service to that part of the year during which climatic conditions were favorable to outdoor play in sand and swings or upon see-saws; (5) location in densely populated sections of the city and on tenement courts, settlement or school yards, and parks in one city, while on vacant lots and school and settlement yards in the other four; (6) support by philanthropic societies and individuals, although using public land in four cities; (7) activities including both free and directed play, the latter being chiefly manual or folk and singing games

lyn seem to have occurred after 1897, since the committee conducting the City Park Playground in that year stated, "So far as we are aware, the City Park Playground is the first one to have been established in Brooklyn."—Cf. *Park Department Annual Report*, 1897.

TABLE III

A Comparative Analysis of the Structure and Function of Provision for Play in Boston, New York, Chicago, Providence, and Philadelphia Between 1885 and 1895

Cities	Age	Season	Period	Equipment	Location	Support	Activities	Motive
Boston	Under 12 years	July and August or during vacation	Generally afternoons	Sand pile, swings, see-saws, mostly*	Congested districts	Societies and individuals; Mass. Emerg'y & Hygiene Ass'n	Sand and apparatus, games, manual work, songs, toys†	To keep children off street and out of mischief and vice
New York City	Under 12 years	July and August or during vacation	Generally all day	Sand pile, swings, see-saws, mostly*	Tenement districts	Societies and individuals as Parks & Playgrounds Ass'n	Sand and apparatus, games, manual work, songs, toys†	To keep children off street and out of mischief and vice
Chicago	Under 12 years	July and August or during vacation	Generally all day	Sand pile, swings, see-saws, mostly*	Congested district	Hull-House and land donated by individuals	Sand and apparatus, games, manual work, songs, toys†	To keep children off street and out of mischief and vice
Providence	Under 12 years	July and August or during vacation	Generally afternoons	Sand pile, swings, see-saws, mostly*	Congested districts	Union for Practical Progress, Kindergarten Ass'n	Sand and apparatus, games, manual work, songs, toys†	To keep children off street and out of mischief and vice
Philadelphia	Under 12 years	July and August or during vacation	Generally afternoons	Sand-pile, swings, see-saws, mostly*	Congested districts	Societies and individuals: Civic Club, City Park Ass'n, etc.	Sand and apparatus, games, manual work, songs, toys†	To keep children off street and out of mischief and vice

*Outdoor only.   †Free play in sand and on apparatus.

adapted from kindergarten programs; (8) motive primarily to keep the children away from danger incident to play in the streets, by inducting them into activities designed to promote certain behavior.

A further analysis of the concept of the function of the play movement at this stage, discloses three explanations for the provision of the sand gardens common to each of the five cities. The first and most frequently mentioned reason for providing sand gardens was the belief that the streets were unsuited to play, since they were narrow, hot in summer, unclean, poorly surfaced for games, and even dangerous to the health, life and morals of children. Attention was called to the many accidents that happened to children at play in the streets. Parents, consequently anxious for the safety of their children while playing in the streets, welcomed the sand gardens in settlement yard, tenement court, or school grounds. A second explanation was the statement that children were frequently annoying, both to their parents and their neighbors, in their unsupervised activities on the street. They were often noisy, destroying property, and injuring one another. Consequently the sand court was accepted as a way of escape from childish disturbances. A typical statement of these two explanations is the following:

Both for the sake of the children and for the convenience and comfort of the community at large, such local pleasure grounds are essential. The children are thereby given resorts where they are safely engaged in their sports without danger to themselves or annoyance to others. The street is too often the only playground for the children of crowded neighborhoods throughout the entire metropolitan district. It is evident that such use of the street is inevitably attended by danger to life and limb, not to mention the equally serious moral dangers, while it is a source of discomfort and annoyance to the entire population.[6]

The third explanation, a corollary of the first and second, was a sense of the maladjustment of childlife to the social situation in congested districts of the cities, evidences of which were seen in the delinquent behavior of children. A good statement of this view was made by the committee on parks and playgrounds appointed by Mayor Strong of New York City.

In the original plan of the City of New York, the children seem to have been forgotten . . . . leaving the children no other place to play but in the public streets. . . . . A sense of hostility between children and the guardians of the public order had arisen, leading to the growth of a criminal class.[7]

They (the sand gardens of Boston in 1887) are maintained in the interest of hygiene and amusement. Though but a poor compensation for fields and flowers, they are full of enjoyment to the children who, without them, would have neither sand nor earth for dirt-pies and miniature forts.[8]

This third explanation accounts in large measure for the fact that the earliest provisions

[6]*Annual Report Metropolitan Park Commission*, Boston, 1893, p. 67.

[7]*Annual Report New York Park Department*, 1902, p. 12.

[8]*Annual Report of Massachusetts Emergency and Hygiene Association*, 1887, p. 18.

for play in each of the five cities were made by philanthropic societies and in connection with settlements.

The residents of social settlements could count the human cost, as few others could, of the failure to provide opportunities for wholesome play. They could not rest without doing something, however little, to meet the problem.[9]

The adjustment attempted by the play movement during its first stage of development was related to the welfare of little children. This was concerned with removing them from the physical and moral dangers of the streets, with ridding the community of the annoyance which their behavior caused, and with the reduction of delinquency among them, and was based upon two assumptions that were not questioned: first, the right of little children to wholesome play, and second, the absence of opportunities for them to do anything else (since they could no longer assist their parents at work, industry having become specialized and removed from the home).

B. *The "model playground" stage, 1895-1900.* While sand gardens were being established for the first time in Pittsburgh in 1896, in Brooklyn, Baltimore, and Milwaukee in 1897, and in San Francisco, Cleveland, Minneapolis, and Denver in 1898, the movement in Chicago, Philadelphia, New York, Boston, and Providence passed into a second stage of development inaugurated by the "model playground." This stage disclosed

[9]Graham R. Taylor, *Annals of American Academy of Political and Social Science,* March, 1910, p. 306.

for the first time, a criticism of the method of
providing for play in urban communities and
gave rise to a change in both the structure and
the concept of the function of the movement. It
was of short duration, experimental in nature,
and added several permanent traits. The "model
playgrounds" of each of the five cities in question are herewith described. A comparative
analysis is also made of their structure, of the
concept of their function, and of their permanent
contribution to the play movement in the United
States.

The first time that the term "model playground" was used seems to have been in connection with a provision made by Hull House, in
1894, on land donated for play use by Mr. William
Kent. It contained about three-quarters of an
acre, being 300 by 100 feet with an L approximately 50 by 50 feet. It was open to both children
and youths. The sand garden type of apparatus,
sand pile, swings, building blocks, and giant
stride, was provided for the children, while the
boys of adolescent age played handball and indoor
baseball.[10] An experienced kindergartner and a
policeman supervised the playground; the latter,
detailed by the city, usually umpired the indoor
baseball games.

[10]Indoor baseball was invented in Chicago as a substitute
for regular practice by professional ball teams during inclement weather. The ball used was a soft one about five
inches in diameter, thus adapting the game to the small
quarters of the average gymnasium. It has since been a great
favorite on all boys' playgrounds of small size.

Highly Organized Sand Garden, "Model Playground" Stage, Boston

[courtesy miss ellen m. tower]

In 1896 a similar and somewhat larger playground was started under the auspices of the Northwestern University Settlement. A police officer also directed the team games of the older boys. His action, however, was voluntary and was performed with a view to its value in maintaining order in the neighborhood. In June, 1898, the University of Chicago opened the third playground of this type in Chicago.[11] It was about the same size as the one at Hull House and contained fifty dollars worth of apparatus. It was supervised by a kindergartner and a policeman, the latter being wholly responsible after five o'clock. The grounds were kept open until nine o'clock. Children, youths, and adults attending this playground, for adults were encouraged by benches furnished for mothers, and games interesting the fathers on Sundays, made free use of a public bath house provided by the city and located across the street, and, during inclement weather, of an indoor gymnasium constructed at a cost of $9,000 and forming a part of the plant of the settlement. The season during which this playground was open extended from June 25 to October 1.

Simultaneous with the development of model playgrounds in Chicago, similar events charac-

[11]Other playgrounds, of the established sand-garden type, were opened about this time in Chicago. The West Side District of Associated Charities provided the first, on the Washington schoolyard in 1897. In 1898 the first public funds were appropriated by the city and amounted to $1,000. To this individuals added $750. Six schoolyard playgrounds were added under the auspices of the committee of women's clubs.

terized the movement in Philadelphia. The
work was begun by the Culture Extension League
organized in the spring of 1893, but which did
not decide to establish a "model playground"
until in the autumn of 1895. At that time, John
Dickenson Square, an undeveloped small park of
about three acres, was selected. The city authorities granted the league full control and
appropriated $5,000 for its equipment. Its struc-
ture contemplated an open circular area in the
center which was flooded for skating in winter and
used for team games during the remainder of the
year. Surrounding this central area was a bi-
cycle track fenced for safety, and outside of this
equipment, tennis courts, swings, parallel bars,
swinging rings, sand piles, and a music stand comprised the chief facilities for active outdoor play.
A promenade encircling the entire area so that
"mothers may wheel baby carriages," rows of
seats "to invite the visitor to rest," and "over-
hanging shade trees" completed the outdoor
equipment. For winter use two small buildings,
pavilion type and steam heated, were placed on
opposite sides of the play field. Two supervisors,
a man and a woman, were in charge. This playground was opened in 1898,[12] and was the most
completely equipped of its kind in the United

[12]Two sand gardens were opened, without supervision, in
Philadelphia under the auspices of philanthropic individuals
in 1893. In 1895 four school yards were equipped as sand
gardens and opened by the board of education, the city council appropriating $1,000. Cf. chap. iii, footnote 4.

States at that time. Commenting upon it, Tsanoff said:[13]

But what really counts is the use made of the playground, and the supervising care is to be intrusted to playground leaders. These teachers are to study the nature of the child and to so conduct the play as to guide the children and not unnecessarily restrain them. New games are to be invented, old ones revived, foreign ones introduced, and all necessary modifications made to answer the natural and growing taste of youth. A thorough co-operation with the home, the school, and the church is to be had for achieving the highest ends. The parents and the teachers in the neighborhood are to direct the children to the playground after school hours, and not let them drift into the streets as they do now. From the churches in the locality many are expected to come who will assist the teachers in playing with the children and exert their influence upon them. Thus the playground will become the center of delight, and of moral and social culture in the neighborhood.

The movement for provision for play in Providence, R. I., passed into the second stage of development in 1897. While sand gardens had been established three years earlier and "after investigating what was done in Boston," playgrounds of the "model" type were not constructed until 1897, after the public school authorities granted the use of several school yards and basement rooms in school houses. The Providence Free Kindergarten Association organized and maintained the work. Miss Helen P. Howell was appointed superintendent and given a staff containing fourteen kindergarten and primary

[13]Stoyan Vasil Tsanoff, "Children's Playgrounds," *Municipal Affairs*, 1898, p. 578.

teachers. Of the nine grounds opened, from July 7 to September 8, two were of the "model" type and provided for larger boys. One of these was equipped with gymnastic apparatus. This feature was probably copied from the Charlesbank Outdoor Gymnasium of Boston, since the beginnings of provision in Providence were preceded by an investigation of the plan being followed in that city. And while the term "model" was not used locally to describe these two playgrounds for adolescent boys, the fact of two provisions such as these is evidence of the recognition of their place in the concept of the function of the movement as it was understood in Providence at that time.

The first "model playground" in New York City became a fact on June 3, 1899, when the Outdoor Recreation League opened the Seward Park playground as a demonstration to the city. The events leading up to this experiment and the final completion of the park in its present form constitute perhaps the most dramatic chapter in the history of the play movement in the United States. They comprise, in large measure, the general anti-slum agitation, as Lee[14] has pointed out and of which Riis[15] has written. The origin of this effort to improve the tenement districts of New York dates from 1857, when a legislative committee inquired into their conditions. Nothing

[14]Joseph Lee, *Constructive and Preventive Philanthropy*, p. 164.

[15]Cf. Jacob Riis, *How the Other Half Lives*, and *A Ten Years' War*.

came of this inquiry and a new effort was begun in 1879. This resulted in the appointment of the Tenement House Commission in 1884. In 1887, an act of the legislature authorized the City of New York to spend $1,000,000 a year for the construction of "small parks," but it was not until 1894 that action was taken in the exercise of this power. That year, Mulberry Bend Park site was acquired. It contained two and one-half acres and cost $1,700,000. But while "the playground was assumed to be an essential part of the park," as stated by Mayor Hewitt, author of the law of 1887 under which the site was obtained, the commission in charge were content with merely securing a "breathing place" and no provision for play was made, nor has any been made there since that time. For a year, indeed, after the buildings were torn down, no further work was done and the unsightly spectacle of abandoned cellars partly filled with debris constituted the visible result of ten years of effort to improve the living conditions of the poor by providing public parks. When, in 1895, a wagon, parked in this open space as was the custom of the local teamsters, rolled into one of the cellars and injured some children playing about it, Jacob Riis was given the material for a newspaper story that aroused such a popular protest that the authorities were compelled to act. Mulberry Bend Park was then finished, but it contained only grass plots, bounded by intersecting concrete walks and dotted with signs bearing the warning "Keep off the Grass!" No space was allotted to children for play nor to youths for sports. Thus the first attempt in New York to provide facilities for the play of both children and youths ended in failure. Mulberry Bend Park was a "breathing place" only.

The second site to be acquired under the provision of the law of 1887 was located in the angle between Division and Canal streets, one of the most densely populated sections of the east side. It is now Seward Park. It comprises two and five-eighths acres and cost $1,800,000 for grounds alone. At the time the land was secured it contained five- and six-story tenement houses. In 1894 the commission recommended that these buildings be removed. Their recommendation became a law in 1895 and provided that the construction of the park should begin within three years. The grounds were not cleared, however, until 1898. Nine months more elapsed before the site was leveled suitable for play. By this time further work was prohibited by lack of public funds, although the plans of the Park Commission called for its ultimate development on lines similar to those followed in the construction of Mulberry Bend. The exact language used by the commission was:

These plans contemplate a small park in the natural style with lawns and shrubbery covering as large an area as possible.

The declaration aroused the Outdoor Recreation League which had been organized in 1898 and comprised nineteen societies. It wished to avert a repetition of the blunder of Mulberry Bend by demonstrating the value of a playground in this locality. At its own expense and guaranteeing to pay any costs that might accrue to the city through accidents involving damage suits, the league opened a "model playground" on June 3, 1899.[16] Outdoor apparatus and instructors were provided. The experiment was a success. Thousands of contributions of from one to five cents each were made by the residents of the neighborhood toward its maintenance. Still the park commissioners hesitated revising their plans, but under pressure they consented to devote one-tenth of the area to a playground. The friends of the children and youths of the neighborhood would not accept this decision and the commissioners finally yielded. Streets were closed, a stadium laid out, gymnasium and baths constructed, and the spring of 1903 saw completed a public playground costing over $2,000,000.

In addition to the provision of gymnastic apparatus and instructors, the experimental playground at Seward Park was characterized further by traits common to "model playgrounds," as indicated by the following:

At Seward Park, a great attraction, always surrounded by a large crowd of grown men, is the kindergarten platform. One of the matters about which the league has taken special

[16]Cf. Joseph Lee, *op. cit.*, pp. 164–167; *The Playground*, April, 1915, pp. 5–6; Chas. Zueblin, *American Municipal Progress*, pp. 298–300; Jacob Riis, *A Ten Years' War*, pp. 169 ff.

pains is to provide for the spectator, in order that fathers and mothers may come there, and that the playground may be a neighborhood affair, and not merely a place for boys. This is done with an eye also to loafers of the district, who can thus be all watched at once.[17]

Further significance of the "model playground" at Seward Park is disclosed by comparing its structure and function with contemporary provisions in the city. In this way, its superior adaptation is strikingly shown. While as many as seventy provisions were listed by the school committee in 1899, none were as complete as that at Seward Park. Among them were thirty-one schoolyard playgrounds of the sandgarden type and under the administration of the school committee. Of these, ten were conducted as vacation schools in the forenoons, the control of vacation schools having been taken over from the Association for Improving the Condition of the Poor, in the previous year. Other forms of provision were:

Five open air gymnasiums, five "kindergarten tents," six recreation piers, three "sand gardens with kindergarten games," in Central park, seven roof gardens, ten swimming baths, and six "evening play centers."[18]

The Outdoor Recreation League taught the park commission how to construct the small parks,[19] as it demonstrated to the entire city a method of adjustment which comprised a more adequate provision for outdoor activities of both

[17]Joseph Lee, *op. cit.*, p. 175.
[18]*Ibid.*, p. 127.
[19]*Ibid.*, p. 175.

youths and children, and made a place for adults as spectators.

In the last city to be studied in this section, Boston, three events must be considered: the Charlesbank Outdoor Gymnasium of 1889-91, the purchase of Franklin Field in 1894, and the North End Park playground opened in April of 1900. Of these three provisions, the first fulfilled the requirements of a model playground as far as equipment and supervision were concerned, but was limited somewhat in activities and was not used as an experimental agency. The second was without supervision except that which police alone gave to it, and was limited in both equipment and activities since it contained no facilities for little children and was devoted exclusively to team games. It may be compared to the Washington Park "meadow," Chicago, described above in the discussion relative to the origin of the play movement. The third event, however, was a conscious attempt to provide a model playground with respect to equipment, supervision, and activities. It was conducted under the auspices of the Massachusetts Civic League. It contained three sections: one for the children of pre-adolescent age known as "the children's corner," and one each for the older girls and older boys. The structure and the concept of its function are graphically described by the committee in charge as set forth in the annual report of the League for 1901.[20]

[20]Cf. *Annual Report of Massachusetts Civic League*, 1901.

There is a wooden shelter with a bench for the mothers and two sand boxes, each six by twelve feet, four swings (to which we have recently added two teeter ladders), a number of carts, and material for kindergarten work, sewing and cutting out.

For the older girls the teachers have introduced besides sewing, baseball, and a number of other lively games.

Chiefly as a means of attracting the boys to the playground, we have had put in by the Naraganset Machine Co., at a cost of $150.00, the following gymnastic apparatus: two horizontal bars, three teeter ladders, two sets of flying rings, two trapezes; and at each end there is a slanting ladder and a pair of slanting poles. These last seem to be, if anything, the most used, a continuous procession of boys climbing up the ladders and sliding down the poles from early in the morning until dark.

Further analysis of the structure and the concept of the function of this playground discloses the following facts distinguishing it. It sought to develop a spirit of loyalty in the youths through team games, emphasizing indoor baseball, while it aimed at being a neighborhood playground, by interesting the men in quoits and handball. The latter was very popular with the longshoremen who lived in the neighborhood. It attempted, furthermore, to determine what type of equipment was best suited to playground purposes, making use of traveling and swinging rings, climbing ladders and sliding poles, horizontal and parallel bars, among other pieces of apparatus. It attempted to classify games according to the ages of those attending the playground and organized inter-scholastic competition between teams representing the various grammar schools of the neighborhood. In administering this work, it required certificates of good standing in deportment and scholarship of all competitors and awarded the prizes to the schools rather than to individuals. It encouraged class work on the gymnastic apparatus. It made use of quiet games and construction work including gardens, of which 400, of about two and one-half feet width and eight feet length, were placed along two of the sides of the playground.

An analysis of the facts relative to the "model playground" stage of the movement as presented in Table IV discloses a change in both the structure and the concept of the function of the movement. Provision is made for participation by youth as well as childhood, in each of the five cities, and either participation or spectatorship by adults is encouraged in all but one of the cities. Instructors with training are employed in each city, but activities are limited, as in the previous stage, to physical and manual or constructive interests. An effort seems to have been made in each city to discover what equipment, including both extent of area and apparatus, supervision, and activities were appropriate. As expressed by a contemporary observer and writer:[21]

The ascertaining of precisely what supervision is necessary or desirable, and what apparatus and what methods are most effective, is the function of the model playgrounds of which a number exist.

[21] J. Lee, *Constructive and Preventive Philanthropy*, p. 172.

TABLE IV

A Comparison of "Model Playgrounds" in Chicago, Philadelphia, Providence, New York, and Boston, Between 1894 and 1900*

Characteristics—	Cities				
	Chicago	Philadelphia	Providence	New York	Boston
Dates of establishment	1894	1895–98	1897	1899	1900
Under philanthropic control	x	0	x	x	x
On private grounds....	x	0	0	0	0
On public school yards.	0	x	x	0	0
On public park grounds	0	x	0	x	x
Including sand gardens	x	x	x	x	x
Containing provision for youths	0	x	x	x	x
Encouraging attendance by men and women	x	x	0	x	x
Open throughout the year	0	0	0	x	x
With apparatus for children only........	x	x	0	0	0
With apparatus for youths and adults....	0	x	x	x	x
Connected with schools, either on grounds or in activities	0	x	x	0	x
Having or using indoor equipment in summer or winter	x	x	x	0	0
Supervised by trained instructors	x	0	x	x	x
Assisted in supervision by special police, detailed	x	0	0	0	0
Organizing team game competition, local or extra mural	x	x	0	x	x
Providing for other than physical activities, as construction work, gardening	x	x	x	x	x

*Plans for a model playground were formulated by the Park Board of Louisville in 1899 although the playground in question was not completed until the following year and then partook of the nature of the "small park" stage of the structure and organization of the play movement. The plans called for a division of the grounds into two spaces, the one to contain a children's playground with wading pool and shelter house, the other a grass covered "play field" surrounded by a macadamized walk. While other "model playgrounds" were conducted upon public lands, this one had the distinction of having received financial support as well from public funds. For this reason it was more of an experiment than a demonstration.

In carrying out the attempt to solve these problems, four conclusions were reached for the first time in the evolution of the play movement: first, that play has an educational value as well as a recreational or amusement benefit upon the participant; second, that facilities for youths as well as children should be provided on the same site; third, that provision for the play of both children and youths should be made throughout the year, although the concept of indoor equipment was not developed; and fourth, that provision for play must be made by public, not philanthropic resources.

As stated by another contemporary writer:[22]

It (the model playground) means open spaces of sufficient area under the management of proper instructors, and equipped with all the means of attracting, invigorating, and guiding the youth of a community or neighborhood in their open air enjoyments during the whole year.

The inquiry concerning the nature of supervision, equipment, and activities requisite to adequate provision for play, constituted the first motive of the model playground. A second motive was that of awakening the interest of municipal officials and of demonstrating to them the form of provision for play best adapted to the needs of children and youths. This explanation is given in one of the Massachusetts Civic League reports:[23]

[22]S. V. Tsanoff, "Children's Playgrounds," *Municipal Affairs*, 1898, pp. 578 f.

[23]*Annual Report of Massachusetts Civic League*, 1901.

Our object is to get the city to introduce similar work in all the public playgrounds; our function being merely to carry the work through the experimental stage.

In another report of the League, expression of both the first and second purposes given above is made as follows:[24]

In short, among city children, brought up as they have been without playgrounds, the forces of anarchy are stronger than the forces of order; such children are unable, accordingly, to use even such playgrounds as are provided unless some supervision is provided with them. To show what can be done by proper supervision in the way of making a playground useful to the children, and by so doing to bring about public supervision of all our city playgrounds, is the object of the work of this committee.

C. *The "small park" stage, 1900–5.* A third stage in the evolution of the play movement in the United States is disclosed by the construction of "small parks" and "squares" varying in area from three to ten acres, equipped with outdoor gymnastic apparatus, ball diamonds, athletic fields, comfort stations, and occasionally pavilions, and beautified by trees, shubbery and lawns after the manner of the structure of the municipal parks of their day. Any discussion of their structure and function is incomplete if their relation to the origin and purpose of the city parks of the United States is not considered, since the "small parks" were adaptations of "park service" to the changed social situation in urban communities at the close of the nineteenth century under the initiative of the play movement.

[24]*Annual Report of Massachusetts Civic League,* 1901.

Municipal parks in the United States developed from the town commons of Colonial times. While the primary purpose of the commons was pasturage, their recreational uses by the youths for team games, by the militia for the October "training,"[25] and by the village folk for various gatherings on holidays, date from their founding. During the nineteenth century, the term "sport field" came to describe that portion of the commons, which had then become city parks, in which team games were permitted. Gradually, however, as the congestion of population in the cities increased, the ratio of park area to numbers of population became less and the traditional uses of the parks for play were more and more restricted. During the last quarter of the century, the refusal of all privilege of playing upon the "green," the only vestige of the commons, in the parks was threatened. The concept of the function of the park had changed. Horticulture had largely displaced "sports" in the parks as the "sport field" had succeeded the "pastures" of the commons. Trees and shubbery, flowers and lagoons, walks and carriage drives occupied an increasing proportion of park area. Placards, reading "Keep off the Grass," "protected" the lawns. The majority of the parks became "breathing places," where, as Jacob Riis wittingly remarked, "one could do little else."[26] This

[25]Joseph Lee, *Constructive and Preventive Philanthropy*, p. 123.

[26]Jacob Riis, *A Ten Years' War, supra.*

concept of "park service" explains why most of the sand gardens and model playgrounds[27] were constructed upon private lands, such as settlement and mission chapel yards or vacant lots, or upon schoolyards, all of which were usually barren and unattractive, instead of in the shady nooks or inviting "meadows" of the parks.

The experience gained in the conduct of model playgrounds, however, give rise both to a new concept of playground equipment and function on the one hand, and to a changed idea of "park service" upon the other: the "small park idea." This plan of adjustment involved a correlation of park and playground structure and function. The former regained its traditional uses, while the latter was given aesthetic development.

The prototype of the "small park" was the Charlesbank Outdoor Gymnasium constructed in Boston in 1889-91. This was the first attempt in the United States in playground landscaping[28] as it was the earliest conscious effort by a park board to provide primarily for play uses. A narrow strip of unsightly river bank, ten acres in extent, and bordered on the land side by a slum section of the city containing two horse stables, a foundry, a factory, a saloon, a blacksmith-shop, a restaurant, a lumber-yard, the Suffolk jail, the Massachusetts General Hospital, and a few tene-

[27]Cf. the discussion of "sand garden" and "model playground" stages above, chap. iii, A, B.

[28]A. and L. Leland, "*Playground Technique and Playcraft,*" p. 59.

Tennis Players, Washington Park, Chicago
[COURTESY SOUTH PARK COMMISSIONERS]

ments and cheap rooming houses, was made into a small park containing outdoor gymnasiums for men and women, respectively, at opposite ends, with trees, shrubbery and lawn between and about the spaces allotted to play. The fence enclosing the women's gymnasium was concealed by shubbery. A decade passed, however, before this type of park, or playground, was copied in other cities, with the exception of Boone Park Playground, Louisville, Kentucky, which was designed by the same landscape architects, the Olmstead Brothers, in 1892, although New York had passed an enabling act permitting the purchase of land for park purposes two years prior to the construction of the Charlesbank Outdoor Gymnasium. But nothing was done in New York toward taking advantage of this act until 1895, because of lack of public opinion to support it. In the language of a member of the city administration in response to the inquiry of Jacob Riis as to why the legislation had not been enforced, "No one down here seems to take any interest in it."[29] This remark, however, furnished Riis with his text for the newspapers, and public opinion was soon formed upon the question.

The "small parks" of New York originated in conjunction with the general anti-slum agitation in that city. Their development, however, was directed by the play movement, while they in turn added features of permanent value to

[29]Jacob Riis, *A Ten Years' War, supra.*

both the structure and the concept of the function of the playground. As a result of the work of the Tenement House Commission in 1884, model tenements were constructed and sanitary regulations were introduced, but it was over a decade before it came to be realized that tenements must be destroyed, "not to make way for other tenements, even though they might be 'models,' but for playgrounds"[30] of the "small park" type.

This adjustment was proposed in 1887, when the State Legislature authorized the expenditure of $1,000,000 a year for the acquirement of land for "small parks" in lower New York. But eight years passed before land for the first park was acquired. Two years were consumed in filing a map of the proposed park according to law, and eight, in condemning forty-one pieces of property. When in 1895, this park, Mulberry Bend, was finally finished, however, it contained no facilities for play as stated above.[31] The prevailing ideal of a city park, "a breathing place" wherein the urban dweller could "rest the eyes" by viewing "natural beauty" of trees and shrubbery, lawn and flowers, prevented the first "small park" in New York from being equipped for play uses. But before improvements had been made upon land secured for the second one, the influence of the play movement was beginning to be felt and the concept of the "small park" was changed. The

[30]Cf. Charles Zueblin, *American Municipal Progress*, p. 298.
[31]Cf. discussion of Mulberry Bend Park above.

"model playground" conducted by the Outdoor
Recreation League upon the site for the second
"small park" during the summer of 1899 proved
so popular with the people of the neighborhood
that the society was able to induce the Park Department to accept its plan of improvements which
included extensive facilities for outdoor play.
Similar improvements for other sites were also
agreed to by the department as lands were
acquired, so that by 1902, the construction of the
first four "small parks," proposed or in process,
was described in the annual report for that year
as follows:[32]

In Hamilton Fish Park, located at Houston,
Stanton, and Sheriff Streets, containing 3.67
acres, and in which, "through co-operation with
the Department of Education, a playground, kindergarten, and (outdoor) gymnasium were operated during the summer" (of 1902), the proposed plan of development included,

The construction of a running track, kindergarten
grounds, the erection of an ornamental iron fence around the
playgrounds and a pipe iron fence around the lawns, the
asphalting of the plaza in front of the building, reshaping the
grounds, spreading the garden mold, sodding, preparation of
tree plots, remodeling of the public comfort station, the
removal of existing connections with street water mains and
properly capping the pipes, and the laying out of a gymnasium and equipment of the same with parallel bars, swinging rings, vaulting horses, and other apparatus.[33]

[32]*Annual Report, Department of Parks*, City of New York,
1902, pp. 35–45.
[33]*Ibid.*

In De Witt Clinton Park, Fifty-second to Fifty-fourth Streets, Eleventh Avenue, and the Hudson River, containing 7.37 acres, and in which ''a tent was erected for nature study classes and a plot of ground was set aside for children's gardens'' during the summer of 1902, since the buildings had only been removed during the spring of that year and no appropriations had yet been made for further improvements, the plan for development contemplated,

The construction of playgrounds, gymnasiums, farm gardens, and a park building to contain comfort stations and shower baths, all to be constructed upon lines now recognized as producing the very best results for small parks in crowded sections of large cities, ... at an estimated cost of $200,000.[34]

In Thomas Jefferson Park, One-hundred and Eleventh, One-hundred and Fourteenth Streets, First Avenue, and East River, a site which had been acquired in 1900, and in which, during the summer of 1902, the park department had ''erected a number of large tents, placed settees and other park fittings upon the grounds, laid out a baseball diamond, and opened the whole for temporary use during the heated term,'' the plan of development comprised,

Laying out the lands in playgrounds, outdoor gymnasiums, running tracks, walks and lawns, and a fine park building to contain shower baths and comfort stations.

In William H. Seward Park, Canal, Hester, Suffolk, and Division Streets, a site which was

[34]*Annual Report, Department of Parks,* City of New York, 1902, pp. 35–45.

acquired in 1897 and in which the memorable "model playground" was conducted by the Outdoor Recreation League in 1899, "the laying out of a children's playground, a gymnasium ground, a nine lap track, lawns, walks, and drainage was practically completed in 1902," while the most elaborate equipment up to that time was completed in the following year, enabling the people to "celebrate May Day, 1903, in a public playground,"[35] a "play park" as well as a "small park." Speaking of the improvement of this park, while it was still in the process of completion, the park department said:

A splendid park building to contain bathing facilities, locker rooms, comfort stations, and other features will be begun early in 1903.

In laying out this park the Department was confronted with the proposition of devoting a large part of the area to playground purposes and still preserving the usual park features.

The pavilion in William H. Seward Park will be a structure 138 feet long and 50 feet wide, the main floor consisting of a large recreation room or a playground. It will also serve as a shelter to view the games in the park, and will be separated from the street by offices and retiring rooms. The portion facing the park will be approached by a wide flight of steps and terraces.

On the main floor will be built public comfort stations at either end, for men and women, and baths, twenty-one baths for women and thirty for men. The stalls to separate the baths will be of marble, the floors and walls will be tiled and special care will be given to proper ventilation. The water will descend at an angle from each shower bath and each

[35]Charles Zueblin, *American Municipal Progress*, 1916, p. 300.

bathroom will be divided into two compartments, providing a small dressing room. This type of bath is believed to be the most sanitary, and it will permit the greatest number of people to bathe at a given time with the least expense for attendants.

The building will also contain a cellar, in which will be the boilers, hot-water tanks, coal vaults and storage-room for materials used in the park.

The building is a light arcaded structure, constructed of brick with terra cotta arches resting on polished granite columns. The color is very light gray. It is arranged so that in the winter time temporary sash enclosures may be erected, permitting the building to be used throughout the entire year.

The (outdoor) gymnasium will be equipped with an iron pipe frame 80 feet long, 20 feet wide and 16 feet high, attached to which will be portions of the apparatus, such as climbing poles and ropes and inclined poles, chest bars, traveling rings and flying rings; also with parallel bars, horizontal and peak ladders, captive tennis balls, merry-go-rounds or giant strides, basket balls and goals and other apparatus. On the playground smaller apparatus, such as the giant strides, teeter ladders, balance beams, captive tennis balls, large and small swings, sand courts, croquet sets, golf and shinner sticks and a round football will be installed.

The detailed statement above of the proposed plan for the completion of William H. Seward Park, discloses the concept of the function and structure of the play movement during the "small park" stage of its evolution. While relating to New York, it was typical of the developments in seven other cities also, notably Boston, Louisville, Chicago, St. Paul, Canandaigua and Rochester, N. Y., and Philadelphia. The more important events in the evolution of the play movement in these cities will now be cited as evidence that the "small park" concept of the structure and function of both parks and playgrounds as developed in New York, was not peculiar to that city, although in some respects it was more highly elaborated and more expensively provided, but on the contrary, it was sufficiently general and permanent to represent a stage in the evolution of the play movement in the United States.

In addition to Boone Park playground of 1892, the pioneer attempt to build a "small park" in Louisville described above,[36] by duplicating in a measure the Charlesbank Outdoor Gymnasium of Boston of 1889-91, and as an outgrowth of the "model playground" planned for Louisville in 1899, also described previously,[37] three "small parks" were completed shortly after 1900. Their names, dates of construction and plan of equipment are respectively as follows:

Triangle Park, a modification of the "model playground" of the same name of 1899, was completed in 1900 at a cost of approximately $55,000 exclusive of its site. The equipment comprised a children's playground, a shelter house containing comfort stations and one centrally located play room, a wrought iron picket fence enclosing the grounds, a generous number of trees, shrubs planted about the edges of the park, and a wading pool. This was the first instance of the incorporation of a wading pool in a "small park."

[36]Earlier in this chapter.
[37]Consult footnote to Table IV, p. 68.

A "park guard" acted as supervisor of the grounds.

Central Park, modification of a public park of the traditional type which had been maintained for several years by the Park Department on the Dupont estate and that became the most elaborate of the Louisville "small parks," was begun in 1900. The site contained fifteen acres formerly the grounds of a private residence. It was thickly covered with an old grove of elm and other shade trees and was located in the residential district. On the one side dwelt a foreign population in what was popularly known as "the Cabbage Patch," while on the other side were American families in many of the most expensive homes of the city. A referendum measure authorizing the expenditure of $90,000 toward improvements was approved by the voters in 1900. Although several years were consumed in establishing its legality, the question was finally decided favorably by the supreme court of the State. Here, as in New York, a recreation league recently formed was instrumental in securing the success of the approval and defense of the referendum measure. The plan proposed by the park department in 1900 for the construction of Central Park included: open air men's and women's gymnasiums, the former containing a running track; a children's playground with a sand court and a wading pool, a central plot for games and the usual swings and teeters; a field house containing comfort stations, and a shelter house from which attractive pergolas extended on opposite sides, and many trees and shrubs enclosing lawns and plots encircled by graceful walks.

Baxter Square, opened in 1900, was the third of the group completed during this stage of the movement, in Louisville. It contained two acres, was designed primarily for small children, and was supervised by a "park guard." It was enclosed by an iron picket fence inside of which shrubbery and trees were planted and a macadamized walk was placed. The equipment comprised a wading pool, and a central grass plot with the usual apparatus for child play.

One general provision made in connection with the "small parks" in 1901, was the appointment of a supervisor of playgrounds assisted by a man and a woman instructor at each park.

A society known as the Small Parks Association was formed in Philadelphia in 1888. The original object of this organization was similar to that of the Metropolitan Public Gardens Association of London which was formed in 1884, because of the familiarity of some of Philadelphia's leading women with the work of that association. Consequently "small parks" for play purposes were not contemplated at first, although this concept of their function was eventually accepted as a result of the influence of the development of the play movement upon the City Parks Association, successor to the Small Parks Association. The two events having the most direct influence were the equipment of Waterview Park in Germantown for play purposes by the Twenty-second Ward Branch of the Civic Club in 1903, and, of Starr Garden, an unimproved city square, by the Starr Center in 1904. The latter enterprise was "the first step toward the Municipal Recreation Park, which now occupies that site at Seventh and Lombard Streets."[38] This "small park" was not completed, however, until July 8, 1911, although the Playground Association supported a playground on this site during the interval. A Public Playgrounds Commission, created on May 27, 1909, assumed control of all private playgrounds in October, 1910, "and let contracts for the construction of the First Municipal Recreation Building at Starr Garden Park."[39] Thus, Philadelphia lagged behind New York and Louisville but eventually surpassed them in elaborate indoor equipment in her "small parks." In the discussion of the succeeding stage in the evolution of the play movement, the development of these "recreation parks," as they have been known in Philadelphia, will be described.

While the city of Boston did valuable pioneering work in the development of the playground parks fully a decade before the play movement in other cities attained the "small park" stage,

[38]*Annual Report of the Board of Recreation of Philadelphia*, 1913, pp. 30–31.
[39]*Ibid.*

as disclosed by the construction of the Charlesbank Outdoor Gymnasium in 1889–91, subsequent
events related to and contemporary with those
of the cities studied in this section necessitate
consideration here in order to complete the survey of this period herewith presented. These
events comprise two groups of facts: first, those
pertaining to the provision of other parks similar
to that of Charlesbank and the work of the Metropolitan Park Commission appointed in 1892; and
second, those involved in the development of public baths and indoor gymnasiums.

The multiplication of the "small parks,"
"squares," and "open air gymnasiums" was
made by the Board of Park Commissioners of
the City in harmony with the recommendations
made by the Metropolitan Park Commission (appointed by the Governor of the State) in its first
annual report, 1893, in which fourteen pages were
devoted to a discussion of plans for the development of various sites. By 1905 there were several
"small parks" of the "open air gymnasiums"
type and of the children's playground type being
administered by the Board of 'Park Commissioners of the city.

The provision of shower baths and swimming
pools, however, was made by a separate department of the city government called the Bath Department, organized in 1897. During 1903 this
department maintained seven beach baths, one
river bath, two swimming pools, nine floating

baths, five gymnasiums, and the Dover Street bath house, an experimental building containing free baths for men and women throughout the year, the second of its kind in the United States (the first having been built in Milwaukee, in 1890). In 1899, work was begun on the first public indoor gymnasium, that of South Boston.

While events relative to the development of "small parks" in Chicago between 1900 and 1905 do not disclose the construction of playgrounds that compare with the "small parks" of New York, Louisville, or Boston, they precipitated results that outdistanced the recreational attainments of those cities and ushered into the play movement another stage in its evolution.[40] They must be considered then in connection with a discussion of the achievement of other cities during this period because of their relation to those events and their contribution to subsequent developments, both in Chicago and elsewhere.

A Special Park Commission was appointed by Mayor Harrison in the autumn of 1899, as a result of the agitation for playgrounds of the "small park" type that had begun as an outgrowth of the publication of a report prepared by the Municipal Science Club the preceding spring. This commission was composed of nine aldermen and six private citizens. The objects of this committee were three: (1) to establish municipal playgrounds in the congested sections of the city

[40] Reference is here made to the "recreation center" stage developed in the subsequent section, D, this chapter.

as rapidly as finances permited; (2) to study the
need of playgrounds in these districts and disclose ways for meeting those needs; and (3) to
study the three park boards of the city with a view
to defining their relation to the play and recreational problems of the community.

In carrying out its first object, the commission
established five playgrounds in 1900 and assumed
charge of the numerous small parked areas within
the city limits, such as triangles formed at street
intersections and squares, since the large parks
of the city were as now under the jurisdiction of
the South, West, and Lincoln Park Boards, respectively.

The annual appropriations for the work of
this commission for the first five years were as
follows: 1900, $11,500; 1901, $10,000; 1902, $15,-
000; 1903, $20,000; 1904, $20,000; 1905, $23,000.[41]

In seeking to achieve the second and third
objects, the commission disclosed the inefficiency
of recreational opportunities provided by the
three park systems of that time because of the
inaccessibility and insufficiency of the parked
areas. It pointed out, that one-third of the total
population of the city lived more than a mile from
any of the large parks and could make slight
use of play facilities should any be installed
therein; and, that those sections which were most
deficient in park space were also those in which
population was most congested. It was in those

[41]Proc. of Playground Association of America, Vol. II,
p. 256.

neglected sections that the five municipal playgrounds of 1900 were located, and the ultimate object of their operation was to develop public opinion that would demand the creation of permanent playgrounds of the "small park" type by the three park systems of the city.

"The way in which one part of the city is favored at the expense of another," said a contemporary writer, "may be best indicated by observing that the eleven wards which contain the bulk of the park and boulevard system include 1,814 acres of park space, the population being about 425,000; this means 234 people to each acre of park space. The remaining twenty-three wards of the city with a population of over a million contain 228 acres of parks or 4,720 people to each acre of park space. This second division includes, of course, some sparsely settled districts, where the need for parks is not so great; if we were to compare, however, the eleven favored wards with eleven wards along the river, we should find the proportion even more startling.

"It is in this large, neglected area that the municipal playgrounds have been established, which it is hoped are but the beginning of an extended movement in favor of small parks and possibly a central boulevard system connecting the river districts with the outer zone of boulevards and parks."[42]

That the Special Park Commission was successful in attaining its second and third objectives is indicated by the following admissions by the president of the largest park system, the first to respond to the recommendations made concerning the creation of additional playgrounds of the "small park" type.

[42]Charles Zueblin, "Municipal Playgrounds in Chicago," *American Journal of Sociology*, Sept., 1898, pp. 145–58; Cf. A. W. Beilfuss, "Municipal Playgrounds in Chicago," *Proc. of Playground Association of America*, Vol. II, pp. 255–63.

Each of these bodies (the three park boards in Chicago) has received suggestions as to small parks from the Special Park Commission, a city organization which has established (1905) nine small playgrounds for children and has studied general local park needs.

The first step taken toward the present park expansion was to amend the Illinois law which permitted additions to recreation area only contiguous to existing parks and boulevards. Since 1869 (the date of the establishment of the three park boards of Chicago) new centers of population have developed. The great stockyards district, with 100,000 people (1900) was without park facilities. The region of Englewood with more than 150,000; the great manufacturing district of the Calumet region, with a population of 100,000; and the congested river wards of the West and North Sides, were all without parks.

When the statute had been amended by the Illinois General Assembly of 1903, the people authorized Chicago Park Boards to spend $6,500,000 for new parks.

The South Park Commissioners were the first to act.[43]

Thus in Chicago, as in Louisville and the three eastern cities discussed above, the play movement attained the "small park" stage of structure and the concept of its function, although the full significance of the evolution in idea both of park and playground service did not become apparent here until after 1905 when the first of the "small parks" were completed and open to use. While the park boards were slower to act than those of Boston, New York, or Louisville, they made excellent use of the experience gained by those cities and eclipsed their highest achievements in play provision. This will be shown in

[43]Henry G. Foreman, "Chicago's New Park Service," *Century Magazine*, Feb., 1903, pp. 610–20.

detail in the discussion of the "recreation center" stage of the play movement to follow; but it is sufficient for the establishment of the proposition discussed in this section to note that the "small park" idea of provision for play dominated the play movement in Chicago between 1900 and 1905.

Before entering upon a study of the motives that gave rise to the "small park" stage, there is further evidence of the nature and extent of the "small parks" to be seen in the developments in St. Paul in 1904, in Denver in 1908, and in Canandaigua and Rochester, New York. The parks developed in the latter two cities were among the best examples of playground landscaping of the period. In the former two, while action was modeled after park developments in Louisville, the playgrounds themselves would not compare favorably with those of any of the cities studied.

TABLE V

A STUDY OF THE CONCEPT OF THE FUNCTION OF THE PLAY MOVEMENT DURING THE "SMALL PARK" STAGE OF ITS DEVELOPMENT AS SHOWN BY SEVEN CITIES

Motives giving rise to the "small parks"	New York	Louisville	Philadelphia	Boston	Chicago	Canandaigua	Rochester
Greater utility of parked spaces	x	x	x	x	x	x	x
Increase in parks and playgrounds in congested sections of cities	x	x	x	x	x	0	0
Recognition of municipal support of playgrounds.	x	x	x	x	x	x	x
Desire to beautify playgrounds by landscaping or parking..	x	x	x	x	x	x	x

An analysis of Table V discloses at least four motives that were common to all of the cities in which "small parks" were provided, or proposed, during the period between 1900 and 1905: (1) that public parks should be open to the play and recreational uses of the people; (2) that their number and area should be adequate and their location accessible to the homes of the city; (3) that playgrounds should be provided at least in part by municipal support and control; (4) that playgrounds should be attractive by virtue of their shade, lawns, flowers, as well as play apparatus, and thus stimulate the aesthetic appreciation of the public.

The first three motives are disclosed by the following statement from the annual report of the park department of New York:

The principal feature of park work in the boroughs of Manhattan and Richmond (congested areas) during the year of 1902 has been the development of playgrounds and kindergartens and the extension of the recreation areas in the larger parks. Playgrounds are being constructed in four new parks in crowded sections of the city, and an effort is being made to build these parks upon lines recognized as best accomplishing the purposes for which the lands were acquired.

The fourth motive is expressed by contemporary observers and writers, such as the following three statements from advocates, landscape architects, or playground administrators:

To my mind the whole playground conception has heretofore been wrong. We have taken as our ideal a bare city lot equipped with paraphernalia for children's exercise. The truer ideal would be an acre or so of natural looking country, which we should create if necessary, with "the flowers of the fields and blossoms of the woods" and "pleasant waters" —a chance for the city child to know the delights of a real outdoors, of a place where in the night there might be fairies, as there never would be in the ordinary city playground.[44]

The time is rapidly coming when we will no longer consent to accept as a suitable place for a playground, a ground that is not beautiful as well as fully equipped with apparatus and playground material.[45]

It had never occurred to us that any defense for beautifying the playground was necessary. We had always supposed that the reason why many of them were not beautiful was on account of lack of money rather than absence of desire. . . . . The first playground we ever saw was Columbus Avenue, Boston, which at that time was a desolate waste of cinders without a tree or speck of green upon it. Our impression was that if we should be obliged to play there it would have to be under compulsion.[46]

TABLE VI

AN ANALYSIS OF THE STRUCTURE AND ORGANIZATION OF THE "SMALL PARK" STAGE OF THE PLAY MOVEMENT AS SHOWN BY THE SEVEN CITIES STUDIED

Features added to sand garden stage. 1900-05	New York	Louisville	Philadelphia	Boston	Chicago	Canandaigua	Rochester
An open space for athletics.	x	x	x	x	0	x	x
A "field" house or "shelter".	x	x	x	x	x	x	x
Aesthetic treatment of site.	x	x	x	x	0	x	x
A wading pool.	0	x	0	0	0	0	0
Shower baths.	x	0	0	x	0	0	0
Area increased.	x	x	x	x	x	x	x

[44]Charles Mulford Robinson, "Landscape Gardening for Playgrounds," paper read at second annual meeting of Playground Association of America.

[45]George D. Chamberlain, address at second annual meeting of Playground Association of America.

[46]A. and L. Leland, *Playground Technique and Playcraft*, Doubleday Page and Co., New York, 1913, p. 54.

D. *The "recreation center" stage, 1905-12.*
The "recreation centers" in the public parks and
the "social centers" in the schools were the first
attempts in the evolution of the play movement
to make provision for all ages of people throughout the year, in indoor as well as outdoor activities. The former type of provision developed
the "field house"; the latter, "the wider use of
the school plant." Incidentally each involved
provision for more varied forms of play than was
made in either of the three preceding stages of
the movement. To the manual play of the "sand
gardens" and the physical and manual activities
of the "model playgrounds" were added three
other types, namely, (1) the social, including
convivial expressions of the gregarious instinct,
such as parties, dances, clubs; (2) the aesthetic,
including story telling, dramatics, both junior and
senior, choral and instrumental musical societies
and programs; and (3) the civic, comprising
lectures on public questions, health exhibits, and
the holding of elections in some of the recreation
centers, especially the "social centers" in the
public schools.

With the wider field of activities came a more
adequate equipment. In Chicago, the "small
park" agitation resulted in the evolution of the
most complete type of physical structure, comprising areas of 10 to 60 acres, fully equipped
with outdoor gymnasiums after the Charlesbank
plan, athletic fields after the Franklin field type,

swimming pools of a new design, and the most elaborate form of fieldhouse of the period containing indoor gymnasiums for both men and women, an assembly hall, two to four clubrooms, a lunchroom, and a branch of the public library. In Los Angeles, somewhat less elaborate facilities were constructed, but these contained all of the essential features of the Chicago plan. Here the word "clubhouse" was used to describe the building. In Boston, the "gymnasium" was developed in some instances; in others, the "public baths" in place of the "fieldhouse or clubhouse." In Rochester, the public school plant was utilized, slight alterations of a more or less temporary nature being made at first. Later, as the idea gained in favor, a change in the architecture of school buildings throughout the United States resulted; assembly halls, indoor gymnasiums, swimming pools, clubrooms, and kitchens being added to the traditional plan. Chicago, Los Angeles, Boston, and Rochester each developed a distinct method of providing "recreation centers." They were the four pioneering cities of the period.

The "recreation center" stage, then, was essentially a turning point in the play movement. Its scheme of equipment, activities, supervision, and support was a culmination of preceding stages and fundamental to all later developments. It was a more accurate answer to the questions that gave rise to "model playgrounds," namely, what supervision, equipment, activities should the playground comprise, as it was the matrix out of which the present concept of the function of "community recreation" evolved. While, in a measure, each of the two preceding stages had served a dual purpose, completing the previous stages and opening the way for a subsequent one, this stage discharged that function more completely than any before or since. It was the adolescent period in the play movement, giving rise to the features of mature life that have since characterized it, as the "sand gardens" represented the period of infancy, and the "model playgrounds" and "small parks" the periods, respectively, of early and later childhood. The motives giving rise to the "recreation centers," and the forms of expression which arose in the various cities will now be analyzed.[47]

The most notable expression of the "recreation center idea" was that completed by the South Park Commissioners, Chicago, during the summer of 1905, when ten "play parks" as they were first called were opened to the public. The story of the origin and nature of these parks has been told many times in print. It was characterized at the time, by President Roosevelt, as the greatest civic achievement by any municipality in America. Briefly the principal facts are as follows: The South Park District was created by acts of the State Legislature of Illinois, approved

[47]See Table VI.

February 24, and April 16, 1869. These acts authorized the organization of a board of park commissioners to consist of five members, each to serve five years, the term of one member expiring each year, and to be appointed by the circuit judges of Cook County, in which the district is located. The original purpose of the board was to acquire, develop, and maintain parks and boulevards. In order to perform this work, the board was made a separate and distinct municipal corporation, independent of the City of Chicago in every respect, and empowered to exercise exclusive control of all lands acquired for parks and boulevards, to levy taxes for their construction and maintenance, to create and maintain its own police force, and to enact ordinances and other regulations for the control of the public while using its facilities. By virtue of their unique organization, the South Park Commissioners have, from the first, enjoyed a reputation of freedom from political bias and corruption in the conduct of their office. The South Park District has contained, from the first, 92.6 square miles. Its population in 1905 was nearly three-quarters of a million. A $5,000,000 bond issue, approved by the voters of the district in 1903, made possible the inauguration of the "new park service" which gave forth the "play parks" of 1905. The motives giving rise to their construction were well stated by Mr. Henry G. Foreman, then President of the Board, in describing the action of the Commissioners after the agitation of the special park commission of Chicago for "small parks" had resulted in the approval of a bond issued for small parks, as follows:

The South Park Commissioners were the first to act. In the crowded quarters they found hordes of dirty and poorly clothed children swarming in the public ways, their playground. They found mothers with no green spot near by to refresh them and their little ones. They found young men and women in many localities with no neighborhood centers where they could meet and enjoy beautiful uplifting pastimes. They found men weary from hard labor, with few places for beneficial recreation to break the monotony of their lives, but with avenues of disastrous amusements on every side.

Local stagnation blighted many districts. There was little or no neighborhood patriotism while the public schools educated children only; they were open certain hours five days to the week and about nine months to the year. The churches for the most part were in service one day in the seven; they were tireless in their religious work, but were unable to provide facilities for physical culture.

The commission had started out to provide simple parks; but the conditions showed that such places, to be serviceable in a city where seventy per cent of the people live in contracted quarters, must be more than breathing spaces with grass, flowers, trees, and perhaps a pond and a fountain. They must afford gymnasiums, libraries, baths, refectories, clubrooms, and halls for meetings and theatricals. They must be useful day and evening, summer and winter. The public must receive a continuous and ample return upon its investment: daily dividends in happiness, health and progress.

Thus the idea of the fieldhouse or neighborhood-center building had its birth.

In the quotation above, three distinct aims are mentioned: (1) that of a continuous service to the public, since the facilities must be open day and evening, summer and winter; (2) a contribution to the development of cleanliness, and a sense of order and beauty in life, as typified by the parked playground and the public baths; (3) a supplementation of the school, the church, and other social agencies by facilities for the promotion of health, sociability, morality, and the enjoyment of art.

The equipment of each of the ten new parks was two-fold: an indoor and an outdoor plant. The indoor plant, the "fieldhouse," contained an assembly hall with stage and cloak rooms, a men's and a women's indoor gymnasiums with locker rooms, shower baths and toilets, two to four clubrooms, a refectory, and a branch of the public library. The outdoor plant contained: (1) a children's playground, for boys and girls under ten years of age, equipped with swings, teeter-totters, giant strides, wading pool, sand bin, lawn and flowers, a free game space, all surrounded by an iron fence concealed by shrubbery; (2) a men's gymnasium equipped with the regular gymnastic apparatus, an iron pipe frame supporting traveling rings, climbing ladders, poles, and slanting beams; pits for jumping, shot putting, and pole vaulting; a cinder running track; both an indoor-ball diamond and a basket-ball court, and quoits; (3) a women's outdoor gymnasium with swings, an iron pipe frame similar to that of the men, an indoor-ball diamond, jumping standards, tennis courts, and quoits. Both the gymnasiums were surrounded with iron picket fences concealed by shrubbery. Each gymnasium also was provided with shade trees and lawns. (4) In front of each fieldhouse was placed a music court, a grove of elms, in which a band stand was erected. The front platform of the fieldhouse also provided a stage for the presentation of outdoor dramatics, musical, and gymnastic exhibitions. (5) In the center of each park was located the "play field," or "ball field," containing one or more baseball diamonds, and football, soccer, and hockey fields in season. This was flooded in winter and skating provided, toboggans being included the first years, but afterward removed because of accidents resulting from their use. (6) Encircling both the ball field and the whole area of each park was an iron fence and rows of trees, banked by shrubbery and surrounded by lawn. (7) The paths in each park and the playing surfaces of the outdoor gymnasiums and ball field were surfaced with "torpedo sand," that is, a layer of coarse sand one stone deep over a bedding of clay. In later years this was oiled annually and was thereby never dusty nor muddy. Hemp rope was used in the swings. Croquet, and tennis, and picnicing were permitted on the lawns, when tennis courts were not provided elsewhere. (8) Nine of the parks contained an outdoor swimming pool of approximately 85x150 feet with lockers, dressing booths, shower bath, spring boards, and diving stands.

The supervision of the recreation centers was somewhat inadequate at first; trained play leaders being provided only in the gymnasiums, an indoor instructor in each indoor gymnasium who also supervised the outdoor athletic equipment for his sex during the summer. This involved all-year employment for the instructors and made possible a closer attachment between them and their neighborhoods. But no direction was given, during the first five years, to the assembly hall and clubroom activities. Permits to use same were issued free upon written application by the South Park Office. In 1909, and 1910, this condition was corrected by the appointment of "Fieldhouse Directors," in each of the parks, to be "head, promoter, and guide to all activities" in the assembly hall and clubrooms. In 1912, the word "Fieldhouse" was dropped and the title became simply "Director," of the park. From that time on, he was responsible for all activities, for the cleanliness and care of the physical plant, for the discipline of both patrons and employees (with exception of the police, the engineer, and the ground foreman who cared for the lawn, shrubs, and trees), and for everything that affected the good name of the park. This was the beginning of the process of decentralization of administration that led, in 1915, to the adoption of "neighborhood organization" as an integral

part of the scheme of support and control of the
uses made of the parks, and that gave rise to the
sixth stage in the evolution of the play movement
in Chicago. The complete staff of employees
located at each small park, after 1910, comprised
the following: one director; two gymnasium instructors, a man and a woman; two assistant
gymnasium instructors, first throughout the year,
but, after 1912, only during the school vacation
period; one head fieldhouse attendant; two locker
and shower room attendants for the men's gymnasium, and two women attendants for the
women's gymnasium; two additional men's and
two additional women's attendants during the
summer while the swimming pool was in operation; two janitors (men) throughout the year,
one additional during the swimming pool season;
two librarians in charge of the branch library
(paid by the public library); one attendant (man)
in the children's playground (to keep it clean and
tidy, not to supervise, that being done by one of
the instructors); one engineer and one fireman
(employed throughout the year on account of the
necessity of heating water for the shower baths
in summer as well as heating the building in
winter); three or four lifeguards while the swimming pools were operated; two policemen, working in shifts with both on duty during the
afternoons; one ground foreman and two to four
laborers as occasion required. In addition to the
above staff there were regular visits at each park

by the landscape gardener, the electricians, the laundry wagon drivers (the South Parks maintain their own laundry, washing all towels, bathing suits, and attendants' and janitors' uniforms), the supply wagon driver, the carpenter, and the "gymnasium rigger" (as was his title) or man to repair gymnastic apparatus.

The cost of each of these recreation centers varied from a quarter to a half million dollars. Armour square, ten acres in area, cost $50,000 for land, $94,000 for fieldhouse and swimming pool, and $76,000 for other equipment; a total of $220,000. Maintenance of this park was $30,000 annually. Some of the parks involved a greater expense both in the original construction and the annual maintenance. Sherman park required $50,000 annually for maintenance. Thus the South Parks demonstrated expenditure for public recreation.

The activities in which the public engaged in the use of the South Park recreation centers were of five groups: (1) The physical, involving indoor gymnasium classes for children, youths and adults from October 1 to May 1, games, apparatus and track and field events during the outdoor season, and inter-park athletic competition in basket-ball, indoor baseball, playground ball, volley-ball, and track meets in their respective seasons. Many baseball teams, organized outside the parks, reserved the use of the ball diamonds on Saturday and Sunday afternoons, playing under the supervision of the police. (2) The manual, connoting sand modeling, kite making, building with blocks. (3) The social, comprising dances, parties, banquets, and club meetings in the halls and clubrooms. (4) The aesthetic, including theatricals, choral and orchestral programs, artist recitals and concerts in vocal and instrumental music and readings, and folk and interpretive dancing on exhibition programs. (5) The civic, or citizenship, activities including lectures on public questions, mass meetings, meetings of local improvement associations, child welfare and similar exhibits, and meetings of women's clubs. The only events prohibited were religious meetings of a sectarian character, political meetings of a partisan nature, advertising, charging admission to entertainments or social gatherings, soliciting funds for benevolent or charitable purposes, playing cards, betting, or smoking while using the facilities. These restrictions were imposed both to elevate the moral standards of those using the parks, and to shield the public from innumerable schemes of exploitation; in short, to emphasize wholesome play, or moral "activity for its own sake."

The concept dominating the organization of activities in the South Park "recreation centers," first in the gymnasiums and later in the entire park as direction was added to the uses made of assembly hall and clubrooms, was that of active recreation rather than passive amusement;

recreation "of the people and by the people" as
well as "for the people," to employ a familiar
phrase. A clear expression of this point of view
was given by Mr. E. B. DeGroot,[48] General
Director of Fieldhouses and Playgrounds, in one
of the annual reports of the commissioners.

Young folks of this day have substituted passive pleasure
for the active play and recreation of the corresponding period
of youth of their parents. "In the old days" most of the
recreation pursuits called for putting hands, head, and heart
and imagination into the effort which gave pleasure. Now
young folks merely put the hand into the pocket for the
nickel, dime, or greater sum, which buys pleasure. One was
wholesome, active recreation, rich in expression; the other is
nearly always passive recreation and is not only lacking in
opportunity for self-expression, but is socially and econom-
ically expensive. . . . .

We need the public playground and recreation center to
restore to children and young folks facilities, programs, traditions, and opportunities for the pursuit of active recreation
as opposed to passive pleasure. The "high cost of living"
is not more real and alarming than the high cost of pleasure.
The secondary effects in the latter case are often more serious
than are indicated in the mere investment of money by the
pleasure seeker.

Next to the South Park Commissioners, Chicago, in the extent of provision made was the
work of the Board of West Chicago Park Commissioners created in 1869 by the same acts of
the State Legislature that authorized the South
Parks. It was distinguished from the latter, however, by two facts. It numbered seven members
instead of five, who were appointed by the gov-

[48]*Annual Report of South Park Commissioners* for 1910.

ernor of the State, for a term of four years each. But, like the South Parks, it was an independent municipality having its own policing, lighting, taxation, and maintenance systems, and the authority to fix ordinances and regulations for the control of those using its facilities. The West Chicago Park District is co-extensive with that portion of the city west of the north and south branches of the Chicago river. By the accident of fortune, the source of revenue for the maintenance of parks and playgrounds by this district has been less productive than that of the South Parks because of the fact that the "loop district" of the city lies wholly within South Park territory; hence, an inequitable apportionment of the taxes went to the respective park commissioners. This fact was largely responsible for the second place which the West Chicago Parks have held in the provision of facilities in comparison with that of the South Parks.

On May 18, 1905, the voters of this district approved a $1,000,000 bond issue for the construction and maintenance of the first three "recreation centers": the B. A. Eckhart Park containing 8.12 acres, opened August 1, 1908; the Stanford Park, 2.89 acres, opened February 22, 1910; and the Dvorack Park, 3.85 acres, opened June 25, 1908. Holstein Park, the fourth recreation center, was completed in June, 1912. In equipment, supervision, and field of activities, these parks were essentially duplicates of those

of the South Park Commissioners, providing
facilities for indoor and outdoor play and recreation by all ages of people every day in the year,
and thus conforming to the concept of the "recreation center" stage.

Second only to the South Parks of Chicago,
was the pioneering work of Los Angeles in the
development of its "recreative centers." By
ordinance of the city council, in September, 1904,
a board of playground commissioners was
created. This board was composed of five members, of whom two were women, appointed by the
mayor, and who served without compensation.
During the first years of its history, this board
expended $137,000 for recreation purposes. In
1912 it became a department of the city government.

The first recreation center was opened in
June, 1905. By 1912 five others had been added.[49]
In addition to these all-year provisions, there
were nine vacation playgrounds and one summer
camp. The distinctive features of provisions for

[49]The following is a table of Los Angeles Playgrounds in
1912:

Name	How acquired	Area	Cost	Opened
Violet Street...	Purchased	2.02	$10,372.00	June 10, 1905
Echo Park.....	Granted by Parks	4.70	11,611.00	May 18, 1907
Solano Avenue.	Granted by Council	0.60	113.06	May 14, 1907
Recreation Center	Purchased	0.55	29,117.00	Oct. 10, 1908
Slausen Avenue	Granted by Water Dept....	4.71	17,814.00	Mar. 12, 1910
Hazard	Granted by Council	10.98	11,409.35	Apr. 29, 1911
Downey	Granted by Council	3.00	7,649.59	June 24, 1911

play in Los Angeles during these seven years
were identical with those of Chicago; facilities for
all ages, open every day in the year, and affording opportunity for participation in play of a
physical, manual, social, aesthetic, and civic
nature.

The playgrounds of Los Angeles, although officially
bearing the title, are more than the name implies. In reality,
they combine the usual playground features with forms of
social activity most often found at the settlement house.
Hence, ''recreative centers'' will be found the more fitting
term.[50]

The equipment of each recreative center involved a division of the area into three spaces:
one for the little children, one for boys and men,
and one for girls and women. The apparatus in
the children's playground consisted of sand bins,
swings, teeters, and blocks; that in the girls' section, of swings, see-saws, maypoles, and basket-
ball, volley-ball, croquet, and tennis courts; for
the boys, facilities for baseball, handball, basket-
ball, track and field, and the usual playground apparatus frame. Under the apparatus frame, tan
bark was used for surfacing the grounds. Shower
baths were usually provided for both the boys' and
girls' sections, and a ''summer house'' in connection with the children's section ''for the mothers
. . . . where they may sit and read or watch
the children at play.'' Another unique feature
of the outdoor equipment was the gardens;

[50]Bessie D. Stoddart, "Recreative Centers of Los Angeles,"
The Annals, March, 1910, p. 427.

forty-five in the first recreative center. The indoor equipment consisted of a "clubhouse" or "fieldhouse," generally of the bungalow type of architecture, containing an assembly hall with stage, clubrooms, storerooms, a kitchen well supplied with dishes, and a home for the director of the center, located in one corner of the playground. The most elaborate indoor equipment was that provided at Recreation Center playground. The motives prompting its erection and the nature of the building are described by Miss Stoddart:[51]

The Playground Commission early felt that the municipality should afford special recreational facilities for the working young men and young women and the adult population. It was determined to build what was termed a recreation center, to distinguish it from the playgrounds proper, as affording better means for indoor play, a house that should offer something of what the social settlement or the Y. M. C. A. building furnishes. A corner lot, 200 by 120 feet to an alley, located in a central industrial district, was secured, costing less than $9,000. Of this amount, $1,000 was subscribed by two industrial companies. Here was built a handsome brick-and-plaster structure of the Spanish Renaissance style so prevalent in Southern California. . . . .

The main feature of the building is a fully equipped gymnasium, measuring 44 by 74 feet, with windows on three sides. On the fourth side a large stage opens, for the gymnasium is also meant for use as an auditorium. Ordinarily the stage is closed off with rolling doors and is used as a clubroom. The gymnasium is two stories in height, a gallery furnished with a running track being located at the second story.

[51]Bessie D. Stoddart, *supra.*

Other features of the building are, briefly, as follows: Ten marble shower baths, modern locker-room, storeroom and furnace-room, two model bowling alleys, district nurse's headquarters, kitchen, two clubrooms, library; physical instructor's office, where measurements are taken and records kept; trellised roof-garden, which commands a magnificent panorama of the city and mountains and is equipped with sand box and building blocks for children, and with electric lighting for evening socials; and last, but a very important factor, a pleasant five-room apartment for the manager. For here again the home rounds out the work of the center and establishes helpful relationships.

From the first, the direction of all activities was given by trained supervisors. In 1912 the staff of the department included one superintendent, one secretary, two supervisors, twelve directors, twenty vacation directors, ten substitute instructors, one manager of Recreation Center, one accompanist, two mechanics, one gardener, seven caretakers, and two vacation caretakers. Usually each all-year playground was provided with two directors, a man and a woman, throughout the year and two additional directors, a man and a woman again, during the vacation months.

The field of activities contained active and passive play. The children were divided into four groups according to age and ability, namely, the kindergartners, juniors, intermediates, and seniors. The directors gave their personal attention to each group during a certain portion of the day, keeping watch of all visiting the grounds. Thus organized and definite play was encouraged.

The nature of the play of each group is indicated by the following description:[52]

Active plays and games, alternating with quiet games and certain forms of handicraft work, occupy the time of the children. The small boys and girls play kindergarten games, use the simple apparatus, and enjoy to the fullest extent the wading pool, the sand courts, and building blocks. Story telling, paper cutting, and scrapbook work also interest them.

The older girls are interested to a certain extent in the play apparatus, but most of their time is occupied with field games, such as croquet, tennis, volley-ball, basket-ball, and playground ball. Each year the game of playground ball is becoming more popular and in a short time this game may be to the girls what baseball is to the boys.

The large boys are kept busy with the more active games such as soccer football, tennis, handball, playground ball and baseball. The outdoor gymnasium is used for play and the performance of "stunts." In order to maintain the interest and enthusiasm of the boys, local leagues are organized, athletic meets are conducted, and teams travel to other grounds to compete. Saturday is usually a big day for match games. These games attract many visitors and provide good wholesome amusement during leisure time.

Legal holidays are celebrated at each playground in a manner suitable to the occasion.

Some of the "clubhouses" contained branch libraries open two afternoons and one evening each week and circulating 1,500 books a month. On days when the library is open, checkers, authors, and other quiet games are played in the buildings. At Violet street, and Recreation Center, rooms were fitted-up as headquarters for district nurses. Here supplies were kept, calls for nurses registered, and dispensary service given.

[52]*Annual Report Los Angeles Playground Commission*, 1912.

Voting booths were erected in many of the "club-houses" and used in connection with the municipal elections. Less extensive uses were made by the adults than by the children and youths, but this was due rather to the limitations imposed by the nature of the physical facilities than to the concept of the function of public recreation held by those administering it.

The next two cities to follow the example of Chicago and Los Angeles in the development of "recreation centers" were Pittsburgh and Philadelphia, respectively in order of time. The first "fieldhouse" in Pittsburgh was opened in Washington Park in 1910.[53] Among the organized groups meeting there regularly during its first year were two Jewish clubs, a colored women's civic club, a colored young men's civic club, an athletic club, two Italian clubs, and a high-school boys' club. The cosmopolitan nature of these uses of the indoor facilities attests the concept of the function of a public "recreation center" that prevailed in that community at the time. Space does not permit full details of the development of recreational provision in Pittsburgh. It is significant, however, that before 1912, four other "recreation centers" were completed: Lawrence Park of 5.72 acres, Ormsby Park of 2.25 acres, South Side Park of 1.75 acres, and Arsenal Park of 11 acres. Each of these four parks was equipped with a "fieldhouse," a ball field, a chil-

[53]*Annual Report Pittsburgh Playground Association*, 1912.

dren's playground, a boys' and a girls' outdoor gymnasium. Lawrence and Ormsby had swimming pools, and the former also a wading pool. The activities of the Pittsburgh "recreation centers" were representative of the prevailing concept of the function of the play movement, involving the physical, manual, social, aesthetic, and civic uses that were common to the South Parks and the Los Angeles recreation centers described above.

In Philadelphia,[54] the first "recreation center" was completed in 1911, the Starr Garden Recreation Park, opened on July 8, and dedicated on October 16. The area was 1.43 acres; the value, $232,041.58. The indoor plant consisted of a small "fieldhouse" containing a gymnasium and assembly hall combined, shower baths for both men and women, a number of small club and games rooms. The outdoor equipment contained space for ball games, the usual playground apparatus, and a wading pool with sand beach. The activities consisted of classes, dances, and entertainments as well as the customary outdoor games and athletic events. The administration was committed to the Board of Recreation of Philadelphia. Attendance at this center totaled over 300,000 annually.

During this period similar provision was made in four other centers: the Disston Recreation Park of 1.25 acres, opened in 1912; the Sherwood

[54]*Annual Report Board of Education*, Philadelphia, 1913.

of 2.70 acres, completed in 1912; the Happy Hollow of 4.25 acres, completed in 1913; and the Athletic of 4.18 acres, completed in 1913. The last contained a larger fieldhouse than any of the earlier recreation centers, having two gymnasiums, an auditorium with stage, and several clubrooms, modeled after the South Park designs of that date.

Other cities to follow the example of Chicago during the period between 1905 and 1912 were Minneapolis, which opened its first "fieldhouse" at Logan Park, in 1912, and Oakland, California, Louisville, Kentucky, and St. Paul, Minnesota, immediately afterward.

In Boston, the provision of indoor gymnasiums in connection with public baths instead of the fieldhouse type of building limited the indoor activities to those of a physical or aquatic nature. Provision for social and civic events was made by the School Board by the organization of social centers in the public schoolhouses. The relation of the public gymnasiums of Boston to the fieldhouses of Chicago is indicated by the following sentence from one of the annual reports of the bath department:[55]

It is a matter of particular interest that we have been able to give important assistance to the Chicago authorities in connection with the development of a remarkable system of gymnasiums and baths in a number of the city's small parks.

In New York, four parks of the recreation-

[55]Seventh Annual Report Bath Dept., Boston, 1904-5, p. 2.

center type were finished at this time; the first
being Seward Park, referred to above under both
the "model playground" and the "small park"
stages. Here the essential features of equipment,
activities, and leadership were similar to the Chicago small parks, although the greatest development of public provision for indoor recreation
in New York has always been in the use made
of the school buildings.

While several cities followed the lead of the
South Parks of Chicago, in the provision of
"recreation centers" in parks, or on new sites
acquired for play purposes, many more chose to
expand the public uses of their school plants, adding evening recreational activities to the traditional day classes. The pioneering work of this
nature was done in New York City, but the
demonstration that attracted nation-wide attention
was performed in Rochester, New York, during
1907-9. The first step toward this achievement
was taken on February 15, 1907, when delegates from eleven organizations met in the Cham-
ber of Commerce and formed themselves into the
"School Extension Committee." The next step
was the securing of an appropriation of $5,000 for
the maintenance of the work during the first year.
The third act was the decision to place all responsibility for the inauguration of the work upon
the school board of the city. The fourth step was
the selection of a supervisor, even before any
work had been organized or any facilities con-

structed. This supervisor, Mr. E. J. Ward, was sent to both Chicago and New York to inspect the recreational work of those cities and bring back to Rochester recommendations concerning the method of procedure. Concerning his visits, the report of the League of Civic Clubs states:

He visited Chicago and there made a careful investigation of the great South Park system. . . . . Later in the season he spent a week in visiting the recreation centers and studying the great public lecture system in New York City. . . . . He came back . . . . firmly convinced that the City of Rochester should not follow the lines of the work done in either New York or Chicago, but should profit by the experience of both of those cities, mark out a new path for itself, and that so it might make a real contribution to the progress of municipal development.[56]

The contribution which Rochester made was essentially twofold: economy and democracy in method of provision. It was pointed out that the fieldhouses duplicated the schoolhouses, entailing unnecessary financial expense, since the former were used almost entirely during the evenings and late afternoons while the latter were idle. It would be economy, therefore, to extend the uses of the school plants instead of constructing additional facilities after the manner of the small parks and recreation centers of Chicago. Making the schoolhouse and surrounding grounds a starting point, additional features of equipment could be added at much less expense than required to purchase new sites and erect new

[56]*Rochester Social and Civic Centers*, Rep. of Civic Clubs, 1909.

edifices; hence, the effort toward economy. In studying the recreational activities in operation in New York schools, it was seen that more participation by the individuals using the evening recreation centers was desirable. This led to the plan of introducing further democracy in administration of the Rochester social and civic centers than existed at that time in either New York or Chicago. The very title, "social and civic centers," suggested an emphasis upon citizenship in a manner more direct than prevailed in the other cities studied. There, recreation was still "for the people" as far as its administration might be considered; here, the ideal was to introduce more general participation by the public in the selection and regulation of its recreational pursuits. More freedom and with it greater collective responsibility. At no time in the evolution of the play movement is the effort to make an adjustment to the changed social situation of modern times more self-evident than in the motives and explanations given by the people of Rochester for their attempt to develop "social and civic centers." An eloquent declaration of this fact is contained in the following statement:

On July 5, 1907, a joint meeting of the Board of Education and the School Extension Committee was held. At this meeting the whole matter of the policy of the social centers was thoroughly discussed and the plans of the work were definitely laid. In that meeting it was decided that the spirit that should be striven for in the social centers should be the democratic, friendly spirit of broad acquaintanceship,

which made "the little red schoolhouse" in the country the
fine community gathering place that it was. . . . .

The social center was not to take the place of any existing institution; it was not to be a charitable medium for
the service particularly of the poor; it was not to be a new
kind of evening school; it was not to take the place of any
church or other institution of moral uplift; it was not to
serve simply as an "improvement association" by which the
people of one community should seek only the welfare of their
district; it was not to be a "civic reform" organization,
pledged to some change in city, or state, or national administration; it was just to be the restoration to its true place in
social life of that most American of all institutions, the
Public School Center, in order that through this extended use
of the school building, might be developed, in the midst of
our complex life, the community interest, the neighborly
spirit, the democracy that we knew before we came to the
city.

In carrying out this program it was decided to
organize opportunities for physical activity by
means of gymnasiums and baths, for passive
recreations by means of table games, for intellectual activity by means of libraries, and lectures, and entertainments once each week, and
for the exercise of citizenship by self-governing
clubs for men, women, and children. It was
further decided to permit the discussion of all
questions at the public meetings, even those pertaining to religion and politics, a privilege denied
by the South Parks, although granted in New
York City.

The outstanding features of the "social center" type of provision for play and recreation as

expressed in Rochester were thus economy and democracy. The former was the more instrumental in furthering the plan of using the school plant as a base from which to work out an adequate scheme of recreational provision. In many cities the problem of finances immediately handicapped the development of "small park" recreation centers, while the small cost of alterations and additional use of heat and light appealed to many in those cities just awakening to the new sense of recreational values. The outcome was a gradual transformation in the architecture of the schoolhouse and a demand for the extension of playground equipment upon school grounds. Perry's[57] volume on "the wider use of the school plant" summarized the materialization of the movement in this stage of its evolution, while the New Trier Township High School, at Kenilworth, Illinois, and the more recent school plants of Gary, Indiana, typified the limit of development of the physical equipment of "recreation centers" of this type. In each of these cities, tracts of five to twelve acres were secured as sites for school plants and then developed so as to comprise all the essential features of a "model playground," a "small park," a "fieldhouse" and a school building of the traditional type combined in one whole devoted to the education and play of all ages, throughout the year, and in physical, social, civic, aesthetic, and manual activities.

[57]Clarence A. Perry, *The Wider Use of the School Plant*, Russell Sage Foundation, 1910.

New Trier Township High School, Kenilworth, Illinois

In Table VII the extent of the use of school-houses as "recreation centers" is disclosed, first, for the period of 1910 to 1912 inclusive, and second, for the five subsequent years which overlap the fifth and sixth stages of the movement and lead to the current one. This table also discloses the fact that the use of the school plant for recreational as well as educational purposes was not a transitory feature of the movement but one that became permanent.

TABLE VII

PROGRESS BY YEARS IN THE DEVELOPMENT OF RECREATION CENTERS
IN SCHOOLS

	1910	1911	1912	1913	1915	1916	1917
Number of cities.....	31	48	71	152	97	127	113
Number of centers...	201	248	278	629	573	663	757

Total number of cities providing centers, 1910-12............   150
Total number of cities providing centers, 1913-17............   489
Total number of centers provided during 1910-12............   727
Total number of centers provided during 1913-17............ 2,622

The facts relative to the "recreation center" stage of the play movement have now been analyzed. It has been found that the structure and the concept of the function in this stage of its history was characterized by the following features: (1) play and recreational opportunities for all ages; (2) throughout the year by the use of both indoor and outdoor facilities; (3) in physical, manual, aesthetic, social, and civic activities; (4) involving participation versus amusement, whereby individuals and groups made their recreation rather than received it, and thereby enjoyed a certain measure of self-expression in the use of their physical and mental powers, opportunities which too frequently urban life had not previously provided and which could only be seized by group or collective effort in the use of public facilities at hand, both in parks and school plants.

E. *The "civic art and welfare" stage, 1912-14.* During the previous stages in the evolution of the play movement, efforts were directed primarily toward the provision of specific facilities for play in the more congested districts of cities, and secondarily toward the organization of play activities on those respective sites. As a result of this concept of function, the movement developed successively the "sand garden," the "model playground," the "small park," and the "recreation center." Each of these structures was an attempt to provide opportunity for play on a given locality, the "playground." The last named type of facility, the "recreation center," represents the development, to date, of the physical structure of provision for play and recreation for children, youths, and adults, upon a given locality. No modification or addition of a fundamental nature has been made in the physical aspect of the "recreation center" since the close of that stage of the movement. Developments since that date have been social rather than physical, involving the organization of activities on the one hand, and the method of supervision on the other. This fact characterizes the "civic art and welfare'' stage and the succeeding ones, as well, and distinguishes them from the preceding four.

The presence of this change became marked with the incorporation in the movement of attempts either to regulate or organize play ''outside the playgrounds.'' These efforts were flanked on the one hand by municipal regulation of commercialized amusement and on the other by state recreational legislation, both permissive and mandatory, for the provision of facilities and activities. They occurred with great frequency throughout the country during the years between 1911 and 1915, and involved both a general utilization of the dramatic, musical, and dancing arts, and an injection of social welfare propaganda sufficiently to modify the concept of the function of the play movement so as to constitute a distinct epoch in its history. This period the writer has entitled the ''civic art and welfare'' stage. At this point the play movement becomes conscious of a wider field of action than any heretofore perceived. It becomes aware that it must not only provide ''playgrounds,'' as it had been doing for the preceding quarter of a century, but also that it must raise the standards of the popular amusements by the use of both restrictive and constructive measures. The former comprised efforts to regulate existing recreations, principally commercialized amusements; the latter, ''municipal music,'' ''municipal theatres," "municipal dances," and "community dramatics, festivals, and pageantry."

Among the musical expressions of the period were the "municipal orchestras" of Boston, Cleveland, Denver, Milwaukee, and San Francisco, the "municipal bands" of Chicago, and Houston, Texas, and the increase in the number of public band concerts in many cities (New York appropriating $100,000 for the services of seventy bands in one season, while the South Park Commissioners of Chicago annually expended $20,000 on twenty bands that gave a total of 100 concerts in the open during the months of July and August). The most notable expression, however, was the organization of the Civic Music Association of Chicago, chartered by the State of Illinois in the spring of 1913, "to promote and encourage the understanding of the art of music and the development of musical talent throughout the community."[58] This association arranged artist recitals and orchestral and choral concerts in the recreation centers and school auditoriums of the city through the generosity of philanthropists and musicians alike, the latter donating their talent. Programs given in the fieldhouses were free, on account of a rule of the respective park commissioners forbidding the charging of admission fees, while those elsewhere could be heard by the payment of ten cents at the door. Simultaneous with

[58]*First Annual Report of Civic Music Association of Chicago*, 1913.

the development of "civic music" in Chicago, came the rise of "community singing," notably in Wisconsin,[59] in connection with the extension department of the State University. While at first "community music," both in Chicago and elsewhere, was *for* the people, it soon became music, also, *of* and *by* the people, as choruses, and orchestras, and bands were formed in local cen- ters for the study and enjoyment of music, often the folk-songs and dances, the music *of* the peo- ple. In order to counteract the tendency to play and sing the current compositions of the class popularly known at that time as "ragtime," ap- proved lists of songs were written and distributed, the first list[60] containing only eighteen, the sec- ond,[61] fifty-five. Also the selection of vocal or instrumental numbers to be given at the early concerts were approved beforetime. Thus the standard of the performances was kept sufficiently high to induce a satisfying response by the pub- lic to the ideal of "civic music" or "community music," namely the understanding, enjoyment, and participation by the people in the production of music that met with the requirements of art.

More extensive than the efforts to raise the standard of musical appreciation, perhaps, were those in behalf of a higher form of dramatic ex-

[59]*University of Wisconsin Extension Bulletin.*

[60]*Eighteen Songs for Community Singing,* compiled by the Music Supervisors' National Conference, C. C. Birchard, Boston.

[61]*Fifty-five Songs and Special Choruses for Community Singing,* compiled by the Music Supervisors National Confer- ence, C. C. Birchard, Boston.

pression. Among the many events were the construction of municipal theatres in Pittsfield and Northampton, Massachusetts; Concordia, Kansas; Hennessey, Oklahoma; Richland Center, Wisconsin; and Red Wing, Minnesota. Some of these institutions were administered by the municipalities; others were leased to responsible companies; but in all, the purpose was to raise the standard of dramatic performance, morally and artistically. Auditoriums for similar uses were constructed in Denver, San Francisco, Houston, and other cities. In addition to these events were other constructive efforts such as the organization of the Drama League of America, the Drama League of New York City, the Chicago Drama League, the New Theatre and the Little Theatre of New York, the Toy Theatre and the Drama Society of Boston, and the Wisconsin Dramatic Society. The latter sought to unite groups of amateurs throughout the State and "to raise the standard of dramatic appreciation," while the drama societies of the large cities sought "to promote in public schools, social centers, settlements, churches, and other agencies, amateur dramatic performances having an educational value,"[62] and to bring to bear on the commercial stage the influence of a refined public opinion which would demand productions of a more desirable nature from both the artistic and the moral standpoint. This opinion was to be

[62] Cf. *Constitution and By-Laws*, New York Dramatic Society.

formed by an educational process that involved participation by the public in amateur theatricals on the one hand, and the exercise of a mild censorship of commercial playhouses by the local committees on the other, demanding clean plays by helping to advertise the more acceptable shows.

Festivals increased in great numbers during 1912–14. The "play festival" held in connection with the first annual meeting of the Playground Association of America in Chicago, June 7, 1907, gave suggestion to many communities on account of the newness of the Chicago recreation centers and the great interest manifested in them at the time. From that day onward, "play festivals" multiplied in playgrounds and small communities not yet supplied with facilities bearing that name. Dancing, both aesthetic and folk, constituted a large measure of the programs. Spring, autumn, and Christmas festivals were among the more common types, and in their production many quaint old customs of England and Continental Europe were revived.

Pageantry came into prominence during the years of 1911–14. While the Pageant of Education, in Boston, in 1908, may properly be regarded as the first of the series to be incorporated in the play movement at this time, and while Duxbury Days, An Historical Pageant, given in Duxbury, Massachusetts, in 1909,[63] was probably the first attempt of this series to present the history of a

[63]Cf. "List of Pageants," *American Pageantry Association.*

community out of doors, the number of cities reporting pageants as a feature of their provision for play was 41, in 1911. The number steadily increased thereafter as seen in Table VIII,
below. Among the more notable pageants were
the MacDowell Memorial Pageant, Peterboro,
New Hampshire, in 1910, which first attempted to
"treat music seriously as a creative factor in the
making of a Pageant"; the Historical Pageant
of Philadelphia in 1912, in which 6,000 participated; the series of New England rural pageants
beginning with that of Thetford, Vermont, 1911,
and including those of St. Johnsbury, Vermont,
in 1912, and Meriden, New Hampshire, in 1913;
and the St. Louis, Missouri, Pageant and Masque
in 1914, in which 7,500 participated on each of
five successive nights, from 6:30 until 10:30, before 125,000 spectators nightly, and costing $125,-
000 to produce.

TABLE VIII
INCREASE IN CERTAIN ARTISTIC EXPRESSIONS IN THE PLAY MOVE-
MENT DURING 1911 TO 1915, INCLUSIVE

Years	1911	1912	1913	*1915
Number of cities reporting supervised playgrounds	257	285	342	432
Number reporting instrumental music	27	38	51	69
Number reporting dramatics	37	37	61	93
Number reporting pageants	41	44	52	102
Number reporting singing	78	84	96	150

*The Playground Association published no report for 1914.

An analysis of Table VIII shows a significant number of cities making use of "civic art,"
including music, both instrumental and vocal, dramatics, and pageantry. In each type the absolute

number increased during the period; and while in some instances the percentage of the whole number of cities declined, that fact was due to the rapid increase in the number of cities providing for play for the first time, whose activities therefore were not as varied as in those communities in which provision was of longer standing.

Among the many efforts aimed directly at the promotion of public welfare through constructive measures relative to the social recreations of the people were the "municipal dances." These dances were organized and conducted by various departments of city governments as a possible solution of the moral problems arising in connection with "public dance halls." They were generally held in halls other than those in the recreational centers and followed the prevailing plan of the commercialized dancing pavilions with the exception that greater effort was made to supervise the patrons. Chaperones were provided, minors under seventeen years of age usually excluded when unaccompanied by parent or guardian, no liquor was sold in connection with the dance, and "no improper conduct allowed." Milwaukee seems to have been the first city to provide such a dance, under Mayor Seidel's administration. Twenty-five cents a couple was charged for admission to the hall. On defeat of the Mayor for re-election, in 1912, however, the dances were discontinued with the return to power of a reactionary administration. In Cincinnati, the

Women's Civic Committee conducted public dances during 1913 in the music hall, open to adults on Saturday evenings and to children on Saturday afternoons. Twenty-two dances, attended by 14,000 people at an admission fee of fifteen cents a head, brought a slight profit to the committee. Soft drinks and ice cream were sold by concessionaires. No return checks were given to those leaving the hall while the dance was in progress, since it was customary for young people to leave the commercial dance halls in order to frequent nearby saloons during intermissions between numbers on the program.

The most successful city was probably Cleveland. This was due to the peculiar situation that existed at the time of the opening of the first dance. Thirty-two commercial halls had just been closed by city ordinance because of insanitary or immoral conditions. The school board hesitated in granting the use of school auditoriums for social purposes. Mayor Baker met the emergency by organizing the first "municipal dance" at the Edgewater pavilion, in August, 1912, at which he and Mrs. Baker led the grand march. Three cents was charged for a dance of five minutes length; in opposition to the commercial halls which asked five cents for a three minute dance. During the first year, $350 were received from 11,630 dance tickets, while during 1914, receipts from the dances netted a profit to the city of $15,000. Afternoon sessions were held for chil-

dren, while minors under eighteen years were excluded, unless chaperoned, after nine o'clock P. M.

The first "municipal dance" in Chicago was
held on December 2, 1914. That day the newspapers printed the following invitation to the
public:

The City of Chicago invites you to attend the first
municipal dance to be given under the auspices of the Department of Public Welfare at Dreamland Hall, West Van
Buren and South Paulina Streets, tonight at eight o'clock.
Admission, fifteen cents.

CARTER H. HARRISON, *Mayor.*

Mayor and Mrs. Carter H. Harrison led the
grand march. Five thousand danced the waltz
and two-step that night in one of the largest commercial dancing academies in the city. While this
first ball was restricted to the "old dances," later
ones permitted the "new steps." The admission
fees were twenty-five cents per couple or fifteen
cents for each individual attending. These dances
were under the general supervision of the Public Welfare Bureau of the city of Chicago and
are to be distinguished in many ways from the
dancing parties conducted for the preceding nine
years in the fieldhouses of the South, West, and
Lincoln Park Commissioners. In the latter, no
admission fees were charged, attendance being by
invitation of those giving the dance who paid for
music, programs, and refreshments if any were
served and who were forbidden to advertise or
solicit funds for any purpose, or use liquors in
connection with the use of the fieldhouses.

The "municipal dances" of Boston were held in the city indoor gymnasiums under the Park and Recreation Departments of the City, while in San Francisco both the new civic auditoriums and the streets were used for "municipal dances" under the supervision of the police. An admission fee was charged at the dances given in the auditorium, while those in the streets were free. The hours were from eight until eleven o'clock. Attendance was promiscuous.

Closely related to the "municipal dances" were the efforts made by many cities to supervise the commercialized halls. A typical case is that of Kansas City, Missouri, as stated in one of the annual reports of the Board of Public Welfare of that city:[64]

During this, the third year of supervision of dance halls, more dances were supervised at less cost . . . . the standard of conduct in the halls was much better than in the preceding year. This was largely due to an order prohibiting any manager from permitting patrons to leave the hall and later return. This order has finally met the approval of the dance hall managers and reduced the amount of disorder resulting from the free use of intoxicating liquor obtained by passing out of the hall to a nearby saloon. . . . . This rule eliminated to an extent, a class of young women who stayed in the hall only long enough to meet a man, leave with him and later return.

The inspectors watch carefully for young girls who appear to be under the age of seventeen. They are not permitted to remain in the hall unless accompanied by their mother, father or lawful guardian. The following day a

[64]*Fourth Annual Report of Public Welfare Board*, Kansas City, Missouri, April 22, 1913, p. 329.

woman investigator calls on the parents, who are charged with keeping the girl away from the halls. If this method fails the parents are summoned into the Juvenile Court and an effective arrangement is made by the Court.

During 1913, the Public Welfare Board of Kansas City, issued 669 permits for dances, revoked three, inspected 2,670 dances, reported and investigated 246 young girls, and tried eight cases in court. Equal attention was given to other forms of commercialized amusements, notably motion pictures and skating rinks, both in Kansas City and other cities where popular opinion was formed on the subject. In all, a total of 158 cities attempted to regulate commercialized amusements by ordinances and inspections.

Both the restrictive and constructive phases of the "civic art and welfare" stage were represented in the state and municipal legislation of the time which sought to prohibit what was believed to be insanitary or anti-social and to provide new opportunities for the expression of wholesome play and recreation interests. Ordinances by cities either made certain forms of recreational behavior unlawful, or provided for the constructive facilities and the organization of activities of a moral character. Legislation by states involved both mandatory and permissive acts. The former made provision of public recreation obligatory, the latter, possible, by communities within the state. This period in the history of the movement was one of great activity in recreational legislation as shown by Table IX which gives the number of legislative acts by years and the number of states by which legisla= tion was enacted each year from 1889 to 1915.

TABLE IX
RECREATION LEGISLATION ENACTMENTS BY YEARS AND STATES

Year	No. of acts passed by states	No. of states en-acting for 1st time	No. of states legis-lating by years
1889	1	1	1
1893	1	1	1
1907	2	2	2
1908	3	1	2
1909	3	3	3
1910	1	0	1
1911	14	6	9
1912	3	2	3
1913	24	8	15
1914	4	0	3
1915	18	4	13
Totals	74	28	53

An analysis of Table IX discloses greater activity during the period from 1911 to 1915, inclusive, than during the preceding twenty-two years. Sixty-three bills were passed during these five years by eighteen states and Congress, out of a total of seventy-four bills by twenty-seven states and Congress, passed since 1889.

By 1915, also many cities had passed ordinances pertaining to play and amusements. A report by the Russell Sage Foundation[65] contains those by sixteen cities, although the total number of cities enacting ordinances relative to rec-

[65]*Recreation Legislation 1913*, Russell Sage Foundation pamphlet, No. 106.

reation was estimated by Edwards[66] at 158. Of
the sixteen mentioned by the report, New York
was first, in 1895, with a law requiring the construction of a playground attached to or used in
connection with each school building erected thereafter. Boston followed in 1907; Hartford, Con-
necticut, in 1909; Buffalo, New York, Charleston,
South Carolina, and Oakland, California, in 1910;
Cleveland, Los Angeles, and New Britain, Con-
necticut, in 1911; Holyoke and Worcester, Massachusetts, Newport and Providence, Rhode Island,
in 1913; and Brockton, Massachusetts, Detroit,
Michigan, and Syracuse, New York, in 1915.

TABLE X

RECREATIONAL LEGISLATION BY SUBJECTS, SHOWING NUMBER OF
STATES AND CITIES WITH LAWS PERTAINING TO
EACH SUBJECT BY 1915

Subjects	States	Cities	Subjects	States	Cities
Board of Recreation	0	1	School Playgrounds	10	5
Athletic Fields	1	2	Public Parks	10	2
Baths	5	2	Recreation Buildings	4	6
Commercial Recreation	2	1	Recreation Commissions	4	11
Concerts	3	1	Recreation Surveys	1	1
Dance Halls	2	2	School Gardens	1	0
Holiday Celebrations	2	1	Social Centers	19	3
Juvenile Commissions	0	1	State Park Commission	1	0
Local Planning Boards	2	0	Sunday Recreation	1	0
Public Playgrounds	22	13			

An analysis of the preceding evidence relative
to the "civic art and welfare" stage discloses
three objectives which shaped developments: (1)
the desire to incorporate the dramatic, musical,

[66]R. H. Edwards, *Popular Amusements*, p. 176.

and dancing arts in the field of public provision for play and recreation in order to counteract the deleterious influences of the commercialized theatre and motion picture; (2) the impulse to regulate, not destroy, commercial amusements so as to conserve the social values potential in them; (3) the belief in the efficacy of city-wide organization for the promotion of art and welfare through activities conducted on a larger scale and open to promiscuous attendance, but inspected and chaperoned by public officials, in the place of the preceding smaller efforts in localities where attendance was limited to neighborhood groups. The first two objectives remained as a permanent contribution to the concept of the function of the movement, but the third was transitory and the disillusionment which followed it gave rise to the distinguishing features of the "neighborhood organization" stage of the movement.

The first of the three outstanding features of the "civic art and welfare" stage was the recognition of the legitimate desire of the people for drama, music, and dancing, on the one hand, and on the other, of the exploitation of that normal desire by commercialized amusements which "debased art for profit," as Percy MacKaye[67] pointed out, while the philanthropic and religious societies generally "ignored art" although seeking to benefit society.

[67]Percy MacKaye, *The Civic Theatre in Its Relation to the Redemption of Leisure*, 1912, p. 31.

Now in organized leisure certain facts are to be noted. First, our leisure, where organized for amusement, recognizes art, but debases it for private profit. This is true of our commercial theatres, vaudeville houses, moving-picture shows, dance halls, etc. Secondly, our leisure, where organized for "education or religion," ignores art entirely while seeking to uplift the public without it. This is true of our public schools, universities, churches, libraries, etc. The notable exceptions are the playground associations, institutions for public music, and our sporadic festivals and pageants.

The second characteristic of the period was the increase in knowledge, by communities, of conditions which prevailed in the leisure pursuits of the public as set forth by private studies, such as that by M. M. Davis, Jr.,[68] in New York City, and public investigations such as the recreational surveys conducted in Kansas City, Milwaukee, Cleveland, and elsewhere. These disclosures led directly to the injection of both restrictive and constructive measures designed to promote more wholesome conditions and a keener appreciation by the people of the true values in recreational activities. Consequently inspections increased, ordinances were passed by city councils, agitation for state recreational legislation made, and lectures, exhibits, and moving pictures introduced in increasing numbers into the existing recreation centers.

The third distinctive feature was the immediate reaction to the situation disclosed by the

[68] M. M. Davis, Jr., *The Exploitation of Pleasure*, Russell Sage Foundation.

preceding two. The local centers were neither sufficient in number nor generally equipped with leadership and financial resources necessary to promote art or conserve the recreational values of the city at large. The existing facilities and organization were supplemented by city-wide action both restrictive and constructive. City and county festivals and pageants were presented, municipal dances were conducted, state and city ordinances regulating commercialized amusements or providing public recreations were passed, public welfare bureaus incorporating the provision of play facilities or the inspection of existing recreations as one of their functions were organized, and municipal theatres and auditoriums were erected. But the populations concerned were too large, the situation too complex, for so simple a solution. The majority of provisions were examples of recreation *for* the people rather than that *of* and *by* them as prevailed in both the preceding and the subsequent stages. It became more and more apparent that men live in groups and must play in groups, as Gulick[69] pointed out, and that a reorganization of the method of administering the local recreation centers, instead of a city-wide attack upon the recreation problem independent of them, was necessary. Its development constitutes the history of the subsequent stage.

[69]L. H. Gulick and others, Minority Report, *Memorandum on Recreation* to New York Board of Estimate and Apportionment, 1913.

F. *The "neighborhood organization" stage,
1915–18.* A sequel to the "civic art and welfare"
stage of the play movement was that of "neighborhood organization." The methods of the former in manifestation of the growing interest in
community welfare, as exemplified on the one
hand by municipal dances, civic music, community drama, and pageantry, and on the other by
recreational legislation and the regulation and
supervision of commercialized amusements, met
with only moderate success as measures for the
conservation of leisure in adjustment of the contemporary social situation. The city-wide method
of control and provision of recreational activities
came far from yielding all that was expected of it.
Among the restrictive measures, for example, the
public inspection of commercial dance halls and
the chaperonage of "municipal dances" was soon
declared an ineffectual scheme for solving the
"dance problem."

The supervision of dance halls tends to establish public
confidence in these places. Supervision only gives the halls
a "surface" decency, and no kind of supervision can reach
the evil influence of mixing unknown bad characters with
those who are seeking innocent amusement.[70]

Commercial recreation has signally failed to meet the
demands of the people during the leisure period. Public
recreation consciously aiming at the things agreed as best in
our social organism, we feel, must take its place.

Commercial recreation is charged with: debasing the
tastes of the people; offering passive recreation only; anti-
social tendencies in breaking up the family groups seeking

[70]*Fourth Annual Report Department Public Welfare,* Kansas City, Mo., 1913, p. 329.

pleasure; consorting with vice; levying a terrific tax—
perhaps over a hundred and fifty million a year in Chicago;
never attempting developmental or educational programs.[71]

Not only on the restrictive side, but with
respect also to the constructive features of the
"civic art and welfare" stage, were the attainments disappointing. The groups involved were
too large and the events too infrequent. Gradually the inadequacy of the scheme was discerned
and a decentralized plan of organization conceived. This plan was regional as well as functional. Its dynamic was the idea of locality; and
the neighborhood in place of the city, as in the
former stage, was chosen as the unit of population and area upon which effort should be
centered. The residents of the respective neighborhoods, corresponding in both area and population to the school districts of city and country,
were asked to participate in both the control and
the support of the scheme of provision for play
undertaken in the vicinity of their homes. Administration of the recreation of the community
was thereby decentralized, localized geographic-
ally, and made democratic. By this adjustment,
it was hoped, a general participation by adults
as well as youths and children would result, and
a greater number of centers, a more flexible program, and more frequent activities become possible on account of the aid secured in leadership
and financial support.

[71]J. R. Richards, Superintendent of Playgrounds, South
Park Commissioners, Chicago, in unpublished general letter to
Park Directors, Dec. 9, 1914.

The following is a contemporary statement of the concept of the function of "self-supporting" and "self-governing" recreation centers:

The leisure of our people has been handed over to commerce. This has broken up the family circle. The father finds his happiness in the saloon; the boy seeks his pleasure in the poolroom, or with the gang; the daughter succumbs to the lure of glittering dance halls. The only force that will rebind the disintegrated family ties, insure the integrity of the home, concentrate domestic interests, is the school center. . . . .

The centers reach an average total of fifty thousand people per night (in New York). A small portion of the entire population of the city is thus served at the present time. If recreation is to be augmented so that it will reach ten times as many as it does now, it would cost the city in the neighborhood of $500,000 a year. . . . .

A close analysis of the operation of the recreation centers discloses the fact that the greater part of the monetary appropriation is divided between the cost of supervision and the cost of equipment. . . . . "Self-government" may partly replace expert supervision, and "self-support" may partly supply the financial sinews for the operating expenses.[72]

The sense in which the terms "self-government" and "self-support" were used requires explanation at this point since neither was taken literally. Each was applied in a limited manner; thus, in the financial support of public education and recreation the original cost of both school buildings, parks, and playgrounds was met through taxation, as was the expense of heating, lighting, cleaning, and maintenance of properties.

[72]E. C. Gibney, *Twentieth Annual Report of Superintendent of Schools*, New York City, 1918, pp. 58–59.

In the government or administration, likewise, public officials, both on general boards of control and in local centers as expert leaders, exercised the right of veto of any action taken by a local group when the same was believed to be deleterious to the larger welfare. As one observer[73] expressed it when speaking of city neighborhood organizations:

Self-government and self-support cannot be absolute. There must be an official body that is responsible for public properties, which formulates salient policies, which stimulates local interest, which standardizes the mechanical aspects of the system through reports, permits, etc.

In the "neighborhood organization" stage of the play movement there was a revival of the underlying concept of the "recreation center," but there was added to that instrument a new meaning and a more efficient method of operation. While making use of the same physical plant, the small park fieldhouse or the public-school building, it utilized the principle of participation by all the residents of the locality in the support and control of the center as a "single, all-inclusive, organized society'"[74] for deliberation and action upon all questions relative to their common life, play being one. The contribution of "neighborhood organization" to the "recreation center" was nowhere more clearly stated than by Ward[75] who consistently used the term "social center"

[73]E. C. Gibney, *Twentieth Annual Report of Superintendent of Schools*, New York City, p. 74.
[74]E. J. Ward, *The Social Center*, p. 253.
[75]*Ibid.*

to describe the type of organized neighborhood that was receiving attention at this time.

In America, where the basic essential of society is its democratic sovereignty, the term ''social'' center is properly used only of an institution built upon a foundation of democratic expression. The social center of any community is the place where the members of that community have their headquarters of expression as a single, all-inclusive, organized society. . . . . The polling place is the center, and all the center there is, in most communities. When the schoolhouse is made the headquarters of the community organization, either for voting or for deliberation, or both, then, and only then, does it become the social center.

While the schoolhouse used as merely a recreation center is not immoral, as the privately run pleasure resort is likely to be, neither is it positively moral. It is a negatively good institution. In order to be positively good, in order to be constructively moral, it must be democratic, for positive moral development comes only with self-expression under self-restraint, that is, with democracy.

So extensively was the plan of ''self-government'' and ''self-support'' of recreation through ''neighborhood organization'' applied that the prevailing plan of ''public'' administration was altered as ''over-head'' organization developed in the form of advisory committees representative of the respective local centers. These committees co-operated with the public officials appointed by government to administer playgrounds, parks, or school plants, and devised ways and means for a more efficient financial assistance on the part of the respective ''neighborhood associations.'' Here for the first time

in the history of the play movement did the provision of facilities and the organization of activities come from the people, "from the bottom up
instead of from the top down," as one writer
expressed it.[76]   The first of these overhead organizations to be effected was that of the Community
Center Conference of Chicago, established in
April, 1916, while the most complete was probably
that of the League of Neighborhood School Centers of New York, formed in February, 1917.[77]

The outstanding feature of this stage, however, was the "neighborhood council" or, as it
came to be known later, the "community council," in connection with "neighborhood associations" at first and "community organization" in
the end.   Local societies and institutions were
correlated in the "councils."   Both departments
of government, as those of health, recreation,
public welfare, police, etc., and city, state, and
national voluntary associations of a philanthropic
character, co-operated to mutual advantage.   As
a result of these connections, the field of activities
of the "recreation centers" was greatly widened.
Among the types that were newly organized or
greatly extended were the "community forum,"
the "town meeting," the "community press,"
the "welfare exhibits," lectures on civic themes,
motion pictures, "social surveys," "co-operative
stores," "co-operative banks," and "community
days."

[76]E. C. Gibney, Cf. *20th Annual Report of Superintendent
of Schools*, New York City, 1918, pp. 72, 79.
    [77]*Ibid.*

The origin of the concept of the structure and function of the "neighborhood organization" stage may be traced to two sources: the one, theoretical; the other, practical. These sources furnished the explanations and the types of activities, respectively, of this stage of the movement and brought it into a functional union with scientific study of the problem of community organization on the one side and with the traditional community institutions and heritages of American life on the other. The former pertained to the re-valuation of the neighborhood by students of political and social science, the latter to the revival of the neighborhood relation under the changed social situation. As the nineteenth century had wrought a deterioration of the neighborhood, so the twentieth was to work out its reconstruction. The neighborhood, it was pointed out, could no longer be disregarded by either the politician or the social worker. Its function in the complicated society of today was held to be comparable[78] to that which it performed in the evolution of society, and welfare movements includ-

---

[78]Cf. Robert A. Woods, "The Neighborhood in Social Reconstruction," *Proceedings and Papers of the American Sociological Society*, 1913. "It is, I believe, one of the most important, and one of the most slighted, considerations affecting all the social sciences, that the neighborhood relation has a function in the maintenance and progress of our vast and infinitely complicated society today which is not wholly beneath comparison with the function which it exercised in the creative evolution of that society. But there are today signs of a wholly new emphasis, both theoretical and practical, upon the function of the neighborhood as affecting the whole contemporary social process."

ing that of play and recreation must work *from* it as well as *toward* it, *by* it as well as *for* it. The process by which this end was to be attained was designated "neighborhood organization" or "neighborhood reconstruction" at the outset and, "community organization" after the plan of adjustment was perfected. The organization of the residents in the respective local districts was known variously as the "neighborhood association," the "neighborhood" or "community council," or the "organized community."

Among the theoretical contributions involving a re-valuation of the neighborhood by students of social science was that of Cooley,[79] in 1909, who designated the neighborhood as a "primary group" instrumental both in producing human nature and in molding institutions. Another widely read monograph was that of Wilcox,[80] in 1911, in which the deterioration of the "local centers" of social organization in urban communities was deplored and their reconstruction, recommended. In 1911, also, Woodrow Wilson,[81] in a

[79]C. H. Cooley, *Social Organization*, Chas. Scribners and Sons, pp. 23 ff.

[80]Delos F. Wilcox, *The American City*, The Macmillan Co., chaps. i, viii.

[81]Woodrow Wilson, "The Social Center, A Means of Common Understanding," *University of Wisconsin Extension Division*, Bulletin. "It is necessary that simple means should be found by which . . . . we may get together . . . . bring all men into common counsel and so discover what is the common interest. That is the problem of modern life which is so specialized that it is almost devitalized, so disconnected that the tides of life will not flow. There is no sovereignty of the people if the several sections of the people are at loggerheads with one another. Sovereignty comes with co-operation."

paper read before the first national "social center" conference at Madison, Wisconsin, pointed out the necessity of bringing "all men into common counsel and so discovering what is the common interest"; while Gulick,[82] that year, declared in New York, that "the people themselves through the effort of organized voluntary groups, shall make their own recreation, govern it, and pay for it," in their uses of public playgrounds and school plants.   In 1913, Ward[83] stated that it was "of the greatest importance to point out the truth that without a basis in self-government, there is no positive moral training in the recreational use" of public facilities provided for that purpose, but it remained for Woods,[84] December,

[82]Luther H. Gulick, "Memorandum on Recreation Addressed to the New York Board of Estimate and Apportionment, by its Sub-committee," *The Survey*, August 23, 1913. "Those men and women who are members of private clubs insist on being allowed to spend their social hours with their own group, among people who want what they want in the way they want it. The great mass of people, who have no private clubs, are entitled to these same privileges. They too are entitled to pay for their own recreation, to govern their own recreation, and to spend their leisure hours with their own social group. The social center, whether it be on school property, park property, or other property, is such by reason of the very fact that it gives this kind of right to the average man, woman, or child. . . . . The aim of the social center is that public money shall provide simply the basic physical opportunity for recreation, while the people themselves, through the effort of organized voluntary groups, shall make their own recreation, govern it, and pay for it. The social center is not a form of paternalism, for it merely provides the channels through which the social life can flow, just as the street provides the channel through which the physical city is able to move."

[83]E. J. Ward, *The Social Center*, Appleton, 1913, pp. 252 ff.

[84]Robert A. Woods, "The Neighborhood in Social Reconstruction," *Proceedings of the American Sociological Society*, 1913. First read before the meeting of the American Socio-

1913, to indicate precisely the concept of the function of the neighborhood in the recreational provision of the community.

The neighborhood is large enough to include in essence all the problems of the city, the state, and the nation. . . . . On the other hand, it is small enough to be a comprehensible and manageable community unit. It is in fact the only one that is comprehensible and manageable; the true reason why city administration breaks down is that the conception of the city breaks down. The neighborhood is concretely conceivable; the city is not, and will not be except as it is organically integrated through its neighborhoods.

Among the practical sources of the origin of the concept of "neighborhood organization" were the many manifestations of community spirit and the collective capacity of the common people in the history of America. The foremost example was probably the New England "town meeting." This institution was often cited as the prototype of the self-governing and self-supporting plan of administration of recreation. An instance follows:

Americans are growing too prone to participate in national affairs only during political campaigns. The passing of the old town meeting has created a crying need for some vehicle by which the static citizen may be converted into the dynamic citizen by constant participation in public affairs.[85]

logical Society at Minneapolis, December 27, 1913, but given also before the City Club of Chicago, December 31, following. At this meeting a number of recreation administrators were present, and Mr. E. B. DeGroot, Secretary of the Playground Association of Chicago, and formerly Superintendent of Playgrounds and Sports of the South Park Commissioners, presided. Here was a point of contact between the scientific and the practical groups.

[85]Eugene C. Gibney, *20th Annual Report, Superintendent of Schools*, New York, 1918.

Even the term "town meeting" was used by some to describe the conduct of an organized neighborhood in conjunction with a school or park recreation center.

Another prototype was the neighborhood recreational gatherings of the nineteenth century which had become less frequent and in some communities abandoned entirely:

It is generally agreed that there are fewer opportunities for the people of the country to get together and have a general good time than there used to be. There used to be the husking bees, the barn raisings, the threshing days, even the log rollings. There used to be the apple cuttings, the bean stringings, the sugar makings. There used to be the spelling bees, the old-time "literaries," the "heated" debates. There are not so many of these "diversions" today. In many communities all of these have been entirely abandoned. Nothing has taken their places.[86]

The attention of play leaders was directed to the schoolhouse as the more universally accessible facility that might serve as the stage of action for collective recreational pursuits and its place in the neighborhood life of the former generation was recalled.[87] The public libraries were also cited as examples of what could be done by collective effort,[88] while among the more recent attempts were the "Hesperia movement," the

[86]L. J. Hanifan, *Community Social Gatherings*, 1914, p. 6.

[87]E. J. Ward, *Songs of the Neighborhood* (mimeographed collection for use in recreational centers and neighborhood associations).

[88]"The library in almost every instance has grown up as the spontaneous expression of the ideals of the people and of their characteristic determination to realize them."—Joseph Lee, *Constructive and Preventive Philanthropy*, p. 11.

"grange," the "consolidated school," and the "co-operative buying and marketing" enterprises. These movements and institutions were studied by practical workers in the field of playground and recreation administration as types of collective enterprises that offered suggestions for either the content or method of "neighborhood organization."

While it is quite impossible to measure the influence of each of the authors and prototypes cited above upon the development of "neighborhood organization," that both were instrumental is a fact. During the years between 1910 and 1917, in which the present writer was associated with the development of neighborhood and community organization in connection with the play and recreation centers of Chicago, the ideas of these authors and the examples of community effort presented above were discussed at both the local meetings and the national conferences of play directors. Among the latter, special mention may be made of the annual conventions of the Playground and Recreation Association of America; at New York, in 1915, the general subject being, "The Awakening of Neighborhood Life in America"; and at Grand Rapids, in 1916, "Community Building through Play." In this connection, also, attention should be called to three other series of annual conferences, namely, (1) the National Conference on Community Centers, at New York in 1916 and at Chicago in 1917;

(2) the National Conference of Social Work;[89]
(3) the meetings of the National Social Unit
Organization at New York, during the same
period. The personnel of each of these groups
of conferences was much the same, including
many recreational administrators, and their programs voiced the prevailing sentiment of the play
movement between 1915 and 1918.

Among the urban communities in which
"neighborhood organization" was attempted as a
method of administering play facilities, Chicago
and New York City lead, seconded by Philadelphia and Cincinnati. Progress in recreational
provision in these four cities will now be analyzed,
and a survey made of similar developments in
rural communities during the same period. In
this survey special reference will be made to Wisconsin, Massachusetts, West Virginia, Illinois,
and Kansas.

[89]Among the papers read at the National Conferences of
Social Work held during the period from 1915 to 1918 are the
following:
1915, Hanmer, "Organizing the Neighborhood for Recreation."
1916, Harrison, "Community Action Through Surveys."
1916, Burns, "Organization of Community Forces."
1916, DeLong, "The School as a Community Center."
1917, Woods, "The City and Its Local Community Life."
1917, Todd, "Reconstruction of Existing Rural Agencies."
1917, Lindemann, "Boys' and Girls' Clubs as Community
        Builders."
1918, Bellamy, "A Community Recreation Program for Juve-
        niles."
1918, Burchard, "Community Councils and Community Cen-
        ters."
1918, Elliott, "A Community Store in a Neighborhood House."
1918, Ingram, "A Community Kitchen in a Neighborhood
        House."
1918, Wilson, "Rural Centers of Community Activity."

In Chicago, the development of organized
neighborhoods or "little communities" was effected in connection with the "small park recreation centers" and the "community centers" in
the public schools. The nature of the structure
and concept of the former is disclosed by the following general letter of the superintendent of the
South Park Playgrounds to directors of the
"small parks," under date of December 9, 1914,
setting forth the policy of administration for the
coming year:[90]

Recreation is a word descriptive of all that is done
during the leisure period of the people. It is not one activity, nor a term applicable to one part of the community; it is
so comprehensive that it includes all of the people and all
their recreation, all the time. . . . . It is the aim of each
park to establish this year (1915) a permanently progressive
and constructive policy of efficient service to all the com-
ponent groups of its community. To do this definite organization is necessary, comprehensive and flexible, but precise
enough to accomplish results. The better articulation with
the community is the plan, and the hearty co-operation with
and from the community is asked. Perhaps we must plead,
we must cajole to get it—but we must get it.

The three fundamental and generic purposes to be secured are: (1) preservation of health, (2) raising of civic
and industrial standards, (3) increasing industrial efficiency.

To accomplish, or to begin, the above program the organization of the four, more or less, distinctive groups of the
community is to be made.

Group I. The mature men and women, who are interested in the essential things and are carrying the responsi-

[90]J. R. Richards, General Letter (unpublished) to Directors of Parks, December 9, 1914, "Statement of the Constructive Plan of Community Work to be Established at Each Park."

bilities and paying the taxes; the parents of the children and others. This group must furnish advice and aid in making possible this plan of efficient service. They should be counseled on the way to do a thing and called in to help. They will not furnish ideas or a program at first, but will be impressed with and aid this scheme, if it is put to them rightly.

Group II. Younger men and women, those interested very largely in social pleasures, dancing, etc. This group may be reached by co-ordinating the different social organizations now existing at each park. Organize a senate from their delegates and many things may be accomplished. From them should come dramatic, literary, and musical recruits. They can be educated into real social intercourse and not allowed to dissipate all their energies on the dance.

Group III. The members of gymnasium classes and boys and girls competing in local park athletics. An association with self-governing features and efficient co-operation will be formed. A plan to reward worth, and not winners alone, will be put into operation.

Group IV. Little children. A modified junior city is to be tried, with ideals of mutual helpfulness and self-government. A savings bank is planned to develop thrift and responsibility.

While the organization of the community had been made by one park[91] before the formulation of the policy outlined in the above letter, by the close of the year 1915, seven of the existing eleven all-year centers of the South Park Commissioners had either completed, or were in, the process of organization.[92] During the subsequent two years,

[91]The Hamilton Park Neighborhood Council was organized October–December, 1914.

[92]Cf. *Annual Report South Park Commissioners*, 1915, p. 68. "With a view of articulating the parks with the neighborhood and securing a conscious community spirit and collective effort in solving community problems, we have been busy the

practically all of the twenty-five park recreation centers in the city developed some form of "neighborhood organization." The term chosen by all to designate the organization of each center was "community council."

The form of organization of the respective "park community councils" differed in details. In some the parents of the children formed the nucleus of the community organization; in others, representatives of the existing local societies and institutions constituted the "community council;" while in still others, membership in the "council" was open to the entire neighborhood, including in its "executive committee" some individuals who were representatives of local organizations and others who were not members of neighborhood societies. The "standing committees" or "departments" of the respective "councils" differed in number and name. Those of the Hamilton Park Neighborhood Council were the following: membership, publicity, ways and

---

past year in organizing the various communities of our district. Participation was the keynote of the whole plan as it is with all effective training. Weekly meetings of directors were held and plans thoroughly discussed. Many problems presented themselves, such as the necessity of creating a community sentiment in the park locality before real community effort could be undertaken, and the best way to secure neighborhood counsellors and workers. Of course, directors were not equally responsible, and better work has been done in some parks than others. Progress, however, has been made and organizations of neighborhoods are in existence at Palmer Park, Bessemer Park, Russell Square, and Hamilton Park, and have been started at Davis Square and Mark White Square. Armour Square is getting in shape to begin and the other parks will follow soon."

Midwinter Gymnastic Exhibition, Hamilton Park Neighborhood Center, Chicago

means, program, vigilance, welfare, improvement, home and markets, education, civics, athletics, social, musical, dramatic, literary, arts and crafts, and outdoor life.[93]   The pioneer work of "neighborhood organization" attempted at the "small parks" encountered many difficulties: (1) The population of each "district" was too large. (2) The boundaries of the respective districts were not definitely fixed. (3) The greater number of the parks were arbitrarily located and the respective districts surrounding them possessed, therefore, no natural unity due to geography, industry, or demography. (4) The park commissioners rigidly enforced an antiquated ordinance forbidding political meetings. (5) Another rule prohibited any individual or group to charge admission fees, solicit funds, or sell articles for any purpose, philanthropic, community, or otherwise, while using park facilities. This last named restriction limited the financial resources to membership dues and voluntary subscriptions and proved a great handicap to the work of the "councils."

Table XI discloses the plan of organization of the Hamilton Park Neighborhood Council, typical of those of the South Parks during 1915–18. On the left hand side is a list of the societies and institutions in the neighborhood, and on the

[93]For description of the duties of these committees and full constitution of this particular "council," cf. "Community Organization," C. E. Rainwater, *Sociological Monograph No. 15*, Southern California Sociological Society, 1920.

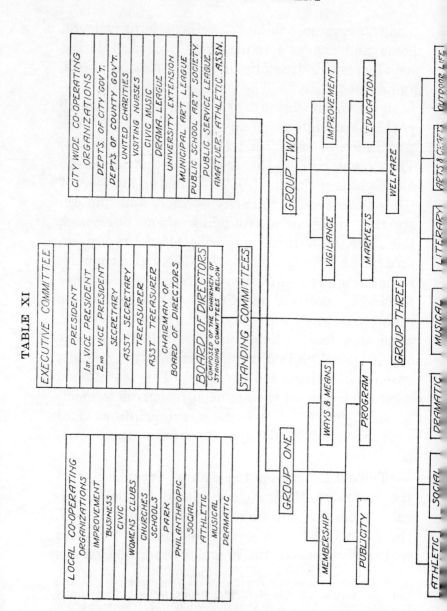

TABLE XI

right hand side are the departments of city government and societies outside the neighborhood, that were correlated with the "council." In the center is the executive committee composed of the regular officers and the chairman and members of the "board of directors," or chairman of the standing committees. The director of the Park was elected annually to the office of chairman of the board of directors. The committees were of three types: (1) those having to do with the maintenance of the "council;" (2) those directly at work on problems of social welfare; (3) those popularly regarded as having "recreational" functions.

"Neighborhood organization" in the public schools of Chicago enjoyed greater resources in securing financial support than were permitted in the parks; but this advantage was offset by other facts, notably the character of the school plants which in comparison with the "small parks" were ill-adapted to community organization purposes. Notwithstanding this handicap there were thirty-nine "community centers," the official name by which the neighborhood organizations were known, conducted in schoolhouses during 1916, the mid-year of the "neighborhood organization" stage. Twelve were opened that season. The number of evenings per week during which the respective "centers" were conducted was two, and the maximum number of evenings for a single "center" was forty-five. Of the twelve new "centers," four were "self-supporting." These were Brentano, Lane, Sabin, and Norwood Park.[94] The Armstrong, the oldest school community center in the city schools, was already self-supporting. In these the Board of Education bore the expense of opening the building, involving heat, light, janitor service, and salary of the

[94]The structure and concept of the school "community centers" is disclosed by the description given of two in the *Annual Report of the Superintendent of Schools*, Chicago, for 1916.

Brentano.—The Brentano Neighborhood Association was formed with annual dues of one dollar per year for the members, the proceeds of the memberships to be used to finance the center. The neighborhood is one in which the same facilities persist from one generation to another. One man was principal of the school for nearly thirty years, and was principal when the center started. The possibilities were in the neighborhood. A leader was found, capable, willing, and able to give the time. He appointed chairmen of the various committees who were enthusiastic and willing to work. . . . .

The programs for the two evenings (during which the center was conducted each week) were different: Monday night for work, and Friday night for play. . . . . The only persons paid were the orchestra and the gymnasium instructor; all others contributed their services. The attendance of young children was discouraged.

Sabin.—In March, at the suggestion of the district superintendent in charge, the principal tried to organize the community for community center purposes. The neighborhood had not asked for the center; consequently it was necessary to get people together who were interested in such movements. From the head resident of Association House on West North Avenue the names were secured of persons who might help. . . . . Several meetings were called at the school, and among those who attended were representatives of Association House, the Juvenile Protective Association, the Eleanor Clubs, the Fifteenth Ward Civic League, the Jewish Educational Alliance, the Y. M. C. A., and the Northwestern Settlement.

A free entertainment was planned at which a prominent judge made an address explaining the purposes in view. The assemblage thereupon formed a permanent organization called the Sabin Community Council, with a president, secretary, several vice-presidents, and a treasurer. . . . . All the helpers were volunteers.

principal, together with a small amount for games and other material, while all other expenses were met by the people participating. The average expense to the school board in these centers was about $16.00 for each night on which they were conducted. In the centers that were not organized for "self-support" and in which the school board met all expenses, the cost was about $28.00 per night. Thus the "self-supporting" centers bore 57% of their expenditures.[95] Commenting on the progress made toward self-government and support, and indicating the significance attached to this feature of the community centers, the superintendent of schools[96] said:

One of the most encouraging features which have attended the work is that of local organization and neighbor-

[95]Financial Report, Brentano Neighborhood Association, from January 1, 1916, to July 1, 1916.

RECEIPTS

From membership dues—580 at $1.00	$580.00
For advertising ads	22.00
Benefit concert ticket sale	61.65
1438 admission fees for dancing classes, 15c	215.70
Total	$879.35

EXPENSES

Gymnasium instructors	$102.50
Music for dances and gymnasium	176.00
Rents to Board of Education*	110.00
Paid lectures	57.25
Printing	194.45
Miscellaneous	194.10
Total	$834.30
Balance on hand July 1, 1916	$ 45.05

*This center used the school building on many evenings in addition to the two per week given free by the Board of Education.

[96]John D. Shoop, *62nd Annual Report Superintendent of Schools*, Chicago, 1916, p. 1.

hood assistance. Many of these centers are managed largely by officials who have been selected by the citizens of the community at large. Local autonomy is recognized as one of the important features of the community center management, and out of this plan of organization an enthusiasm has grown that augurs well for the future use of school buildings as a point at which the interests of the community will center.

The development of the concept of "neighborhood organization" in Chicago led to that of the function of an "overhead" organization as an indispensable adjunct to the local "councils" and "centers," evolving in connection with park fieldhouses and schools. Such an instrument, it was thought, would facilitate mutual aid between "neighborhood organizations," as in the provision of speakers for forums, of talent for entertainments, and the exchange of experiences, and build up a functional relationship between the "councils" and the respective departments of city government and voluntary agencies immediately related to the organized neighborhoods; as for example, the department of health, or the associated charities, as well as the school and park boards. During the previous year many adjustments had become obviously necessary if the efficacy of the organized neighborhoods was to be realized and the scheme of democratic administration of the recreational institutions made successful. Consequently, in April, 1916, representatives of all the organized neighborhoods in Chicago met at the City Club and formed the Community Centers Conference. The function of this conference as defined in its constitution was:[97]

> The discussion of community center organization, administration and maintenance; mutual aid in arranging programs and entertainments; recommendations to public and private agencies upon community center matters, and whatever else may be deemed advisable.

This was the first attempt, as far as the writer is aware, to correlate both officials and private citizens, experts and laymen, in an "overhead" organization, with advisory rather than disciplinary power, designed to promote self-government and self-support through collective neighborhood effort as a method of procedure in the administration of play and recreation. It remained active until the war, when the community councils displaced it.

In New York, the development of "neighborhood organization" as a decentralized and democratic scheme of administration of play was organically related to the "recreation center" stage and made in connection with the small park and public school "social centers,"[98] of which there were about sixty in 1914. The connecting link between the two stages of development was the Social Center Committee formed in 1912 as a result of the national conference on social centers

[97]Unpublished manuscript of the Constitution of the Community Center Conference, Chicago.

[98]The term "social center," as employed in New York at that time, designated a juvenile recreation center rather than "a single, all-inclusive organized society" as defined by Ward. Cf. above.

that met in Madison, Wisconsin, in October, 1911.[99]
The intermediary steps that led to the concept
of structure and function characterizing the
"neighborhood organization" stage included the
following eight: (1) the conduct of self-sustaining public forums in some of the schools of Brooklyn; (2) the attempt to demonstrate a complete
"social center," "self-governing" and "self-
supporting," at the McKinley School, Manhattan;
(3) the organization of "neighborhood associations" in connection with the school social centers as a method of promoting self-government
and self-support, these "associations" being
given the privilege of charging admission fees to
entertainments held under their auspices and of
raising money in other prescribed ways, such as,
membership dues and the sale of articles at fairs,
bazaars, etc.; (4) the holding of a "neighborhood

[99]The situation in New York at this time is described by
John Collier in a monograph entitled "Community Organization and the Great Decision," which appeared in July, 1919,
in the *Seward Park Community Center Magazine*. "Eight
years ago (1911), New York possessed social settlements, half
a dozen forums, two neighborhood betterment societies, and
fifty-five public school recreation centers for boys and girls.
This practically measured the extent of conscious community
organization in a population of five million people. There was
political organization; there were reform societies; there was
organized labor, just becoming conscious of its world power
and its community obligations; there were churches, benefit
societies, secret societies, racial groups. There was an expenditure of one hundred million dollars a year by New York City
in educating, healing, and otherwise modifying human beings.
New York was a labyrinth of labyrinths of special, exclusive,
partial, non-social human organization. The great impersonal,
economic process of factory, and bank, and store did give a
certain unity to the people's life, but it was an unconscious
unity, a unity of cogs, of braces and fly-wheels in an unconscious machine."

workers institute" at the New York School of
Philanthropy in June, 1914,[100] of a seminary in
"community center work" under the auspices of
the New York Social Center Committee, in the
spring of 1915, and the organization of the New
York Training School for Community Workers
with Luther H. Gulick as President, through the
promotion of the People's Institute in the autumn
of 1915;[101] (5) the appointment by the board of
education of a "director of community centers"
in the public schools;[102] (6) the creation of
"health districts" in connection with the "neighborhood associations" in the schools, where a
representative of the health department of the
city co-operated with the neighborhood society in

[100]This institute was conducted for "secretaries of neighborhood associations, leaders of school social centers and
others." Among the topics discussed were "programs for clubs
and classes and the general problem of neighborhood organization . . . . and their relation to a city social program."
This institute was "endorsed by the officers of the National
Federation of Settlements and conducted in co-operation with
the New York Association of Neighborhood Workers." Cf.
Bulletin of New York School of Philanthropy (now the New
York School of Social Work) for 1914–16, General Announcement, pp. 38–39.

[101]The names of the consultants and lecturers for the
second year included among others: Carol Aronovici, Edw. M.
Barrows (Associate Director), John Collier (Director), M. M.
Davis, Mrs. J. Gilmore Drayton (Ex. Secretary), Luther H.
Gulick, Shelby Harrison, Joseph Lee, Percy MacKaye, C. A.
Perry, Edw. F. Sanderson (Director People's Institute) and
Mrs. V. G. Simkhovitch. The first year's attendance was limited to 36, of whom 25 received diplomas, and 17 held positions through the school year in neighborhood organization
and related fields.—The New York Training School for Com-
munity Workers, General Announcement, 1916–17, p. 2.

[102]This officer was Eugene C. Gibney, formerly a director
of one of the public school recreation centers and an alumnus
of the Training School for Community Workers.

adapting the machinery of the department to their needs; (7) the organization of "community clearing houses" in connection with the school centers, where a citizen of the neighborhood might obtain any information concerning the municipal or philanthropic agencies accessible to him in solving a personal or group problem and to which he, too, might bring his own resources in some undertaking of common interest;[103] (8) the organization of "community councils," first on a "personal" and later a "group unit" basis.[104]

About 1915 the term "community center" came into use, in New York, when referring to the agency or instrument through which "neighborhood organization" was being effected. During that year sixteen "community centers" were being developed in schoolhouses alone, but within three years the number had increased to eighty-five, the work having been greatly propagated by the People's Institute. The concept of "neighborhood organization" as formulated at the begin-

[103]The community clearing house developed out of the research conducted by Mildred Taylor for the committee on the unadjusted child. It constituted a stepping stone between the community center and the community council, and was referred to by local workers as "the neighborhood gateway to all the resources of New York." "Here any citizen could find out how to get whatever he needed and how to offer his services for anything he wanted done. At this headquarters any agent of government or of private welfare work could call into service any other agent whose help was needed in any task of discovering and meeting human need. Thirteen city departments joined in a quasi-official way to make effective the work of the community clearing house."—John Collier, *supra*.

[104]For a definition of the sense in which the terms "personal" and "group" unit are here used, cf. p. 163.

ning of this period is indicated by the following:[105]

The neighborhood spirit finds expression through the community center. In general a community center is a place where the people of a locality may unite in their own way for the expression and enjoyment of whatever interests they have in common. It is founded on the schoolhouse, as this is apt to be the only effective building owned by the people together. It leads to the establishment . . . . of every human expression of a neighborhood's interest in behalf of its people.

The vital characteristic of a community center is its absolute democracy. Cities, or schools, or park boards, or private enterprise may evolve elaborate systems for benefiting the people, but these systems are developed externally and applied from the outside, while the community center reflects the spontaneous desires of the people of a neighborhood, is developed by the people themselves, and is maintained through their own leaders in their own way.

It does not belong within the field of this report to write a complete history of community centers in New York City;[106] the references here made

[105]New York Training School for Community Workers, *Announcement* for 1916–17.

[106]If the reader is interested in this line of investigation, he is referred to the following sources as being among the most valuable: (a) *Community Councils of New York City*, Statement of Work and Problems, prepared for the conference held at the home of Mrs. Frank A. Vanderlip at Scarborough-on-Hudson, July 12, 1919; (b) "Community Organization and the Great Decision," John Collier, *Seward Park Community Center Magazine*, July, 1919; (c) *Twentieth Annual Report of the Superintendent of Schools of New York*, 1918; (d) "Community Centers in Social Education," *Papers and Proceedings, American Sociological Society*, Vol. XIII, pp. 111–16; (e) "Community Councils," *Conference of Social Work*, John Collier; (f) *The Community Center*, magazine of the National Community Center Association; (g) *The Community Clearing House*, Mildred Taylor, 1917, a pamphlet published at 227 East 22nd St., New York City; (h) "Why Community Organization," by John Collier, and his discussion of another paper by John L. Elliott on "Some Neighborhood Needs" at the National Social Unit Conference, Cincinnati, October 23–25, 1919.

to them are limited to their relation to the play
movement, that is, to the fact of the development
within the play movement of a "community center" or "neighborhood organization" stage, and
to the community center as a phase of the play
movement. A reciprocal relation existed between
the two, and the field which they occupied in common was that of "neighborhood organization"
for the administration of play. The object here
is, thus, merely to define the structure and the
concept of the function of the "neighborhood
organization" stage as it was manifested in New
York between about 1915 and 1918. The facts of
greatest importance in the discussion here are,
accordingly, those relative to the method of procedure followed in organizing neighborhoods for
the administration of play. These involve (1)
"neighborhood associations," (2) "community
councils," (3) the "overhead" organization of
the "councils." While the "community centers"
and "councils" had a greater significance than
merely that of serving as a medium for the
administration of play, in the sense in which the
term is used in this study,[107] it remains true that
they also had *that* meaning and were originated in
play centers.

An analysis of the development of the method
or technique of "neighborhood organization" in
New York City shows that the first attempts to
organize neighborhoods consisted of the forma-

[107]Cf. pp. 4–8 above.

tion of a number of "neighborhood associations."
These societies were "homogeneous groups"[108]
whose membership comprised persons, living in
the vicinity of the schoolhouse in which the "association" was organized, who participated voluntarily and independently of any connection that
they may have had with a local institution or
society. There was, thus, no functional union of
the "neighborhood association" with local
groups; no members were approved delegates of
organizations already existing in the neighborhood or out of it. Now these "associations," it
was observed, tended to disintegrate after the
original enthusiasm that gave rise to them had
ceased. A realization of this fact led in time to a
reorganization of the "associations," whereby
their control was vested in a "council" composed
in part of delegates from each of the functional
groups of the locality and the respective social
agencies and departments of government active
in that vicinity, and in part from the membership of the association at large. The functional
groups were usually those interested in music,
dramatics, games, athletics, dances, or labor union
activities, while the social agencies embraced the
philanthropic societies and the departments of
government, those of health, education, correction, and recreation. This was the origin of the
"community councils;" and it is clear from the

[108]John Collier, in discusion of paper, "Some Neighborhood Needs," read at National Social Unit Conference, Cincinnati, October, 1919.

nature of the groups correlated with the "neighborhood organization" that the function of the "councils" was predominantly recreational. The "councils" were, primarily, instruments used in the decentralized and democratic administration of play. They were "self-governing" as far as it was possible for an organization using public property to be so, and "self-supporting" as far as the additional expenses necessitated by their use of the schoolhouse were involved. Membership dues, admission fees, and the sale of commodities were the principal sources of their financial income, no public appropriations being made for their maintenance after the second year.

The application of the method of "self-government" and "self-support" of "community councils," as the neighborhood organizations were then called, logically led, in New York as it had done previously in Chicago, to a sequence of attempts in "overhead" organization for the promotion of greater efficiency in the work of the local "councils." Service, not control, was the object, and the correlation of programs and money getting activities was the method of the "overhead" organization experiments. The first step in this direction was the formation of the "League of Neighborhood School Centers" after a series of meetings beginning on February 8, 1917. The objects of this league, as outlined in its constitution were as follows:

(a) To form a closer union between Recreation and Community Centers. (b) To make the school the People's Club.

(c) To develop the Neighborhood School Centers to their maximum of service and efficiency by co-operative treatment of the following: (1) community choruses, orchestras, and concerts, (2) motion pictures, (3) dramatic performances, (4) athletics, (5) forums, (6) clubs, (7) dances, (8) game and reading rooms, (9) such other activities as may develop. (d) To arrange for co-operation between the centers in the following manner: (1) by arranging co-operative money raising activities, (2) by gathering information regarding availability of talent and arranging for the interchange of same, (3) by arranging athletic meets, (4) by arranging for the interchange of equipment, (5) by the publication of a periodical, and arranging for any other desirable publicity. (e) To co-operate with the Council of Community Center workers to the end of securing their advice and assistance.[109]

Subsequently, "district co-operative leagues" were formed, the chairmen of the respective district leagues constituting the executive committee of the League of Neighborhood School Centers. Each local center was represented by a delegate in the district league, of which there were eleven in 1918.[110] On July 1, 1919, "A City Parliament of Councils" was formed, a further elaboration of "overhead" organization.[111]

[109]*Twentieth Annual Report of Superintendent of Schools.* New York City, 1918, p. 79.

[110]*Ibid.*

[111]As stated above, by 1918 the term "community council" had displaced that of "community center" as the name by which the organized neighborhood was known. Consequently, as a result of both that change and the development of "community councils" throughout the nation during the second year of the participation of the United States in the Great War, the method of "overhead" organization was further elaborated. The work of the "councils" organized in response to the appeal of the Council of National Defense (of which there were 180,000 developing by the time the war ceased)

These are the essential facts relative to the development of "neighborhood organization" as a method of administering play in New York City that received greatest emphasis about 1915-18.

In Philadelphia, "advisory councils" were developed in connection with the "recreation parks" that offered all-year facilities for play. These "councils" were composed of adults, either delegates or officers of the respective neighborhood clubs using the indoor recreation centers. They were identical in structure with those in the school centers in New York, although not as large, being composed of representatives of the functional groups of the neighborhoods about the parks. No "overhead" organization was attempted by them, and their self-supporting activities were limited as were the councils organized in connection with the Chicago parks analyzed above, yet they were designed to provide "local self-government"[112] in the administration of play.

was primarily that necessitated by certain war emergencies, and for this work special "overhead" organization had been provided. After the war, peace conditions necessitated a reorganization, and on July 1, 1919, "A City Parliament of Community Councils" with a co-ordinate group of advisory committees was organized. The objects of the "parliament" were similar to those of the "league," and the committees were those on health, recreation, education, and industrial relations.

[112]In the annual report of the Board of Recreation of Philadelphia for 1913, on p. 26, the following statement is made concerning these "councils": The Board of Recreation is anixous to provide in the evening for those who work by day in factory, workshop, and office. The shower baths and swimming pool are more used by adults at night. The grounds are electric lighted and many daylight games are played at night.

In Cincinnati, the most unique experiment in self-government and self-support of play facilities was made in connection with the work of the National Social Unit Organization in the Mohawk-Brighton District, during 1916–19.[113]   A statement of the details of this experiment is beyond the purpose of this report, but it is significant that one of the seven groups represented by elected delegates in the "occupational council" was that of the "recreational workers" of the district in which the experiment was undertaken.   Self-support and self-government were among the distinctive traits of the "social unit" plan.

In rural communities, there was a growing consciousness, about 1915, "that people must work together in these local groups if they seek the best results."[114]   In some respects, indeed, provision for play, in both the open country and the village, was from the first more democratic than that of the cities; that is, more self-govern-

---

. . . . Among older patrons, the club motive is strong.   The officers of each club form a Playground Council which promises to be a governing body of importance.

In the report of 1914, p. 29, is inserted a full page picture of one of the "advisory councils" in session.

[113]For further information concerning the National Social Unit Organization, its structure, history, and function, consult their Bulletins, Nos. 1, 2, 2a, 3, 4, and the papers read at the National Social Unit Conference, Cincinnati, October 23–25, 1919.

[114]Kenyon L. Butterfield, in his Introduction to *Mobilizing the Rural Community*, by E. L. Morgan, Massachusetts Agricultural College Bulletin, No. 23, September, 1918.

ing and self-sustaining.[115] There were fewer institutions that attempted to give service *to* the people, and more that worked *with* them. The "rural life" movement, for example, universally inaugurated activities to be undertaken by the people, such as "community drama" and "community music" developed conspicuously in Wisconsin, North Dakota, and Kansas.[116] Similar events occured in West Virginia during 1913-15, when at the suggestion of the state superintendent of schools, one thousand rural teachers volunteered to undertake the organization of "social centers" of a democratic type in their school buildings. The assistant superintendent prepared a handbook for their use in that work.[117]

But these earlier attempts to provide for play in rural communities were, with possibly only one exception,[118] of the "homogeneous group" type like the early "neighborhood associations" formed in New York,[119] that is, a voluntary society

[115]C. J. Galpin, "Rural Social Centers in Wisconsin," *University of Wisconsin Agricultural Experiment Station Bulletin*, No. 234; and State Superintendent of Schools, Wisconsin, *Report of the Sub-Committee of the Committee of Fifteen*, Bulletin No. 18.

[116]Cf. Peter W. Dykema, "The Spread of the Community Music Idea," *The Annals*, 1916, pp. 218-23; and "Community Music and Drama," *University of Wisconsin, Extension Division Bulletin*, General Series. No. 638, 1917.

[117]L. J. Hanifan, *Community Social Gatherings at Rural Schoolhouses*.

[118]The West Newbury Federation for Rural Progress, West Newbury, Essex County, Mass., organized in the spring of 1909. "It was composed of representatives of some dozen organizations and agencies of the town, including the church, the school committee, and two granges." Cf. E. L. Morgan, *Mobilizing the Rural Community*, p. 7.

[119]Cf. John Collier, *supra*.

performing a definite and limited function, as a "school improvement club" or a "community house association," or an institution that undertook a new service, as a rural church organizing community music, or a township building a community house. An intermediate step in the development of the concept of "neighborhood organization" in rural districts was the formation of a more complex organization with an executive committee consisting of the president, secretary, treasurer, and chairman of the respective standing committees. This bridged the distance between the simple homogeneous group formed for a single purpose and the heterogeneous one composed of representatives of existing institutions who formed a "community council." The clearest anaylsis of this transitional type of rural organization was possibly that of Carver,[120] who proposed an executive committee as described, and two groups of standing committees; the one "business," and the other, "social." The former comprised "farm production," "marketing," "farm supplies," "credit," and "communication," that is, roads and telephones; the latter, "education," "sanitation," "recreation," "beautification," and "home economics." Concerning this scheme, however, he said:

No single plan of organization will suit all communities. . . . . The plan here presented is intended only as a general

[120]Cf. T. N. Carver, "The Organization of a Rural Community," *U. S. Dept. of Agriculture, Yearbook for 1914*, pp. 89–138.

guide, to be followed so far as it seems to meet the needs of any community which is studying the problem of organization. . . . .

It is not a plan for the "uplifting" of the farmer. The farmers are quite capable of taking care of themselves, but they have not yet taken up the work of organized self-help as completely as could be desired.

The function of the "recreation" committee in this plan of rural organization was outlined as follows:

To promote wholesome sports adapted to rural communities, such as swimming, horseback riding, "hiking" games, for old and young, neighborhood fairs.

To promote rural festivities combining threshing, husking, cotton picking, and other seasonal work with social recreation.

To promote neighborhood choral clubs, annual musical events by township, county, and state.

To promote playgrounds, parks, and neighborhood centers.

During the two or three years preceding 1918, a limited number of "community councils" were formed in country-side and "town" districts. These "councils" consisted of a small membership of delegates, usually less than a score, chosen by their respective institutions and societies which generally included the church, the grange, the county Y. M. C. A., the parent-teacher association, the boy scouts, the camp fire girls. These "joint-committees," as they were also called, usually made a more or less thorough survey of their community and outlined a program of development extending over a period of from three to

five years. Provision for play was always a feature of the work of the "councils" and one which
occupied much of its attention. Massachusetts
was one of the first states in which this plan was
adopted on a wide scale.[121] In support of it, a
community advisor wrote, after six years of experience with "councils:"[122]

It has seemed better to unite existing groups for work
than to bring about something new which would be an additional burden to an already overloaded community. The
council leads community committees in a thorough study of
the town, and in the working out of a three to five year plan
or program of town[123] development, made up of special
projects in farm production, farm business, conservation,
boys' and girls' interests, and community life, that is,
education, the home, public health, civic affairs, recreation,
transportation, etc. The carrying out of this program is done
by the local organizations co-operating through the council.

A natural outgrowth of "neighborhood organization" in many rural communities was the acqui-
sition of a building, a "community house," for
recreational and other collective uses. These indoor community plants were usually obtained by
the purchase and remodeling of existing structures, but in some instances by construction, as
in Kansas where a state law permitted town-
ships to vote bonds not to exceed five thousand
dollars for that purpose.[124] A few were donated.

[121]E. L. Morgan, *Mobilizing a Rural Community*, Massachusetts Agricultural College Bulletin, No. 23.
[122]*Ibid.*
[123]The word "town" as here used is equivalent to "community," meaning the New England "town" or township.
[124]W. C. Nason and C. W. Thompson, "Rural Community
Buildings in the United States," *United States Department of
Agriculture*, Bulletin No. 825, p. 29.

The finances necessary for either purchase or construction, when not procured by donation or a bond issue, were raised by the formation of stock companies, by subscriptions, by admission fees to entertainments, and by membership fees, and in part by rentals after the operation of the plant had begun. By 1918 community buildings had been provided in one or more rural districts in forty-one states. During 1915–18, ninety buildings such as these were acquired either by purchase or construction, an average of thirty per year.

The simplest of these buildings, often found in the open country, contained an auditorium with movable seats so that it might be transformed into a dining room, a gymnasium, or dance hall, a stage, and a kitchen, each equipped with the usual apparatus. In the smaller towns there were often in addition to these facilities, a library, a reading room, a game room, a woman's rest room, and clubrooms; in county seats and the larger towns, often an office, cafe, gymnasium, billiard room, agriculture exhibit room, and headquarters for the agricultural agent, visiting nurse, and secretary of the commercial club. From an analysis of the structure of these plants, it is clear that their use was largely that of play.

These buildings have become the centers of their communities for recreational, gymnastic, athletic, social, and welfare work, and often for political, co-operative business, and religious work.[125]

[125]W. C. Nason and C. W. Thompson, *op. cit.*, p. 5.

In some rural communities, efforts toward "neighborhood organization" resulted in the creation of a new public office: the "community secretary."[126] The first one was elected in Osseo, Wisconsin, June 20, 1914, when the school principal was chosen to be "civic secretary"[127] as well as school head, with an increase of one-third of his former salary. Sauk City and Neillsville, both in Wisconsin, soon followed the example of Osseo. Later several rural communities in Massachusetts adopted the plan, although not making use of the heads of the local schools in all cases. Under the personal leadership of the "community secretaries," the local institutions and associations were correlated into a functional and dynamic whole. The control and support of play was a phase of the task of the "community secretary," constituting at least fifty per cent of his work, and involving the management of the social center and the public forum, the making out of a calendar of local meetings and events, the directing of community surveys, and the charting of community needs.

The employment of the "community secretary" in the plan of rural organization was a development rather than a disavowal of the con-

[126]Various titles were employed in designating the office. "Civic secretary," "chairman of the board of directors," "community advisor," and "community secretary" were all in use at first. but the last title finally displaced the others.

[127]E. J. Ward, "The Greatest Office in Any Community," *LaFollette's Magazine*, September 5, 1914; and Graham Taylor, "A Community Secretary," *National Municipal Review*, April, 1915.

cept of "neighborhood organization." It was
followed as readily by local communities in which
"councils" were already active as by others, for
it had become evident that someone must give a
considerable amount of time and thought to a
given enterprise undertaken by any community
if it were to terminate successfully.

As stated by an experienced worker, a community adviser, himself:[128]

In the past we have held to the idea that one of the
greatest needs was to discover and train local people to
assume local responsibilities. While our belief on this point
has not changed, still it has become apparent that the average farmer will not continue to give time to matters of business routine or organization detail which belong to the entire
community. The future is going to see our communities doing collectively a good many things that they have never done
before. This will come merely because it is the most efficient
way of getting those things done which we have in common.
This need, which is everywhere apparent, leads to the suggestion that someone be officially designated and maintained
by taxation as community secretary. The work he could do
would be no mean task.

While no form of "overhead" organization of
"rural councils" or "neighborhood associations"
was developed by the initiative of these groups,
an equivalent aid in their administration was provided by both federal and state agencies. Examples of the former were the U. S. Departments
of Agriculture and the Interior; of the latter,
the state superintendents of instruction, the extension departments of state universities, the

[128]E. L. Morgan, *supra*.

state boards of agriculture, the agricultural and
normal schools. In some instances county-wide
organization through the "county farm adviser"
or the county Y. M. C. A. was effected.[129]   A frequent method of extending assistance and ex-
changing counsel was by way of a "conference."
The "A. B. C. Conferences"[130] of Illinois, were
typical examples. The first was a state convention, held at the State University, June 20–22,
1916. Later, district and local conferences were
held. Play and recreation was always a topic for
discussion at these meetings, and their function
was twofold: to define the method of community
organization, and to interest communities in
accepting the responsibility of solving their local
problems. The question was not whether the people could be entrusted with power, but how they
could be induced to take it, to accept responsibility
for the local welfare. The "neighborhood organization" stage of the play movement, then, was
never, in city or in country, an expression of
unrest in rebellion to constituted authority; on
the contrary, it was from the first a method of
supplementing governmental organization. In
the language of one of the earliest "civic secretaries," in 1914, when speaking of the function of
his office :[131]

[129]*Op. cit.*, cf. pp. 48–54 for an extensive list of sources of
aid to local councils, classified according to the respective
projects.

[130]The letters "A. B. C." signify "A Better Community."

[131]N. T. Buckley, elected at Sauk City, Wisconsin, June,
1914. Cf. Charles Zueblin, *American Municipal Progress*, 1916,
pp. 226–27.

With this work recognized and remunerated as public service; with its administration organized and centered in the State Superintendent's office in the Capitol; and with the Bureau of Social Center Development and the other Bureaus of the Extension Division as ready sources of suggestions, material for discussion, speakers, and motion picture films, I prophesy that the people of Wisconsin will be equipped to get three times the value they have been getting out of their investment in educational equipment—and incidentally will have in their hands the machinery for that genuine home rule which is democracy.

And in the words of another, who developed one of the first successful community centers in New York, the organized neighborhood "is a microcosm of democratic society:[132]

In developing self-governed clubs under the supervision of qualified leaders we are developing two of the essential attributes of citizenship, respect for authority and obedience to the law. . . . . The boy or girl that is affiliated afterwards grows to manhood and womanhood as a member of a political club, a civic club, or a neighborhood association with a definite purpose of benefiting the community. It is the difference between the solitary and the social. The former becomes an adult lacking interest in public affairs, the latter emerges into citizenship with a keen desire to be a dynamic and loyal member of the nation.

The "neighborhood organization" stage of the play movement has now been analyzed. It has been found that its distinctive features were: (1) an emphasis upon "self-government" and "self-support" of play activities in a decentralized scheme of administration in order that the economic resources of government might be made

[132]Eugene C. Gibney, *Twentieth Annual Report of Superintendent of Schools*, New York, 1918, pp. 12–13.

sufficient for adequate provision of facilities in all communities; (2) the selection of the "neighborhood" or "local community" in the place of city or county as the field of decentralized control and support of the play activities of the people; (3) the development first of "neighborhood associations" designed to carry out given projects of common interest, and second of "community councils" to correlate local institutions into a dynamic whole, functionally related to both philanthropic agencies and departments of government; (4) the utilization of the energies of the residents of local communities in the control and support of definite projects under the leadership of trained persons, "community secretaries," elected and employed by the people involved; (5) the designation of schoolhouses, fieldhouses, and "community houses," designed especially for play uses, as meeting places or "centers" of the common interest of which neighborhoods and "little communities" were becoming conscious; (6) the grant to neighborhood groups using public property of the right to charge admission, collect dues, and solicit funds for the support of community projects; (7) the evolution in some localities of elaborate schemes of "overhead" organization for securing co-operation between "councils" and "associations" in handling money getting devices, exchange of talent, and control of athletic and literary competitions, and in other districts, of extensive efforts on the part of government and philanthropy to encourage local autonomy in the solution of community problems; (9) the incorporation in the field of activities of the play movement of certain phases of the "community center," "country life," and similar movements, involving given projects of common interest to the neighborhood group; (10) the co-operation of social workers and students of social science in defining the concept of the function and the structure of the play movement, resulting in the acceptance of less sentimental and more "socio-rational" objectives, as the substitution of autonomy for philanthropy, both public and private, in the support and control of facilities for play.

G. *The "community service" stage, since about 1918.* The mobilization of the military and naval forces of the United States at the beginning of our participation in the Great War gave rise to a changed social situation with respect to play. New problems arose in every community adjacent to army cantonments or naval bases and training stations, and in those industrial centers in which war supplies were being produced on an extensive scale. In some of these industrial districts the population increased 50 to 100 per cent in a few weeks, and consequently living conditions were so abnormal for many new arrivals that the labor turnover amounted for a time to 50 per cent per month; while in the towns and cities near the cantonments the presence of large numbers of soldiers, sailors, and marines flocking in "on leave" created a demand for larger and more appropriate facilities for leisure time activities than existed in any community, even New York. Commercialized amusements seized the opportunity for exploitation, but they were soon opposed by a new adjustment provided by the play movement, the organization of wholesome recreation under the leadership of what was first called both "war camp" and "war workers'" community service. The Playground and Recreation Association of America proposed to the Council of National Defense that their experience of twelve years and the thousands of trained play leaders engaged in administering facilities in other communities be recruited for service in making an adjustment to the social situation in the "war camp" and "war worker" communities. The suggestion was accepted; the Army and Navy Departments approved and "W. C. C. S."[133] was organized. The president and the secretary of the Playground and Recreation Association of America became corresponding officers in "War Camp Community Service."

The method of procedure employed by War Camp Community Service was essentially that of the "neighborhood organization" stage of the play movement, but through the emotional

[133]"W. C. C. S." were the letters generally used during 1918 to designate War Camp Community Service. Its function was related to recreation in communities *near* the camps and training stations, as that of the Y. M. C. A. to the recreational events *inside* the camps.

intensity of the war emergency that medium was raised to the nth power of efficiency. As stated by one writer:[134]

As War Camp Community Service conceived the problem, it could not be solved by any outside agency, no matter how great or how well organized. It had to be met by the communities themselves. W. C. C. S. could only give the benefit of its advice, could only point the way. The work had to be done through the proper co-ordination of the latent recreational facilities of each camp town and the development by the citizens themselves of new facilities where, as in nearly every case, the existing facilities were inadequate.

It was, as W. C. C. S. visioned it, a problem of neighborliness.

. . . .

That's what they (the soldiers and sailors) got, in so far as the earnest effort of thousands and thousands of hospitable people in the camp towns all over the United States could see that they got such home welcomes. There was no coddling, no charity, no philanthropy in the formal sense, no institutional feeling. The idea was that these folks were entertaining the neighbors' boys.

Before the signing of the armistice "War Camp Community Service" had organized the social and recreational resources of six hundred and four communities near the cantonments for the benefit of the military and naval forces of the nation; and about fifty districts in which war industries were being carried on, of which Bethlehem, Chester, and Erie, Pennsylvania, were typical examples. A force of 2,700 trained workers was employed and a volunteer staff of 60,000 addi-

[134]John R. Colter, "The Town That Found Itself," *Community Service* (Incorporated), Bulletin No. 7, 1919, pp. 13–14.

tional leaders of given activities and committee-
men besides those who received soldiers and
sailors in their homes.[135] The field of activities
involved practically all the types of play that had
been previously developed by the play movement
and many new games and stunts arranged to
enable large numbers to participate at one time,
"mass games,"[136] as well as a number of occupations for convalescents in hospitals. Among
the distinctive types of activities were community
singing, pageants, dances, block parties, athletic
meets, motion pictures, artist recitals, game
rooms, and home hospitality. Thus "War Camp
Community Service" was developed during 1918[137]
as a means of conserving the health and morale
of the fighting forces of the nation.

In the attempt to extend hospitality to the
armed forces of the nation, the respective communities in which "War Camp Community Service" operated for the brief season of actual
hostilities and the shorter period of demobilization
became conscious, for the first time in many instances, of the function of organized recreation
administered by a self-governing and self-supporting method. While seeking to serve others they

[135]"Community   Service," *Community   Service* (Incorporated), Bulletin No. 2, p. 3, 1919.

[136] Cf. Edna Geister, *Ice Breakers* (a book of games and
stunts for social gatherings), Women's Press; *Community
Recreation*, International Com. Y. M. C. A., compiled by Geo.
C. Draper; and Neva L. Boyd, *Hospital and Bedside Games*,
Chicago School of Civics and Philanthropy.

[137]"W. C. C. S.—Its First Year," *The Playground*, Vol.
XII, pp. 273 ff.

had gained something new for themselves, for
many of these communities had not yet adopted
the plan of "neighborhood organization" worked
out during the preceding three years.

Hence, the popular demand was made that
"community service" be continued with the return
of peace, adapting its spirit and technique to conditions of the reconstruction period. In addition
to this request other factors emphasized the value
of an agency such as "community service" in
peace as well as war: (1) there was the need of
Americanization, and "community service" was a
valuable method for achieving it; (2) the greater
demand for rural recreation, since many of the
soldiers and sailors were returning to rural
homes; (3) the large place left vacant in the social
life of many communities by the abolition of the
saloon; (4) the increase in leisure time as a
result of "daylight saving" and shorter working
hours in industry; (5) the necessity for greater
attention to the physical development of the people as disclosed by the high percentages of rejec-
tions for physical unfitness by draft boards.[138]
To aid communities, both urban and rural, in solving these five problems during the reconstruction
period, "Community Service, Incorporated," was
organized in 1919, with general offices at 1 Madison Avenue, New York City.[139] A fund of two

[138]*Community Service* (Incorporated), Bulletin No. 2, p. 2,
1919.

[139]Cf. *Community Service* (Incorporated), Bulletin No. 1,
1919, for statement of names of officers, committees, board of
directors, and members of the "corporation."

million dollars was secured with which to start the work as soon as possible in about four hundred communities, selected chiefly from those in which "War Camp Community Service" had operated.[140]   Thus, "Community Service, Incorporated," is the successor to "War Camp Community Service" as it in turn was an outgrowth of the Playground and Recreation Association of America.   The personnel of the central office remains practically unchanged.[141]   An excellent formulation of the concept of the structure and the function of "community service" is contained in the following sentence from one of their bulletins:

Community Service is the medium through which the residents of a community get together and truly become members of the community, with a consequent real interest in community welfare, prosperity, and stability.

According to this statement, the "community service" stage of the play movement has much in common with that of "neighborhood organization." In many instances the application of the former involves the latter, as indicated by the following:

The neighborhood has been recognized as an essential social unit not only through the school centers and local clubs, but by block parties, which are being made a specialty in Philadelphia and elsewhere.

[140]Cf. op. cit., for statement of budget of Community Service (Incorporated), for the first year, 1919.

[141]Joseph Lee and Howard S. Braucher remain president and secretary, respectively, of both the Playground and Recreational Association of America, and Community Service, Incorporated.

But, while directed from a national headquarters and standpoint, the details of its application remain optional with the local communities and involve some form of group organization of the leisure pursuits of the people of those communities. To quote from their own literature again.[142]

Community Service operates nationally, applies itself locally, and thinks in terms of leisure time.

The method of procedure followed by "Community Service" is democratic and constructive. The fund of two million dollars was designed only for use in self-supporting and self-governing "community recreation" in about four hundred localities, allowing about $5,000 to each for the first year. And it was expected that for every dollar thus expended, at least ten would be spent by the local communities in support of the work thus inaugurated.[143] As outlined in 1919:

The method of work will be to send to each city a community organizer to form a representative committee of citizens and start the work. In some cases a song leader or some other specialist may also be provided to start a special activity, but always the aim will be to make the people feel that the problem is their own problem and to hand the work over to them as soon as possible. A constant feature will be the training of volunteers to act as song leaders, as teachers of dramatics, or directors of playgrounds or school centers, as chaperones at dances, or to help in other kinds of work. . . . .

[142]W. F. Edwards, "Community Service, A Positive Force in Reconstruction," *Community Service* (Incorporated), Bulletin No. 1, p. 4, 1919.

[143]Cf. *Community Service* (Incorporated), Bulletin No. 2, p. 7, 1919.

The appeal in each community is made to all the people, not as rich or poor, as native or of foreign origin, but as citizens. . . . .

The aim . . . . will be not to impose a cut-and-dried program from without, but to draw out the strength that is in the people and to make them conscious and efficient directors of their own affairs.

The field of activities promoted by "community service" comprises an extensive list of wholesome leisure pursuits[144] with emphasis upon the following types:

Physical: aquatics, athletics, basket-ball, boating, boxing, camping, field-days, folk-dancing, games, hikes, meets, skating, soccer, street play, stunts, tournaments.

Social: banquets, block parties, candy pulls, clubs, community centers, dances, game rooms, home hospitality, motion pictures, spelling-bees.

Aesthetic: concerts, choruses, dramatics, festivals, oratorios, pageants, recitals, "sings."

Constructive: gardening, pets, sand modeling, sloyd, sewing.

Civic: Americanization, community councils, community days, community Christmas trees, cooperative enterprises, "dry saloons," forums, mass meetings, night schools, lectures, surveys, welfare exhibits, vacation homes for working girls.

The degree of success attained to date is indicated by the following events of the past two years. On May 1, 1920, the report of the first year of "Community Service, Incorporated,"

[144]Cf. *Community Recreational Activities*, pamphlet by Playground and Recreation Association of America, 1920.

showed that sixty-five cities had raised a local budget and had started work, the total amount subscribed during the six months preceding being $700,000, while, since the armistice $27,521,000 has been raised or pledged for "memorial community buildings." At the present writing 129 cities have raised local budgets for the support of "community service." These figures by no means represent the total expenditures of the play movement during the past two years. The emphasis upon the community function greatly aided public appropriations for play facilities and "community service" was in turn benefited by them.[145]

The war has had its effect on recreation, not only through emphasizing the community values involved, but also in the development of the municipal recreation movement which for years has slowly but surely been gaining ground in American communities and which Community Service, Incorporated, seeks to strengthen and enlarge.

Some of the more conspicuous examples of an advance in public provision for play in correlation with community recreation are the following: (1) that the total number of playgrounds and recreation centers publicly maintained decreased only 1.8 per cent during the year 1918 in spite of the war demands, while during that same period the number of year-round workers increased 174 per cent; (2) that a $10,000,000 bond issue was authorized by Detroit, and $500,000 by Portland for

[145]Abbie Condit, "Recreation," *American Yearbook*, for 1920.

small parks and playgrounds; (3) that public appropriations for play were doubled by Memphis, Milwaukee, Newton, Mass., and Sacramento, California; (4) that many gifts were made to public recreation, such as the $2,500,000 Hannan Memorial Hall for music in Detroit, a $10,000 memorial playground in Sacramento, a forty-acre park in Cleveland, and a seventeen-acre tract in Kalamazoo, Michigan; (5) that state legislation was enacted in behalf of both public and community recreation, as the Pennsylvania law which requires boards of education throughout the state to make their school plants available for recreational use upon petition by a given per cent of the adult residents of the community, and the Michigan law known as "An Act Creating a Community Council Commission, County Community Boards and Community Councils" by which an attempt is made to promote the play and community interests of the state by a board of 26 to whom the county commissions and local councils are responsible. The Michigan law was an outgrowth of the work of the Councils of National Defense organized during the war and parallels the work of "community service."

The concept of the structure and function of the play movement at the present time, the "community service" stage, involves emphasis upon the following features: (1) great enthusiasm for neighborliness, an after-glow of the war spirit; (2) financial support for propaganda, in the form

of a huge budget; (3) great confidence on the
part of the public in the practicality of its method
as a result of the success achieved in six hundred
communities during the war; (4) the equivalent
of a voluntary national "overhead organization"
in the function of the national office of "Community Service, Incorporated;" (5) an effectual
correlation of the "neighborhood" with the
"community" in the control and support of a
democratic plan of administration of play, as exemplified in "music weeks," "community days,"
"holiday celebrations," "community singing,"
"community drama" and "pageantry;" (6)
facilities for educating the public in the use of
leisure, as provided by the local office of "community service" whose staff is more engaged in
the work of co-operating with existing institutions
and agencies, in training play leaders, in discovering unused resources and developing facilities
where none exists than in merely administering
more efficiently given plants, such as school or
park "recreation centers;" (7) the formation of
"advisory councils," in the place of the former
type of "local overhead organization," composed
of representatives of all institutions and organizations attempting social work in the local community, such as the Knights of Columbus, Council
of Defense, Y. M. C. A. and Y. W. C. A., Boy
Scouts, Camp Fire Girls, Council of Churches,
Playground Association or Department, Women's
Clubs, W. C. T. U., Parent-Teacher Association,

and Industrial Welfare Employment Departments; (8) the conduct of intensive training courses for community recreation leaders under the initiative of the local organization of "community service" in co-operation with existing institutions, such as a musical college or dramatic league, the first one being offered in Washington, D. C., during 1918;[146] (9) the aiding of financial campaigns, the voting of bond issues, and the authorization of public appropriations for the purchase and equipment of sites for play uses; (10) the development of unutilized opportunities for ,wholesome play by all ages and throughout the year, as noon-hour "sings" in factories, street play, holiday celebrations. In other respects the "community service" stage utilizes whatever may be thought appropriate to the local situation from the technique of the six preceding stages of the play movement.

With this survey of the recent and current emphasis upon "community service" in the administration of play, the present analysis of the respective stages of the play movement in the

[146]Concerning the school at Washington, D. C., Bulletin No. 2 of *Community Service* (Incorporated), states: This is a school for recreation leaders. Here are taught as quickly as possible the rudiments of physical recreation, social recreation, community drama, and community singing. The students learn not only how to present plays, operas, and pageants, but are trained in the making of costumes, the painting of scenery, and even the making of dyes. . . . . At present, the courses are designed to train leaders for social and recreational activities for the government departments, but as the girls give up their work in Washington and return to their home states they will be qualified to teach in community centers all over the United States.

United States is completed. It has been shown that there have been seven stages, each one more or less sharply defined by the incorporation of certain features of structure correlative with emphasis upon given changes in the concept of function. These facts both indicate an evolution and imply the presence of "transitions." The following section presents an analysis of these "transitions."

IV. THE TRANSITIONS IN THE POLICY AND ACTIVITIES OF THE PLAY MOVEMENT

A further analysis of the play movement discloses changes in its method of procedure that are fundamental to its "stages" but are not coterminous with them; changes that in some instances extend cumulatively through several periods giving rise to various "stages"; changes that bear a longitudinal relation to the movement as the "stages" hold a latitudinal position. These alterations are here denominated "transitions," signifying passages from one condition or action to another. A "transition" is, thus, distinguishable from a "stage," as the concepts are employed in this investigation, in that it is an alteration in a process while the latter is a period or degree in a development; that is to say, a "transition" is a modification of the method of procedure, while a "stage" is a state of progress in a process at a given time. The former is dynamic and functional; the latter, static and structural. An analysis of the "transitions" of a movement forms the basis for an explanation of the origin of its "stages" and a definition of the "trend" of the action as a whole. The "transitions" of the play movement, then, are the changes in the methods of procedure which effected an evolution in its structure and the concept of function giving

191

rise to the respective "stages" analyzed in the preceding section, and indicating, in part at least, the "trend" of the movement which will be studied in the subsequent section of this report.

The "transitions" of the play movement are nine in number, as follows: (1) from provision for little children to that for all ages of people; (2) from facilities operated during the summer only to those maintained throughout the year; (3) from outdoor equipment and activities only, to both outdoor and indoor facilities and events; (4) from congested urban districts to both urban and rural communities; (5) from philanthropic to community support and control; (6) from "free" play and miscellaneous events to "directed" play with organized activities and correlated schedules; (7) from a simple to a complex field of activities including manual, physical, aesthetic, social, and civic projects; (8) from the provision of facilities to the definition of standards for the use of leisure time; (9) from "individual" interests to "group" and community activities.

A. *From provision for little children to that for all ages of people.* Accepting the establishment of the sand gardens in Boston in 1885 as the beginning of the play movement in the United States, the earliest facilities were provided exclusively for the use of little children, specifically those of pre-school and primary-grade ages. As was shown above in the analysis of the "sand garden" stage, the same age group was provided

CHILDREN'S SINGING GAMES, HAMILTON PARK INDOOR GYMNASIUM,
CHICAGO

"WOODEN SHOE" DANCE, WOMEN'S GYMNASIUM, HAMILTON PARK

for in each of the five cities conducting playgrounds during 1885-95. In Baltimore, the society inaugurating the movement there was called the "Children's Playground Association" as late as 1897. This title was characteristic of similar societies elsewhere,[1] and was indicative of the structure and the concept of the function of the play movement during its first stage.

Following the initial adjustments made in behalf of little children came a recognition of the need of play facilities for those of the intermediate and grammar grades. The older brothers and sisters of the little children playing in the sand gardens "gathered about in mute appeal."[2] And in response, the sand gardens of Boston were cautiously opened to them when they signified their desire, as the chairman of the committee in charge explained it, "to play with the little ones, to aid the matrons, or to sit quietly by and sew or read or play checkers."

In New York, however, less discrimination was made from the first, as indicated by the sporadic playground opened in 1890 under the auspices of the New York Society for Parks and Playgrounds. This provision was designed for boyhood and girlhood as well as for little children. It was about

[1]Among these were: The Brooklyn Society for Parks and Playgrounds, incorporated in 1889; the New York Society for Parks and Playgrounds, 1890; The Providence Free Kindergarten Association, 1893; and the law of New York of 1888 authorizing the incorporation of "societies for providing parks and playgrounds for children in the cities, towns, and villages."

[2]Joseph Lee, *Constructive and Preventive Philanthropy*, 1902, chapter on "Playgrounds for Big Boys."

an acre in size, located at 99th Street and 2nd
Avenue, and was equipped with apparatus for
"exercise, play, and comfort,"[3] consisting of see-
saws, swings, wheelbarrows, small wagons, footballs, flags, shovels, drums, banners, and a sand
pile.

Recognition of the necessity for making provisions for the play of youths, "playgrounds for
big boys" as Joseph Lee called them,[4] was the
third step in the lengthening of the age of the
group with whom the play movement is concerned. This type of provision was a distinctive
feature of the "model playgrounds" as shown
above, although in New York it was also a part
of the general anti-slum agitation as has been
interestingly told by Jacob Riis.[5] There was no
separation there, at the time, between the two
movements. In 1899 the Massachusetts Emergency and Hygiene Association opened three summer playgrounds in Boston designed especially
for boys between twelve and fifteen years of age.
They were equipped with a limited amount of
gymnastic apparatus and supervised by young
men with some training in physical education.
This experiment was sufficiently successful to warrant its repetition the following year, after which
the school committee took over the playgrounds
conducted by the Association.[6] Pioneering work

[3]Joseph Lee, *op. cit.*
[4]*Ibid.*
[5]Cf. Jacob Riis, "*A Ten Years' War.*"
[6]Cf. Ellen M. Tower, "Playgrounds and Sand Gardens," in
World Wide, Montreal, April 26, 1902. Paper read before the
Montreal Local Council of Women.

had been done, however, by the park department
of Boston, when it opened Charlesbank Outdoor
Gymnasium in 1889-91 and Franklin Field in
1894. The most extensive provisions for the play
of adolescents were made during the "small park"
and "recreation center" stages, of which that by
the South Park Commissioners, Chicago, was the
most elaborate. After the first year of the operation of the South Park "recreation centers," the
opinion of the commissioners on their function
in the life of the youths of the city was as follows:[7]

Playground movements in most cities have been confined
almost entirely to the interests of school children, and to a
short period of the year. In Chicago more than two-thirds
of our children leave school to go to work before, or when,
the eighth grade is reached. Since the dominant interest in
the life of a youth is play and not work, and since the best
growth and development at this age comes from play and not
from work, it seems that more attention should be given to
an all-year playground service and that it should take into
consideration the young working boys and girls quite as much
as the children in school.

The incorporation of facilities for adult play
and recreation in the structure and concept of the
function of the play movement followed that for
youths and children. The beginnings of adequate
provision of this type were made in connection
with the "small park" and "recreation center"
stages, but the social organization of adult play
did not develop until the "civic art and welfare"
and the "neighborhood organization" stages of
the movement. In the latter, play was considered

[7]*Annual Report South Park Commissioners*, 1906, p. 57.

a community function to the extent that its administration could be made efficient only through the operation of facilities that united the family and the neighborhood group of families in common activities for at least a part of the time; that is, the provision for either children or adults involved some activities in which both participated simultaneously. The pageant, festival, neighborhood social dances, entertainments, gymnastic exhibitions, track meets, holiday celebrations, welfare exhibits, community councils, community days, and picnics were examples of attempts to unite the family and the neighboring families in wholesome uses of leisure time.

It should not be overlooked, however, that during the earlier stages of the movement adults were often beneficiaries of provisions primarily intended for youths and that a few sporadic provisions were made in their behalf. There were, for example, the evening recreation centers in the New York Schools, 1895–97, and the city recreation piers in New York, Philadelphia, and Boston, 1897–99. There were the bathing beaches of Boston and a few other cities, in the nineties, during the summer and skating on park lagoons and small flooded areas in many cities in winter, first in the New England and North Atlantic states, and later in the Middle West. There were, also, the ball fields and the athletic grounds in public parks. But the more conscious attempts to incorporate facilities for adults came with the "recreation center'' stage in 1905, although it was a decade before their utilization was fully developed. The tennis courts, baseball diamonds, football gridirons, swimming pools, and outdoor gymnasiums completely equipped and supervised by trained instructors distinguished the outdoor facilities. But ample and beautiful as were these open air features, the fieldhouse erected in each of these new parks was a more dramatic event in provision for mature members of the community. Each building contained an assembly hall, two to four clubrooms, a library or reading room, a lunchroom, a men's and a women's gymnasium with appropriate shower-bath and locker-room facilities. Each gymnasium was in charge of a trained instructor who organized formal classes for all ages as well as arranged interpark team-game competition, while the free use of assembly hall and clubrooms, as well as free admission to all gymnasium classes, stimulated activities in any wholesome manner that might appeal to maturity. Relgious sectarianism, political partisanism, advertising commodities, smoking, and card-playing were prohibited. Los Angeles, Philadelphia, Boston, and New York were first to follow the example of Chicago, and since then, facilities for adult relaxation have been an essential feature of the play movement.

The ''wider use of the school plant''[8] has been the plan of adult provision for play generally

[8]Cf. Clarence A. Perry, *The Wider Use of the School Plant*, 1910, and *Community Center Activities*, 1916.

adopted and involves the opening of the building and grounds after school hours, principally during the evening, for lectures, night school, gymnastics, and dramatic, musical, and civic clubs. Among the latter uses are the "community councils." John Dewey forcibly advocated the wider use of the schoolhouse at the meeting of the National Educational Association at Minneapolis, 1902.[9] It was dramatically tried out on a large scale for the first time in Rochester, New York, during 1907–9, under the personal direction of E. J. Ward and supported by an appropriation of $5,000 by the school board,[10] while during the winter of 1910–11, thirty-one cities reported that their schoolhouses were used as "recreation centers." Twenty-seven contained 201 centers.

In a special statement relative to the progress of the play movement during the year 1910, the secretary of the Playground Association of America, speaking of contemporary developments indicated by reports sent in to his office, said:[11]

More and more the municipal play center is providing for the recreation of the adult members of the community as well as for the children.

So strong was this tendency that in the following year the name of the Association was changed to that of the Playground and Recreation Association of America, so as to be more in accord

[9] Cf. *The Playground*, May, 1915, p. 42.

[10] Cf. *Rochester Social and Civic Clubs*, 1909.

[11] H. S. Braucher, *"Developments and Opportunities in the Field of Public Recreation,"* publication of the Playground Association of America, 1910.

with the transition taking place in the structure and the concept of the function of the movement. In 1912, Percy Wallace MacKaye in a widely read volume on "the civic theatre"[12] advocated an extension of provision for the leisure-time pursuits of adults; in 1913, the Committee on School Inquiry of New York[13] reported that there was greater necessity for an organization of adult leisure than ever before on account of certain changes in the industrial order; while in 1914, the Recreational Inquiry Committee of the state of California,[14] after a survey of the play facilities of the state, declared itself in favor of an extension of those designed to conserve the leisure time of adults. By 1915, as disclosed in the analysis of the "neighborhood organization" stage above, the technique for the conservation of adult leisure was carefully elaborated in the "community council," a self-governing and self-supporting organization of neighborhood recreational resources. During 1918–19 "community service" was established as a modification of the neighborhood organization plan for conserving the leisure of all ages of people in the community. Thus the play movement evolved in its structure and concept of function from an agency for

[12]P. W. MacKaye, *The Civic Theatre in Its Relation to the Redemption of Leisure*, 1912, p. 30.
[13]Cf. *Report on the Economic Utilization of the Public School Plant for Educational and Recreational Purposes*, of the Committee on School Inquiry of the Board of Estimates and Apportionment of the City of New York, 1913, pp. 409–10.
[14]*Report of the Recreational Inquiry Committee of the state of California*, September 28, 1914.

conserving the play of children to a medium for the exercise of the play activities by all ages of people.

B. *From summer to annual provision for play.* The first playgrounds were operated only during the summer. This fact applied to those of both the "sand garden" and the "model playground" stages and was true also of most provisions made during the "small park" stage of the movement. Beside the sand gardens conducted by the Massachusetts Emergency and Hygiene Association between 1885 and 1902, other examples of summer-time provision were the Charlesbank Outdoor Gymnasium, Boston, 1889–91; Boone Park, Louisville, Kentucky, 1892; the first two playgrounds opened in Philadelphia, by philanthropy, in 1893; the first half-dozen New York City playgrounds including the one in 1895 carried on "under a wisteria vine"[15] in the backyard of the Nurses' settlement; the opening of certain schoolyards in Pittsburgh, Pennsylvania, in 1896, at the request of the educational department of the Civic Club of that city;[16] the nine schoolyard playgrounds opened at Providence, R. I., in 1897, under the supervision of the Free Kindergarten Association, the season extending from July 7 to September 8;[17] the first playground opened by the Children's Playground

[15]Joseph Lee, *Constructive and Preventive Philanthropy*, p. 127.

[16]*Annual Report Pittsburgh Playground Association*, 1908.

[17]*Annual Report Free Kindergarten Association*, Providence, 1898.

Association in Baltimore,[18] July 1, 1897, as well as the five additional ones conducted the following year; and many others throughout the country maintained by philanthropic effort.

Not only were the first philanthropic efforts in providing playgrounds limited to summer periods, but the first municipal appropriations also were for the maintenance of vacation playgrounds. In 1895 the city councils of Philadelphia appropriated $1,000 for the equipment of schoolyard summer playgrounds, of which four were sand gardens. The next year the appropriation was made $3,000, remaining at that figure for the next seven years. These playgrounds were maintained during the months of July and August. By 1898 the number had increased to twenty-five. The record of beginnings of municipal appropriations for play in New York parallels that of Philadelphia. In 1897 Mayor Strong's committee on small parks, of which Jacob A. Riis was secretary, reported, "New York has not yet a single municipal playground, and not yet a school playground worthy of the name."[19] As a result of the publicity growing out of this report, the school board at a meeting on June 13, 1898, approved a measure that eighteen school yards be "used for purposes of recreation during the vacation months, the expenditures necessary to be paid from the funds

[18]*Annual Report Children's Playground Association*, Baltimore, 1898.
[19]Cf. Joseph Lee, *op. cit.*

now at the disposal of the board.''[20] The vacation months referred to in the measure were July and August. The following year there were thirty-one ''school play centers'' of which ten were devoted in the mornings to vacation school purposes. The school board also had charge of ''five open-air gymnasiums, five 'kindergarten tents,' six recreation piers, three sand gardens with kindergarten games in Central Park, seven roof gardens, ten swimming baths, and six evening play centers.''[21] Chicago, in like manner, appropriated, by action of the city Council, in 1898, $1,000 for ''temporary small parks.'' The money was entrusted to the vacation school committee of the Women's Clubs[22] of that city. The Board of Education granted the use of six schoolyards, and the Turnvereins loaned portable gymnastic apparatus. Playgrounds were conducted during the summer vacation months only. In Milwaukee, the city park commissioners in 1897 established a playground in West Park as an experiment. And for the next decade the general plan developed by the cities mentioned above was pursued almost literally by all communities making provision for play.

Slowly did the cities adopt the plan of all-year provision for play. For years the custom

[20]*Annual Report Board of Education*, New York, 1898.

[21]*Annual Report, New York City School Board*, 1899, pp. 28–32.

[22]*Annual Report Vacation School Committee*, Chicago Women's Clubs, 1898.

of opening playgrounds only during the school
vacation period was adhered to by even the more
progressive communities, while the joy of the open
schoolyards of summer made eloquent appeal in
contrast with the closed yards of the remaining
ten months of the year—closed by an iron fence, a
locked gate, and an irate janitor, "for fear, apparently," as Joseph Lee, writing at the time,
ironically remarked, "they may be of some use."
And as he further explained:

The reason usually alleged is that the children will do
mischief if they are allowed inside; but it has not yet been
shown either that children can use a playground to advantage
if they are not allowed inside or that they wholly abstain
from mischief when they have no playground. The real reason appears to be that the janitors do not like the trouble
involved in having the yards opened; and, as everybody
knows, the function of the school janitor is to direct the
school committee. Some cities have gone so far as to build
schoolhouses without any yards at all.[23]

The public parks are to be credited with showing the way to all-year provision, which later was
adopted generally by school boards.

The development of the "new park service,"
as it was contemporaneously called, rested on
the custom of playing baseball in spring and mid-
summer and football in the autumn. The first
step was taken when skating was not only permitted but provided for by park commissions both
on lagoons, ponds, and rivers, and on artificially
flooded areas, from the surface of which the snow
and fine ice-cuttings caused by extensive use were

[23]Joseph Lee, *Constructive and Preventive Philanthropy.*

nightly swept, and a new and perfect surface provided the next morning by reflooding and freezing during the night, after the skaters had departed. While sporadic attempts were made in a few places, as in Boston in 1892, for example, when two acres in the Charlesbank Outdoor Gymnasium were flooded by the park department, the movement reached general practice about 1900. At that time many of the northern cities made regular provision of this kind. Boston possessed fourteen municipal skating-places, nine being artificially flooded and ten regularly swept off by a horse-drawn device for the purpose; in all about 130 acres containing seven ice-hockey fields. Chicago had fifteen acres flooded and swept, in addition to nearly a hundred vacant lots with a total of nearly three hundred acres flooded by the fire department but cared for by the people of the vicinity. St. Paul provided five acres; Milwaukee, seven; and Detroit, twelve. Cleveland, New York, Minneapolis, and six other cities, fourteen in all, reported skating[24] provided by their respective park systems. Coasting[25] and tobogganing were also allowed in many cities.

[24]Skating is a close competitor with bathing for the first place in popularity and value among municipal provisions for play and exercise. The ponds in the middle of a city, even those whose surface is planed every morning, are often worn by afternoon or evening until their surface is a mixture of gravel and soft snow; and with their crowds of skaters they look, from a little height, like flypaper at a summer hotel.— J. Lee, *Constructive and Preventive Philanthropy*, p. 233.

[25]"Coasting is allowed in Boston on certain streets and on one of the hills on the common, sometimes on other parts of it. There was a time in Mayor Prince's administration when some

The second step taken by the park departments toward all-year provision of play and recreational facilities was the creation of the "small parks." New York City opened the William H. Seward Park in 1902-3, which contained a building making possible the use of the grounds throughout the year.[26] But the most dramatic event looking toward all-year provision of recreational equipment and activities was the construction of ten small parks containing a heretofore unseen type of public recreational facility, the "field house," by the South Park Commissioners, Chicago, in 1903-5. In these fieldhouses, not only was indoor space heated and lighted and freely offered to neighborhood groups for play, but a definite program of events was established in each indoor gymnasium, led by the same individuals who directed the summer outdoor playgrounds and gymnasiums located in these institutions. Thus, contact by way of leadership as well as physical equipment was here first maintained on a large scale with the neighborhoods of public play centers.[27]   Although the method of

---

of the principal walks were iced by the city and bridges built across them which the solid men of Boston had to climb on their way to business and back, but one or two fatalities resulted in the giving up of the experiment."—*Ibid.*

[26]A description of this building will be found below, where the transition of the play movement from outdoor to indoor activities is discussed. It is significant here that such a proposal was entertained for the purpose of providing some form of more adequate facilities throughout the year.

[27]The further significance of this fact will be shown below under section F.

leadership in these small parks was greatly altered after five years of experience, and further developed after another like period, nevertheless the ten small parks in question revolutionized municipal provision for leisure-time activities. They remain today unique in the history of the movement, although other cities have modeled after them. Los Angeles was first, opening an all-year playground containing a club house in 1905, and with the West Chicago Park Commissioners, the Philadelphia Board of Recreation, and the Boston municipal gymnasiums later, was one of the more perfect examples of an adoption of the South Park plan.

TABLE XII

DEVELOPMENT OF ALL-YEAR PROVISION 'FOR PLAY IN CITIES OF THE UNITED STATES*

Year	No. of Cities Reporting All-Year Provision	No. of Workers Employed All Year	Percentage of Cities Making All-Year Provision
1909	32	....	12
1910	68	....	37
1911	36	377	14
1912	63	655	22
1913	68	337	20
1915	111	1053	25.7
1916	108	675	29
1917	140	1454	29.3
1918	128	1630	34.3

*Compiled from statistics published in the *Yearbooks* of the Playground and Recreation Association of America.

Table XII gives the increase in number of cities providing all-year facilities for play by years, for a period of nine years following 1909, the first year in which statistics on the subject were available. There was an increase from 32 to 128 cities representing respectively 12 and 34.3 per cent of all cities reporting provision during those years. The year 1918 showed 12 cities less than during 1917, on account of the participation of the United States in the Great War, yet the total number of workers that year increased 176 in spite of the demands upon them for "war camp community service."

The transition from provision during the summer only to that throughout the year was accompanied by the following six disclosures in the evolution of the structure and concept of the play movement: (1) that facilities for play are popular in all seasons of the year; (2) that from the hygienic standpoint organized play is more beneficial in winter than in summer because of the greater amount of time spent out of doors during the latter; (3) that it is impossible to administer play with the greatest efficiency by employing different persons as leaders in the same playground for each vacation period; (4) that efficient play leaders cannot be secured summer after summer unless similar employment is furnished them during the remainder of the year; (5) that the efficiency of play-leadership is further increased by continuous employment of a given person in the same community for a period of years; and in like manner, (6) the maintenance of an all-year play center providing activities appropriate to each season on the same site is equally advantageous. Only as this plan is adhered to, is it possible to achieve "neighborhood organization" or "community service." Play is a group function. It remains while persons pass away, and that form of adjustment is best suited to the provision of facilities which is permanent, continued, complete, and unified in one agency, such as a community center in school or fieldhouse. From the days of the "sand garden" stage, administrators of playgrounds and recreation centers have observed the fact that a new play center is more difficult to discipline and organize than one that has long been established.[28] With the passing of time, a routine, a variety of customs and traditions, a structure of social activites, and a concept of function is built up in

[28]Cf. Ellen M. Tower, "Play-Grounds and Sand-Gardens," *World Wide*, April 26, 1902. "The civilizing influences of the sand garden are apparent on the first day of a session—in an old yard the children enter quietly, welcome the teacher with joy, apply themselves at once to their play and occupation, and there is little excitement. For an account of a new yard, may I quote from the report of 1899. In an experience of twelve years we have encountered nothing worse than the systematized depravity of this, to us, new neighborhood. The children were fairly interested with the toys and books, games, gymnastics, songs, and flowers, but the thing that roused the keenest joy, that brought a shout of delight from almost every lip, that left the yard empty in a twinkling, was a street fight among their mothers. The men hung about the sidewalk and egged the boys on to mischief and rebellion and paid them sometimes to carry out their evil suggestions. The women fought with the children, blow for blow, and one day a fierce creature rushed through the gate with a hammer in her hand after a small boy who had, she thought, struck her child.

"Nearly all the sand gardens have been opened with like turbulence, although few quarters of the city are as depraved as the one here mentioned. At Hancock school there was last summer a daily average attendance of 456 children, and only once was there, to use the slang of the day, a 'scrap.' Then the guilty one was a boy of defective mind, who should have been sent to an asylum."

a play center that is continuously operated, especially under the administration of the same persons when they are reasonably efficient.[29] The transition from summer to annual provision for play, therefore, is related in general to the quality as well as the quantity of the service rendered by the movement.

C. *From outdoor equipment to both indoor and outdoor facilities.* Correlative with the development of all-year operation in the place of summertime provision, came the construction of indoor as well as outdoor facilities. This change in the structure and the concept of the function of the play movement constituted a third transition in its evolution; and since a complete analysis involves a consideration of many events previously mentioned in the discussion of the second transition, the study made here may be somewhat

[29]While the present writer was engaged in the administration of Hamilton Park Community Center, Chicago, during 1910-17, he had occasion to observe the influence of continuous all-year provision in one center: groups would assemble daily for the "organized" games and play for hours without supervision or altercations; members of clubs that had disbanded for the summer would re-unite for winter meetings in the fieldhouse; attendants at the gymnasium classes would stand in line by the hundred on the opening day for indoor classes each autumn; numberless people would make inquiries concerning the coming "Flag-day program," or "Fourth of July celebration," or "mid-winter" gymnastic exhibition or "Spring festival," or similar special event weeks before time, and interest such as that facilitates their organization. A certain standard of decorum was also maintained by the group consciousness relative to the behavior of persons making use of the dance hall, the ball field, the library, etc. The park teams adopted "yells," "colors," "uniforms," and other insignia to express their attitude toward the community of interest that abounded.

briefer than would have been possible had it been
presented in advance of the foregoing analysis
of the second transition. But while the second
and third transitions have much in common, their
development was not identical in time nor coterminous in structure. The idea of making provision for play throughout the year did not involve
at first the construction of indoor facilities as in
the "sand garden," "model playground," and
"small park" stages, when, with the exception of
shelters, that might be temporarily converted into
"playrooms" on rainy or chilly days, as in Philadelphia, there was no concept of the "indoor gymnasium," the "assembly hall," the "clubrooms,"
the "branch library," or the "school social center" which characterized the "recreation center"
and subsequent stages of the movement. Thus
the construction of indoor facilities for play began
after the idea of all-year provision had gained
considerable ground, although the full development and widest application of the two ideas were
made simultaneously and in mutual correlation.

During the "sand garden" stage, as shown
by Table III above,[30] the only equipment actually
constructed was that for outdoor uses only,
although in Boston and Providence permission to
use the toilets and the basement of the school
buildings on rainy days, was granted by the school
committees. Similar facilities were also accessible to those using settlement yards. But the

[30]Cf. Miss Towers' description of "sand gardens" above.

apparatus provided primarily for play consisted of sand piles, sand bins, swings, teeters, and in some instances, as in Brooklyn, a tent to shelter from the heat of the sun, although in Boston the "sand garden" was conducted on the shady side of the schoolhouse. During this stage, also, the various attempts to make an adjustment to the play-life of the children were all undertaken by philanthropic people or societies so that the funds were limited and the equipment more or less temporary, the site often changing from summer to summer.

In the "model playground" stage, also, the support and control still remained under philanthropic management, although as shown by Table IV,[31] the playgrounds in four of the five cities conducting "model" examples were located on public property; in three cities the playgrounds were open throughout the year, being used primarily for skating during the winter months by flooding the grounds; while four provided apparatus for youth as well as little children, of which the sand pile was a universal feature. In three cities the "model" playgrounds made use of school buildings as did the "sand gardens" before them, but in only one instance was an indoor equipment of any kind contemplated[32] and this was essentially a shelter which was to be used for play only on days of inclement weather when the outdoor equipment was inaccessible. The

[31]Cf. page 68 above.
[32]Philadelphia.

concept of constructing indoor facilities primarily
as a play provision was not exemplified even in
this case. The recreation piers opened in New
York in 1897 and the roof gardens agitated at
about the same time were both outdoor facilities,
although possessing in some instances shelter from
sun and rain. While the object of the Outdoor
Recreation League, whose very title is significant,
and whose influence upon the movement in New
York was responsible for the "model playgrounds" and the form in which the "small
parks" were finally developed, being composed of
a federation of nineteen societies, was, in part,
to obtain recognition of the necessity for restoration and
physical exercise as fundamental to the moral and physical
welfare of the people; to secure the establishment through
the city of New York of proper and sufficient exercise in
recreation places, playgrounds, and open air gymnasiums for
the people.[33]

During the "small park" stage, likewise, the
concept of the structure and the function of the
play movement involved outdoor activities and
facilities primarily, and indoor equipment only
as a secondary and auxiliary feature. As shown
above in Table V, one of the motives that gave
rise to "small parks" was the desire for greater
utility of existing parked spaces; a second, an
increase in the number of open spaces in the congested sections of cities; and a third, the beautification of play spaces by "parking" or the use of

[33]Cf. Constitution of the Outdoor Recreation League of
New York, 1899.

lawn, shrubbery, trees, and flowers in their construction. And as stated in Table VI, the structure and organization of the "small parks" in
the seven cities studied involved open air facilities, such as (1) spaces for athletics in six cities,
(2) aesthetic treatment of the site in six, and
(3) a wading pool in one; while the only indoor
equipment comprised a "field" or "shelter"
house in each of the seven cities with shower
baths in two, while both features were auxiliary
to the primary purpose of the "small parks."
The. term "fieldhouse" at that time did not con-
note what it does today, for the South Park "fieldhouses," the most complete in the country, had
not yet been erected. The earliest "fieldhouse"
was merely a box in which to store apparatus.[34]
Next it became a shelter for the patrons of the
playground[35] and finally with the construction of
the Chicago and Los Angeles types in 1905, an
elaborate indoor recreational plant. From that
date the "fieldhouse" has been regarded as an
integral part of provision, being of value primarily on acount of the facilities for play which
were added by it rather than because of an auxiliary function which it performed in relation to
the outdoor equipment, as was the concept of
shelters and shower baths during the first three
stages of the movement.

[34]An example of this type was given by the sand gardens
of Boston.

[35]An example of this type was found in Brooklyn in 1897,
and in general throughout the "model playgrounds" and "small
parks."

The dividing line between the two concepts of the function of "indoor" equipment in connection with provision for play marks the inception of the "recreation center" stage of the movement. The growth of the new concept passed through four phases: (1) the park "fieldhouse" period, (2) the "social centers" in public school buildings, (3) the remodeled school plant designed for both "play" and "school" uses, and (4) the use of library, courthouse, armory, and other public buildings for play, as in the "community service" stage.

The most significant contribution to the indoor play equipment was the construction of the "fieldhouse" by the South Park Commissioners, Chicago, in 1905, fully described above under the analysis of the "recreation center" stage. This plan was later found to be uneconomical since it involved the expense of constructing and maintaining a dual system of provision for "play" and "education" with no commensurate gains. Where this plan is followed the "fieldhouse" remains idle during the daytime while the schoolhouse is in use, and conversely, the schoolhouse is unoccupied while the "fieldhouse" is in use. The recognition of this fact led to the utilization of the schoolhouse as a "social center," first in Rochester, New York, in 1907–9, as a means of providing indoor facilities for play throughout the year. The "community centers" in Chicago and New York during 1916–18 were further elaborations of "the wider use of the school plant" which was well begun in 1910, five years after the opening of the South Park "fieldhouse" in Chicago. Table VII above shows that thirty-one cities used their schoolhouses as evening "recreation centers" for the first time in 1910 while during each of the next six years the number was much larger, that of 1913 being 152 and that of 1917, 113, while the total number of centers provided in city schools between 1913 and 1917 was 2,622.

The utilization of school buildings as "recreation centers" led to fundamental changes in school architecture. Those designed for class room instruction were found to be poorly adapted to the function of community centers. A room with fixed seats "gave a formable and stiff appearance"[36] and was suitable only for singing clubs, choruses, debating and literary programs, lectures for small groups, and library and night class uses. The first modifications consisted of attaching the desks to strips so that they could be easily moved either to one side or out of the room and thus give sufficient space for folk and social dancing, games, gymnastic classes, wrestling, and many other activities. In later buildings two rooms were sometimes divided by a folding partition which could be pushed aside to form a small hall for social gatherings, dancing, and gymnastic classes, the desks being removable

[36]*Annual Report, Superintendent of Schools.* Chicago, 1916, p. 24.

as before. Next gymnasiums were included and
used both for gymnasium and assembly hall purposes, but this arrangement was not entirely satisfactory since the demand often developed conflicts between groups who sought to use the room
at the same time but for different ends. After
much experimentation it was found[37] that

> An ideal building is one which in addition to the ordi-
> nary school rooms and domestic science rooms, library, etc.,
> provides one or more large floor space for social dancing, so
> that the young people may feel that their wants are provided
> for and at the same time furnishes a gymnasium for physical
> recreation, and leaves the assembly hall for neighborhood
> gatherings, lectures, and entertainments, and for use as a
> public forum.

Practically all of the "social centers" conducted in 1905–12 were obliged to curtail one or
more activities each evening on account of the
absence of some essential features in the design
of the school plant. The Froebel school, of Gary,
Indiana, was perhaps the first example of "an
ideal building" for recreational and social uses.
It was located on a twelve-acre site with about
seven acres constituting a parked foreground and
the remainder devoted to athletics, games, sand
pile, and gardening uses, while two swimming
pools, two gymnasiums, an assembly hall with a
stage about eighty feet in width and convertible
into a gymnasium as well as adaptable to dramatics and pageantry and other entertainment
uses, beside the library, domestic science, and

[37]*Annual Report, Superintendent of Schools*, Chicago, 1916,
p. 25.

shop equipment constituted the facilities for play indoors. A suggestive plant was that of the New Trier Township High School, Kenilworth, Illinois.[38] In these and similar plans is disclosed the idea of equipment for community center purposes that prevailed prior to the Great War; a combination of facilities for "play" and "education" with distinctive features of the "small parks" added.

Since "war camp community service," the construction of "memorial buildings" and the use of all public buildings, such as armories, libraries, and courthouses in small communities, has developed in addition to the utilization of the school plant as a community center. Memorial buildings have been erected more extensively in rural communities than elsewhere, and exist, or are in process of construction, in five hundred rural communities today. "Township halls," as in Kansas,[39] "community high-school districts" with additions to the school plants that make them more adaptable to the play function, as in Illinois, and consolidated grade schools in many states are other forms of adjustment being applied in rural communities. Thus, briefly, has the play movement evolved in structure and the concept of function from an adjustment that utilized outdoor equipment only to that which comprises both indoor and outdoor facilities.

[38]Cf. *Annual Catalogue of the New Trier Township High School*, 1916.
[39]Cf. *Rural Community Buildings*, Department of Agriculture, Bulletin No. 825, p. 29.

D. *From congested urban districts to both urban and rural communities.* The first adjustments attempted by the play movement were made in those districts of our larger cities in which the greatest congestion of population prevailed. Boston, Philadelphia, Providence, Chicago, and New York were those to which the movement was confined during the "sand garden" stage of its history. These were also the cities in which "model playgrounds" were established, although sand gardens were being introduced contemporaneously in Brooklyn, Pittsburgh, Baltimore, Milwaukee, San Francisco, Cleveland, Minneapolis, Denver, and Louisville. During the "small park" stage likewise, the movement was restricted to cities and in particular to the effort to extend parks and playgrounds into the older and more thickly populated districts. As disclosed above in the analysis of that stage, those in New York were developed in conjunction with the anti-slum agitation, being the final solution of that problem as exemplified by the history of Mulberry Bend Park and the Hamilton Fish, DeWitt Clinton, Thomas Jefferson, and William H. Seward parks.[40] In Louisville, the site of one of the earliest "small parks" was in a section of the city occupied by its foreign population and popularly known as "the Cabbage Patch."[41] In Philadelphia, the first two "small

[40]Cf. pages 73–79.
[41]Cf. page 80.

GIRLS' INDOOR GYMNASIUM CLASS, HAMILTON PARK
FIELDHOUSE, CHICAGO

BRANCH PUBLIC LIBRARY, HAMILTON PARK
FIELDHOUSE, CHICAGO

parks'' were constructed in similar sections, Germantown and Starr Garden.[42]   In Boston Charlesbank Outdoor Gymnasium was originally a narrow strip of unsightly river bank, bordered on the land side by a slum section.[43]   While in Chicago, the first of the three declared purposes of the ''small park'' commission appointed by the mayor to investigate the situation in that city, was to establish municipal playgrounds in the congested sections of the city as rapidly as finances permitted.[44]

In the ''recreation center'' stage, even, the function of the playground in congested districts of urban communities was still more clearly conceived than that in other districts, although it was during this stage that the beginning of the transition occurred.   Thus the progress of the play movement in San Francisco, as in many other communities, was retarded by the report of a committee that the great number of vacant lots made it unnecessary to make municipal provision since there was ample space upon which the children could play.[45]   This sentiment was paralleled by the attitude prevailing until about 1910 with respect to playgrounds in connection with rural schools.   It was thought, thus, that the large schoolyards and the open country surrounding them made it unnecessary to equip and direct rural schoolyard playgrounds.   In some instances, in fact, the recess periods were abolished, so that

[42]Cf. page 82.   [43]Cf. page 72.   [44]Cf. page 84.
[45]*Proceedings of the Playground Association,* 1900.

the children as well as the teacher could go home one-half hour earlier than was otherwise possible. In conjunction with the idea that play facilities were more necessary in crowded districts was the belief that the children of the poor required provision more than did those of the rich, a point of view overlooking the essential fact that play is natural to all normal children irrespective of economic status or geographical location. But gradually, however, the social aspect of the nature and function of play came to be more clearly understood, and consequently (1) that children in comfortable homes may lack opportunities for normal association with playmates of their own age; (2) that all children learn games through membership in a group—through social inheritance not biological heredity; and (3) that plays and games must be taught wherever the channels of communication between persons and groups are not open to normal functioning.[46] As Newell had pointed out in 1911, the children of America had the richest play heritage of any nation of the civilized world until about the last quarter of the nineteenth century. Then our traditions of play began a rapid decline and, unless some adjustment is not quickly made, may be permanently lost because of the isolation in rural districts and the congestion and immigration in urban communities.[47] The function of the play movement, as it

[46]Cf. G. E. Johnson, "Why Teach a Child to Play?" *Proceedings of the Playground Association*, 1909.

[47]Cf. page 9 above.

is conceived with respect to children, is to revive the heritage of play in all communities where it is passing away.

As the social function of play both in childhood and maturity came to be more clearly discerned, the necessity for some adjustment in both the rural districts and the exclusive residential section of the cities as well as the over-populated areas of urban communities became increasingly evident. And, contemporaneously, that adjustment came to be regarded as a community function. Consequently, in the cities the play facilities were distributed in keeping with a plan to place them within reach of every one, irrespective of the economic or social status by which a given district might be characterized. This fact is disclosed by an examination of the playground map of any city today, showing both the location of new spaces devoted to playgrounds and the construction of play facilities in the older parks to be frequently surrounded by the more expensive residences. While in addition to this, as play came to be more generally used in the educational process, schoolyards in both urban and rural communities were equipped and supervised for play during recess and after-school hours.

The leading events indicative of the fact of a transition from crowded sections of cities to all communities throughout the nation comprise the following, all occurring during or after 1906 :[48]

[48]Sporadic attempts that deserve passing attention in this connection were the New York Law of 1895 requiring play-

On April 10–12, 1906, the Playground Associa-
ciation of America was organized in Washington,
D. C., to extend the movement throughout the
United States and Canada. In June of that year
there was held the first annual field-day and play-
picnic of the county schools of Ulster County, New
York. This event served as a model and source
of inspiration to later rural recreational experiments throughout the country; a subsequent one
being the first county fair and field-day in Camp-
bell County, Virginia, 1908.[49] By 1911 twenty-
five counties of that state were holding similar
events. On June 10, 1910, a rural pageant was
held at Ripon, Wisconsin.[50] And in the same
year, the Board of Land Commissioners of Colo-
rado,[51] at the request of the state superintendent
of public instruction, passed a resolution granting
from two to five acres of land for playground
purposes to district school boards when the district board shall agree to expend an amount
satisfactory to the state superintendent of public instruction for playground apparatus and
equipment. Thus many rural schools in Colo-
rado were permitted to secure playgrounds at
slight expense and without respect to economic

grounds in lower New York City adjacent to or used in connection with each schoolhouse to be erected thereafter; and
the statute of New Jersey, of 1902, authorizing the provision
of parks and playgrounds by county action. Cf. Chapter 338,
New York State Laws of 1895, and chapter 227, New Jersey
State Laws of 1902.
    [49]*The Playground*. VI, 261–62.
    [50]*Ibid.*, VII, 240–49.
    [51]*Ibid.*, IX, 44–45.

conditions of the population affected, nor congestion, nor the fact of the existence of large expanses of open territory surrounding school property.

The subject of play for rural communities occupied considerable attention at the fifth annual meeting of the Playground and Recreation Association of America, in 1911. Among the impressive addresses on the theme was that by Liberty H. Bailey who presented the possibilities contained in recreation for rural happiness and the awakening of a more highly organized country life. In that year, also, Hamilton County, Tennessee, and Johnson County, North Carolina, each engaged a supervisor-of-play to direct play activities in all of the schools of the county, while Pierce County, Washington, erected play apparatus and play sheds, constructing a $3,000 gymnasium in District 74.

Efforts to organize juvenile play in rural communities frequently took the form of "corn clubs," "calf clubs" or "pig clubs," respectively, with prizes given to the best product exhibited in competition. During 1912, thirteen hundred "corn clubs" with a total membership of twenty-five thousand were organized in Oklahoma. Since then similar clubs have become common throughout the Middle West.

The provision of facilities in rural communities was not long confined to the play interests of children; adult activities were organized in

the country as soon as, if not before, they were
given commensurate consideration in the cities.
In this manner rural life shared with urban communities in the development of social centers in
schoolhouses. The first "social center" conference in America, it is interesting to note in this
connection, was called by a farmers' periodical
and attended very largely by agricultural
people.[52]   This meeting was held at Dallas,
Texas, February 17, 1911, eight months prior to
the national social center conference at Madison, Wisconsin. In harmony with this gathering,
as stated above in the analysis of the "neighborhood organization" stage, the state superintendent of West Virginia during the summer of
1913, called for one thousand volunteers from
among the seven thousand rural teachers in the
state to organize their respective neighborhoods
into social centers "for the purpose of social,
recreational, and intellectual benefits." More
than a thousand teachers responded. In 1916, a
National Conference on Community Centers met
in New York, and again in 1917, in Chicago.
These meetings were attended by people from
practically every large city and many rural communities. One of the most interesting addresses
at the latter conference was made by the teacher
of a one-room rural school in Missouri, telling
what had been accomplished by her neighborhood

[52]Cf. *Social Centers in the Southwest*, Holman and Murphy,
1912.

in organized play.[53] During 1918, attention was centered on the leisure problems of the war camp and war industry communities; but since that year efforts have become general again attempting to make adjustments in all communities through municipal and county playgrounds and community centers, through "play in education" in both rural and urban schools, and through "community service" and "community organization" emphasizing self-governing and self-supporting play as a group function and irrespective of social or industrial features of particular communities.

From the above survey of developments since 1906, it may be inferred that provision for play is no longer considered a necessity merely in congested sections of urban communities. It is now conceived to be a national problem occasioned by the social maladjustments arising from congestion and immigration in the city and isolation in the country, and culminating in attempts to make adjustments to the changed social situation everywhere. In the words of Joseph Lee,[54] play is an antidote to modern civilization, whether urban or rural, which he conceives may be characterized by

the banishment of ideals through the perfecting of means which could be valuable only in service of them, the cultiva-

[53]Cf. H. S. Curtis, *Play and Recreation for the Open Country*, Ginn & Co., 1914, for specific examples of what has been accomplished in rural recreation.

[54]Joseph Lee, "Play as an Antidote to Civilization," *The Playground*, 1911, pp. 110–26.

tion of utilities at the expense of ultimates, a national disease to be remedied by more opportunity to live as we go along.

And in the words of Robert A. Woods:[55]

The social recreation of young people is in every sort of community a problem of anxious significance.

While Professor T. N. Carver[56] has asserted:

it is now clear that the economic prosperity of the farmer instead of making him and his family satisfied to remain on the farm, only the sooner leads them to move to a town or city. Neighborhood cultural organization in the open country thus appears to be not merely a matter of sentimental interest but of the most substantial concern.

E. *From philanthropic to community support and control.* An analysis of the methods by which the movement has derived financial support and exercised local control of facilities for play discloses a transition from "philanthropic" to "community" administration in which transitory emphasis was placed upon "public" control and support. The "philanthropic" method of administration, as the term is here used, signifies that by which both the original cost of construction and equipment and the subsequent expenditures for operation of facilities are met by funds secured entirely by donations or subscriptions and without subsidy either from the public treasury or by admission fees, membership dues, or other finances paid by those patronizing the facilities. It further implies

[55]R. A. Woods, "The Neighborhood in Social Reconstruction," *American Sociological Society Papers and Proceedings,* 1913.

[56]T. N. Carver, "Rural Community Organization," *U. S. Dept. of Agriculture, Yearbook,* 1914, pp. 89–113.

that both the disbursement of the funds and the
leadership of activities is made by an authority
other than that of the government and of the
people who participate in those activities. The
earliest adjustments undertaken by the movement were "philanthropic." This method prevailed exclusively throughout the "sand garden"
and "model playground" stages.[57]

In Boston, as shown in the analysis of the
origin of the movement above, the sand gardens
were operated by the Masachusetts Emergency
and Hygiene Association, the sand itself being
donated by a certain firm in that city, while the
sites were mission chapel and nursery yards exclusively during the first three years.

Brooklyn did pioneering work in 1889 when
its society for Parks and Playgrounds was incorporated under a statute of New York. The first
playground established in one of its parks was
conducted during the summer of 1897 by a group
of philanthropic people. New York Society for
Parks and Playgrounds opened the first playground in that city in 1890. In 1895 a small
summer playground was opened by philanthropists,"[58] in the back yard of the Nurses

[57]The only possible exceptions to philanthropic provision
during the first two stages of the movement were: (a) the
construction of the Charlesbank Outdoor Gymnasium in Boston in 1889–91; (b) the purchase of Franklin Field, Boston,
in 1894; (c) the acquirement of land for "small parks" in
New York, 1895–9; (d) the equipment of a playground in a
park in Louisville, in 1899. But each of these facilities were
supervised, if at all, by philanthropy.

[58]Cf. Joseph Lee, *Constructive and Preventive Philanthropy*, p. 125.

Settlement, while on May 1, 1896, Miss Grace
Dodge equipped another at the corner of Seventh
Avenue and Thirty-seventh Street. About this
time the Union Settlement maintained a playground on South One-hundred-and-fourth street.
The number of playgrounds in New York, until
1898, was limited to a half-dozen similar attempts, including those made by the Association
for Improving the Condition of the Poor, in connection with their vacation schools. That year
the board of education took charge of the vacation schools and established twenty playgrounds
in connection with them. That year, also, the
Outdoor Recreation League, comprising nineteen
societies, was organized in New York.[59] During
its first year the league conducted the Hudson
Bank playground at Fifty-third Street and Eleventh Avenue, while during its second it constructed the "model playground" at Seward Park.

In Philadelphia and Providence the first playgrounds were established by philanthropic persons and societies. In the former, one was
provided by two people in 1893, while during the
following winter the City Park Association,
assisted by the Civic Club, the Culture Extension
League, and the College Settlement, agitated the
question, opening a playground the following
summer. In the latter city, the first playground
was conducted in 1894 by the Union for Practical
Progress assisted by the Provident Free Kinder-

[59]Cf. Constitution of the Outdoor Recreation League.

garten Association. Playgrounds were maintained by these two societies until 1897, when, upon the disbanding of the Union, the work was continued for several years by the Association.

Chicago established a playground in 1894 on land donated by a philanthropist and under the auspices of Hull-House. A similar provision was made by the Northwestern University Settlement in 1896, through the generosity of a small group of interested persons and the University of Chicago Settlement in 1898. During the summer of 1897, the West End District of the Associated Charities maintained a playground in the yard of the Washington Street school, and during the following five years, another on a vacant lot near Hull-House. Pittsburgh opened its first playgrounds in 1896 under the auspices of the Civic Club of that city and supported by donations. Baltimore began in 1897 through efforts of the Children's Playground Association, a department of the United Women of Maryland. Sand gardens or playgrounds for older children were conducted by Women's clubs in Cleveland, Minneapolis, Denver, and San Francisco in 1898.

The concept of public provision for play received emphasis about 1900, but it was a decade before one-half of the cities maintaining facilities did so either wholly or in part by public funds and management, while in 1915 the extent of public provision had reached only 57 per cent; yet from the "model playground" to the "neighborhood organization" stage, the promoters of the movement urged governmental administration. "Public" provision involves the construction and administration of facilities for play exclusively from finances derived by public taxation and without additional revenue obtained through philanthropic or other sources. It implies supervision by public officials whether elected, appointed, or selected by civil service. This method of provision has included six types of application: (1) the equipment and supervision of schoolyards by boards of education; (2) the construction of both outdoor and indoor facilities in public parks; (3) the formation of "boards of recreation," or equivalent bodies, to develop new facilities and correlate existing agencies into a functional whole; (4) the wider use of the school plant; (5) the regulation of commercial dance halls and the provision of "municipal" dances; (6) recreational legislation.

Permission to construct playgrounds on schoolyards was given by the school committee of Boston as early as 1888, and $1,000 was appropriated by the city council of Philadelphia for the construction and maintenance of four sand gardens on public schoolyards in 1895, yet in 1897 a committee appointed by Mayor Strong of New York[60] reported:

New York has as yet not a single municipal playground, and not yet a school playground worthy of the name.

[60] Abram S. Hewitt was chairman and Jacob Riis, secretary.

The following year the board of education took over all of the playgrounds conducted on school-yards and established others so as to bring the total up to twenty. The next year they increased the number to thirty-one, and in 1900 there were reported to be some seventy facilities of all types, open air gymnasiums, sand gardens, recreation piers, roof gardens, swimming pools, evening play centers. This was the most extensive public provision by any community at that time.

In the construction of both indoor and outdoor facilities for play in the public parks, Boston[61] and New York[62] did pioneering work, but Chicago established the standard concept of public support and control, when, in 1903, the voters of the South Park District approved a $5,000,000 bond issue for the purchase of fourteen tracts of ten to sixty acres each to be equipped as all-year play centers for all ages of people. In 1907 the first outdoor play festival in connection with a modern play center was held in Ogden Park, Chicago, on the closing day of the first convention of the Playground Association of America. This event attracted considerable attention to the South Park method of provision as indicated by the following statement.[63]

[61]Reference is here made to Charlesbank and Franklin Field, Boston.

[62]New York possessed sites for four small parks in 1902, cf. the analysis of the "small park" stage, above.

[63]*Annual Report of South Park Commissioners*, 1909. p. 13.

The possession of so many splendid plants equipped for
social service has imposed a leadership on the South Park
Commissioners, and as a consequence, they are frequently
called upon for advice and information as to the methods
of operation, and for plans and statistics that will inform
and arouse the public in other cities. The South Park fieldhouses, it may be said, are regarded as the laboratories for
the whole country; and they are, in consequence, serving in
a patriotic way the nation, and not the South Park District
alone.

Next to the Playground Association of America, the South Parks have been the greatest force
in molding opinion concerning public responsibility for play. The following statement of their
superintendent of recreation, written eight years
after the first small park was completed, is indicative of the concept of "public" control and
support that was being emphasized during the
"recreation center" stage:[64]

Municipal expenditure of money is largely traditional.
Large public buildings, sums for conventional improvements
such as streets, etc., are accepted as proper even though no
idea of the return is general among the citizens. The public
furnishes educational institutions, books, and teachers for a
few hours of the minor's day, but is not yet familiar with
the needs of the longer period of the life of every individual
in the community. Recreation is a function of municipal
government, and many municipalities are intelligently attack-
ing the need.

The third type of application of the concept
of the "public" method of providing for play,
the formation of special commissions to correlate
existing agencies as well as provide new ones,

[64]J. R. Richards, *Annual Report South Park Commissioners*, 1913, p. 45.

was first made in Los Angeles when a playground commission was created in September, 1904. A board of recreation was appointed in Philadelphia in 1909 and another in New York in 1914. Table XIII gives the number of cities, by years, conducting play centers under a special commission responsible to municipal government.

TABLE XIII*

THE NUMBER OF CITIES CONDUCTING PLAYGROUNDS BY PLAYGROUND COMMISSIONS FROM 1910 TO 1915

Year	1909	1910	1911	1912	1913	1915†
Number	15	17	31	33	31	55
Total reporting...	89	184	257	285	342	432

*These statistics represent only the number of cities responding to requests for information sent out by the Association and in which supervised playgrounds were being maintained.
†The report for 1915 includes that for 1914 also.

The fourth type of application, the wider use of the school plant, was incorporated in the concept of "public" control and support after the development of the "social and civic" centers in the schoolhouses of Rochester,[65] N. Y., in 1907–9, and the discussion of the "schoolhouse as a social center" at the meeting of the Playground Association of America in 1909, while perhaps the most highly organized examples are those of New York.[66] During the school year, 1912–13, one hundred twenty-six cities reported the provision by boards of education of heat, light, and janitor

[65]Cf. discussion of the "recreation center" stage above, for analysis of the Rochester experiment.

[66]Cf. discussion of the "neighborhood organization" stage above.

service incidental to the evening use of school buildings as play centers, while seventy-one reported nearly twenty-one hundred paid workers. Over five hundred schoolhouses were used as polling places, nearly as many for political meetings, more than three hundred for exhibits, and over six hundred for motion pictures.[67] In 1915 the field secretaries of the Playground and Recreation Association of America aided in the establishment of play centers in the public schoolhouses of Milwaukee, and in 1917 the Association met in that city. In 1916 the "social" centers in schools and the outdoor playgrounds of Grand Rapids were placed under one superintendent.

The fifth type of application, the inspection of commercialized recreational institutions and the provision of "municipal" dances, gained greatest popularity about 1912–14; while about the same time, the sixth, that of legislation, also developed. Both were indicative of the "public" method of support and control as analysed in the discussion above of the "civic art and welfare" stage.[68] Table XIV summarizes the development of "public" administration from 1910, the first year concerning which complete statistics are available, to 1915, and discloses an advance from 34 to 57.8 per cent of the total number of cities reporting supervised playgrounds during those five years.

[67]Cf. C. A. Perry, *Social Centers of 1912-13*, Russell Sage Foundation, Department of Recreation, pamphlet No. R, 135.

[68]Cf. pp. 125–29 above.

The earliest "public" provisions were made free of all charges to persons utilizing their respective opportunities. This fact was one of the distinctive features of the method of administration of the South Park recreation centers in which baths, lockers, gymnasium classes, club

TABLE XIV

THE PROGRESS OF "PUBLIC" SUPPORT AND CONTROL IN THE PLAY MOVEMENT

Year	1910	1911	1912	1913	1915*
Total No. of cities reporting supervised play.....	184	257	285	342	432
No. of cities with "public" provision wholly or in part	121	152	193	226	312
No. with provision entirely by the "public" method..	62	88	99	111	182
No. with "public" provision only in part	59	72	94	115	130
Percentage of cities with "public" provision wholly	34	34.2	34.7	34.4	57.8

*No report was published for 1914.

meetings, band concerts, tennis courts, ball fields, and the privilege of reserving the assembly hall were available without either rentals or admission fees. It is only within the last three years that small fees are required for the use of given facilities, and these in the large parks not the small ones. Boston charged two cents for a towel and bath in the "public" gymnasiums; Chicago, ten cents for a suit, locker, and towel at the municipal beaches. In other cities, small fees were asked for the use of the schoolhouse and other public halls. This modification of the "public" method led to the concept of "community" support and control. This plan retains

"public" construction, ownership, and general
management of facilities, but permits both financial assistance and supervision of activities by
local groups, such as "neighborhood associations" and "community councils" organized in
the respective play centers, whose membership is
usually based upon residence in the vicinity
rather than upon the payment of a fee, and whose
objects are non-sectarian, non-partisan, non-com-
mercial. These groups are permitted by the
body in general charge of the centers to receive
admission fees to certain programs presented
under their auspices, to collect membership dues
and solicit funds for community purposes, and to
decide to what use the money procured by their
efforts may be devoted. "Self-support" and
"self-government," as these terms were defined
above in the analysis of the "neighborhood organization" stage, are the two distinctive traits
of the "community" method. The explanations
given by the advocates of this method, as stated
above, were two: justice to other neighborhoods
in the city in which no "public" provision may
as yet have been made, and the supplementation
of the resources of the city so as to make possible
adequate "public" provision in all neighborhoods.[69]

The "community" method was first advocated by M. M. Davis, in 1910, after an investi-

[69]It was estimated by Gulick in 1913, that the "public"
facilities for play in New York were adequate for only 5 per
cent of the population.

gation of play and commercialized amusements in New York under the auspices of the Russell Sage Foundation.[70] Two features characterized the concept as he formulated it: self-government under the general supervision of municipal officials, and financial contribution in rentals toward the maintenance of the "public" property whose facilities organized groups made use of. The following year a committee of play leaders in New York[71] declared the "community" method to be the only satisfactory solution of the leisure problem, since the sum required for "public" provision sufficient for the city was beyond the resources of taxation, however much philanthropy might aid it, because other demands upon the tax-budget were many and increasing; and

[70]Cf. M. M. Davis, *The Exploitation of Pleasure*, Russell Sage Foundation pamphlet, 1910, p. 60. "The administration of the few regular meeting places which have thus far been provided in New York has rarely been such as to render them acceptable to adults. Managing meeting-rooms in the school-building is one thing when they are to be occupied by boys and girls of seventeen, as in the recreation centers; quite another thing when the tenants are men of twenty-five. Here appears a clear line of division between two policies:

"First: In dealing with children and adolescents, where the thought behind the work is educational, the facilities offered should be free, and positive supervision should be exercised;

"Second: In dealing with adults, unless the advantages offered are avowedly educational, like lectures, or classes in English for foreigners, the people should be treated as responsible citizens of a democracy; a rental should be charged for rooms furnished, and only negative supervision exercised (that is responsible city employees always in the building, accessible at need). Deposits in advance should be required when necessary to ensure responsibility."

[71]Memorandum on Recreation, addressed to the New York Board of Estimate and Apportionment by its sub-committee.

since the people were entitled to opportunities
for the creation, government, and support of play
beyond those furnished by "public" provision
at any time. But the recommendation of this
committee was not approved until the "neighborhood organization" stage of the movement. The
Playground and Recreation Association of
America continued advocacy of "public" administration of play as it had since its organization
in 1906, but at the National Community Centers
Conference in New York in 1916, and again at
the annual convention of the Association in
Grand Rapids, Michigan, that autumn, the question of "community" support and control was
the dominant one.[72]   Since the development of
"community service," the method of "community" support and control has been followed in
cities almost as extensively as in rural districts,
as shown above in the analysis of the "neighborhood organization" and "community service"
stages. At present, the leading city is New York.
Thus it has been shown that the "philanthropic"
method characterized the "sand garden" and
"model playground" stages; the "public," that
of the "small park," "recreation center," and

[72]Cf. *The Community Center*, magazine, Feb. 3, 1917, for
reprint of papers read at both the New York and Grand Rapids
conferences including: (*a*) Jean Hamilton, "Self-Governing
Working Girls' Clubs"; (*b*) Pauline Witherspoon, "How the
Louisville Community Centers Grew"; (*c*) L. H. Gulick, "The
Opportunity of the Community Center" and "Freedom Through
Self-Support"; (*d*) Edward M. Barrows, "The Meaning of Self-
Support."   Also consult, *The Playground*, June, 1916, articles
by H. S. Braucher, and J. R. Richards.

A "SELF-SUPPORTING AND SELF-GOVERNING" SOCIAL DANCE,
HAMILTON PARK, CHICAGO

A COMMUNITY SUPPORTED AND GOVERNED JUNIOR DRAMATIC
HAMILTON PARK CAST, "HOUSE OF THE HEART"

"civic art and welfare"; and the "community," that of the "neighborhood organization" and "community service."

F. *From "free play" and miscellaneous activities to "directed play" and correlated schedules.* The earliest adjustments made by the play movement consisted of unsupervised spaces, equipped with simple apparatus, such as sand piles, buckets, shovels, swings, teeters, and designed for "free play"; or that which is unorganized by a leader other than a member of the group involved, although it may be groupal as well as individualistic, taking the form of a game, that is, having certain rules and leading to a conclusion. In this sense of the term, the sand gardens during their first two years provided opportunities only for "free play," each garden being in charge of a woman "to keep watch and ward."[73]

One, a poor little creature, who confessed to having an unsatisfactory husband, and was therefore eager for distraction, gave her whole attention to the care of the children; the others were kindly neighbors, who brought their sewing to their windows and looked out occasionally to utter a reproof when a quarrel was on.

During the summer of 1887, women were employed, for the first time, to supervise the gardens. They were given the title of "matron" because that of "teacher" in Boston at that time signified a person with sufficient pedagogical

[73]Ellen M. Tower, "Sand Gardens and Playgrounds," *World Wide*, April 26, 1902.

training to merit a certificate from the school
committee.[74]   In 1893 a superintendent and corps
of assistants with some kindergarten training
were employed.

Digging in the sand and playing games were the first
entertainments offered. Then kindergarten plays and occupations seemed possible in the open air, and a kindergartner
was engaged for each yard; not necessarily as head matron,
for that position requires more than education. It demands
tact, patience, love of children, a sense of justice, and the
force of character necessary to make these qualities felt, and
to command the obedience of the children.[75]

As late as 1902 the title "matron" was given
to those persons in charge of the sand gardens,
although it no longer described their function.

We designate the caretakers as matrons . . . . but it is
an inappropriate title, as many of them are young and charm-
ing girls, graduates of State Normal Schools, or of Normal
Kindergarten classes, or of Schools of Physical Culture, or
Gymnastics. Others are teachers who need money, or who
become weary of idleness in the long vacation.[76]

The maximum development of the concept of
"supervised" or "directed play" attained during the "sand garden" stage is indicated by the
following description of "one yard in particular":

It would be difficult to find a prettier picture than it presented with its two sunny-haired matrons, one wearing a soft
grey gown and quaint muslin cap, the other hatless, her head
bared to sun and wind, surrounded by their busy, happy children—the cool shadows from the precious trees falling about
them. Not far away, a visitor who came regularly every

[74]Ellen M. Tower, *loc. cit.*
[75]*Ibid.*   [76]*Ibid.*

week, one of Boston's high-born daughters, sitting in the center of a ring of not too clean boys and girls, singing to them and with them, and then listening and watching while they sang their street songs, or some precocious infant did a cake walk.[77]

The early playgrounds for older children, with the exception of the "model" ones, and the "small parks," like the first "sand gardens" were inadequately supervised. Many of these were unsuccessful, as the twenty schoolyard playgrounds opened by Mayor Quincy of Boston during the summer of 1898, and some were closed upon complaint of the neighbors because of antisocial situations created by them,[78] as in Philadelphia, Denver, Indianapolis, and St. Paul. The first explanations given for the failure of the unsupervised playgrounds were such as those of Lee, first, that the more orderly boys were at work during the day, and second, that the number of playgrounds was insufficient;[79] while the

[77]Op. cit.

[78]Cf. Joseph Lee, Constructive and Preventive Philanthropy; A. and L. Leland, Playground Technique and Playcraft.

[79]Cf. Joseph Lee, Constructive and Preventive Philanthropy, pp. 171–2. "The better class of big boys are at work during the day, leaving the less desirable class, made up of those youths of elegant leisure who live on their mother's washing, to act the part of the petty tyrants of the local playground, stealing the little boys' bats and balls, breaking up their games, threatening them with dire penalties if they come there again, and enforcing these penalties when their commands are disobeyed. Possibly another reason why the unsupervised playgrounds in crowded districts are so little used may be because the demand is so far in excess of the supply. Boys interfere with each other, find organized games impossible, and get discouraged. It may be something like trying to fill a tumbler with a fire-engine hose."

opposition to "directed play" was based on the
belief that it was "autocratic," "upopular,"
"less beneficial,"[80] and "unnecessary," since
"children do not need to be taught how to play."[81]
With increased experience, it was discovered that
"free play" alone did not make possible the most
socially productive use of the playground since
the children had lost much of the play heritage of
preceding generations,[82] while "directed play"
was more popular, equally beneficial to those participating in it, and the only method of restoring
the passing heritage and of preserving democracy on the playground.[83] The third annual
meeting of the Playground Association of America, 1909, was largely devoted to a discussion of
the function of "directed play." An outline of
a normal training course for play leaders was
presented by one of the committees of the conference and recommended by the convention to
both schools and playground departments. Since
that date, attention has been given more and
more to leadership instead of equipment in the
concept of the structure and function of the
movement, resulting in the development during
the "neighborhood organization" and subsequent
stage, of a technique for directing play.

[80]Cf. H. S. Curtis, *The Playground*, p. 8, December, 1907.
[81]George E. Johnson, "Why Teach a Child to Play," and
L. H. Gulick, "The Doctrine of Hands Off in Play," *Proceedings
of the Playground Association of America*, III, pp. 289-65,
357-65.
[82]Cf. statement by Newell, on p. 8.
[83]Cf. *ibid*. and L. H. Gulick, "Play and Democracy," paper
read at the first meeting of the Playground Association, 1907.

1. One phase of this development comprised the classification of all persons participating in the activities of the playground. The separation of the sexes in given activities has been followed since the "model playground" stage. While the "sand gardens" were provided for both boys and girls under ten years of age, in the "model playground" and subsequent stages the sexes above that age were separated in physical activities and apparatus and leadership provided appropriate to each. But in social, aesthetic, manual, and civic activities both sexes frequently participate in the same event. Classification according to age has involved four methods of grouping those who participate in play: earliest, and briefest, that by Lee,[81] as shown by Table XV, and second,

TABLE XV
AGE PERIODS OF PLAY ACCORDING TO LEE

Periods	Characteristics
Two to six years...... ("Dramatic Age")	Imitative plays and games based upon the occupations of their elders.
Six to eleven......... ("Big Injun Age")	Self-assertive activities; individualistic games and competitive play.
Eleven and over...... ("Age of Loyalty")	Co-operative play; gang life; team games; with "combination . . . . as a part of the game itself."

that by Johnson, presented by Table XVI. In the former, three groups are made, while in the latter there are five, yet both involve persons under fifteen years of age, and each classification

[84]Joseph Lee, "Play as Medicine," *Charities and Corrections*, August 3, 1907.

is familiar to all who have engaged in the direction of playgrounds. That of Lee has been reprinted as a pamphlet and subsequently incorporated in his volume, *Play in Education;* while Johnson's *Education through Plays and Games* is perhaps the best known book in the library of the movement. In a handbook published by the Playground and Recreation Association of America, in 1919, these classifications have been reprinted, and playleaders referred to the volumes of both Lee and Johnson.

TABLE XVI

AGE PERIODS OF PLAY ACCORDING TO JOHNSON

Periods	Characteristics
Under three years.....	Motor activity and sensory play.
Three to six years.....	Plays of imitation and imagination.
Seven to nine years...	Individual and competitive games; "it" games.
Ten to twelve years....	Group games, competitive, lowly organized.
Thirteen to fifteen years	Co-operative play; group competition; teams.

Since the age periods of both Lee and Johnson do not involve persons above the fifteenth year, while the play movement during the "recreation center" and later stages has included groups of older persons, two classifications have, therefore, been made of all persons attending the recreation centers. That of the school board of New York roughly separates those under seventeen from those over that age, providing "junior recreation centers" for the

[85]Cf. *Twentieth Annual Report Superintendent of Schools*, New York, 1918.

former, and "senior" for the latter.[85] That by
the South Parks, Chicago, makes four age groups
of those attending the neighborhood centers,
eight of those attending the gymnasium classes,
and two of those participating in other activities,
junior and senior, respectively.[86]

TABLE XVII

THE FOUR AGE GROUPS OF PERSONS ATTENDING NEIGHBORHOOD
CENTERS, ACCORDING TO THE SOUTH PARK CLASSIFICATION

Group one.......	Little children under ten years of age.
Group two.......	Those between eleven and fifteen years, attending indoor gymnasium classes and participating in athletics.
Group three.....	Those between fifteen and twenty-five, chiefly attending social, aesthetic, and physical activities.
Group four......	The men and women of the neighborhood, some of whom attend gymnasium, but most of whom are interested in social aesthetic and civic activities.

For each of the four groups a separate schedule of activities is arranged by the South Park
plan of administration of recreation centers.
Table XVIII gives the age divisions made of
those attending the indoor gymnasium classes
conducted from October to May.

An analysis of Table XVIII shows an attempt
to place children below seven years under the instructor in the women's gymnasium, to group
older children of both sexes approximately according to the same age divisions, and separation
of the younger from the older adults because of
the ability of the former for more vigorous games.

Classification according to weight of persons
attending the playgrounds is made so as to insure

[86]Cf. Unpublished handbook for directors and instructors
of the South Parks playgrounds, 1917.

competition between those of like development
and ability. The weights that are employed in
the standard competitions are as follows: in basket ball, 95 pounds grammar school, 95, 105, 115,
125, 135, and unlimited closed, and unlimited
open; in soccer, 90, 110, and 125 closed; in playground ball, 75, 90, 110, and 135 closed; in track

TABLE XVIII
AGE GROUPING OF PERSONS ATTENDING SOUTH PARK INDOOR
GYMNASIUMS

Men's Gymnasium	Women's Gymnasium
Boys 7 to 9 years old.	Boys and Girls, 4 to 7 years old.
Boys 9 to 11 years old.	Girls 7 to 9 years of age.
Boys 12 to 15 years old.	Girls 9 to 11 years of age.
Boys 16 to 18 years of age.	Girls 11 to 13 years of age.
Employed boys of 16 to 18.	Girls 13 to 15 years of age.
Younger business men.	Employed girls of 16 to 18.
Older business men.	Younger women (unmarried).
	Older women (married).

and field athletics, 105, and unlimited closed, and
unlimited open; and in wrestling, 105, 115, 125,
135, 145, 156, and unlimited closed divisions. The
term "closed division" signifies that competition
to which only those who are registered in the
given playground league and have not competed
elsewhere at any time are eligible; that of "open
division" signifies that to which those who may
have competed in a high school, a Y. M. C. A. or
other league are eligible. This is a fourth classification of those participating in playground
activities; while a fifth divides them into two
groups, the "novice" and the "classified"; and,
a sixth into the "amateur" and the "professional." A "novice" is one who has not won a

first, second, or third place in any event; a "classified" person is one who has done so. An "amateur" is one who has never competed for a money prize, nor under a false name nor with professionals, nor where gate money was charged, nor served as a teacher of athletics with salary paid directly or indirectly, while a "professional" is any person who competes under one or more of these five conditions. A seventh classification is that by height, sometimes applied to volley-ball competition by girls, the division being made at five feet.

2. The classification of play leaders, as well as those attending the centers, disclosed a further development of "directed play." Table XIX shows four types of supervisors of play and their respective titles, qualifications, and functions, that apply in all communities in which a system of play centers is maintained by park or school boards, or by a recreation commission or department of municipal government, or where "community service" is established.

3. The training of play supervisors, a prominent feature of the "community service" stage, has nevertheless been practiced by city playground departments and school boards since the publication of the outlines for a normal course of study for play leaders by the Playground Association of America in 1909. Baltimore has trained all its leaders, except its superintendents, in that manner. Sixty-three cities offered normal courses

TABLE XIX

CLASSIFICATION OF PLAY LEADERS ACCORDING TO TYPE, TITLE, QUALIFICATIONS AND RESPONSIBILITIES

Type	Title	Qualifications	Responsibilities
General supervisory capacity.	Superintendent of Recreation or Recreation Secretary.	25 years of age, college education, administrative experience and executive ability, equal to superintendent of schools.	Chief executive and administrator for a play or recreation system, provided by a school or park board, or department or commission of recreation for a city.
Local supervisory capacity.	Director of Playground, Park, or Recreation Center.	21 years of age, of college education, executive ability. Open to men and women.	Head, promoter, and guide to all activities of a single playground or recreation center; collector of statistics of uses of local center.
Detailed leadership. Class A.	Instructor in Outdoor Playground or, Indoor Gymnasium, entirely responsible for section of play center.	21 years of age, of high school or college education, including technical knowledge of games and athletics. Open to men and women.	Leader and coach in all games, calisthenics, athletic competition; frequently also in story telling, story playing, and dramatics.
Detailed leadership. Class B.	Coach, Teacher, Instructor, or Social Worker. Responsible for given activity.	21 years of age, possessing technical skill in particular subject taught.	Coach or director of dramatic club, chorus; or teacher of domestic science, social dancing, or other special types of play.

during the winter of 1910–11. Cleveland enrolled over three hundred in evening classes in 1913. The most elaborate scheme of normal training was developed in Pittsburgh, in 1915, through the co-operation of the local playground association and the University of Pittsburgh. Since the Washington, D. C., school for "community service" workers in 1918, practically all cities in which "community service" has been organized have conducted classes in community singing, community drama and pageantry, or other activities. Courses of study have also been organized in a great number of colleges, normal schools, kindergarten training schools, and schools of physical education, and of social work, while a few private schools have been organized for the training of play directors. During 1910, seventeen schools and colleges reported the use of the "normal course in play" prepared by the Association.

4. The organization of amateur athletic and team game competition is another phase of the development of "directed play." This field of activities involves contests between teams from the various playgrounds and recreation centers of a city, or park department, or public school system. City championship series are often played. Baseball, indoor-ball, soccer, hockey, tennis, cricket, swimming meets, track meets, wrestling, and apparatus work are the usual events included. It was in conjunction with this phase of developments in supervised play that the classification of competitors as "novice" or "classified," "open" or "closed," and as "amateur" or "professional" was made, as defined above.[87]

[87]Cf. Appendix B for a statement of the method by which athletics are organized in a given recreation system, the South

5. The "efficiency test"[88] was another device employed in the direction of play. It comprised a given number of events in which the boy or girl, for it is designed for both sexes of adolescent age, is required to compete against a given "standard" rather than against other contestants. It was designed to stimulate a more educational use of the common playground facilities than that of unorganized or "free" play upon them. Its list of events, therefore, are "stunts" on the apparatus frame, "dashes" on the track, and jumping. The "standards" defined for each event are of three types, arranged in an ascending order of difficulty in performance so as to accommodate the scheme to the changing ability of the group for whom it was designed. A "badge" or token of some kind is awarded each contestant who successfully meets the requirements of each event in one or the other of the three groups of "standards"; that is, he must meet the requirements of each event of a given group before receiving a reward of any kind, notwithstanding any special ability he may have in performing some one of the "standards" in any other group. While the particular playground or system of recreation may differ in its choice of events as in its requirements for each,

---

Parks, Chicago, also Appendix H gives athletic calendar followed in interpark competition.

[88]Other terms by which this test is known locally are: "badge test," "button test," "individual test," "athletic test."

the Playground and Recreation Association in
1913 adopted a standard test as follows:[89]

STANDARD EFFICIENCY TEST FOR BOYS
First Test:
 Pull Up (chinning the bar)......... 4 times
 Standing Broad Jump............. 5 ft. 9 in.
 60-Yard Dash .... 8 3-5 seconds
Second Test:
 Pull Up .... 6 times
 Standing Broad Jump............. 6 ft. 6 in.
 60-Yard Dash .... 8 seconds
 Or 100-Yard Dash................ 14 seconds
Third Test:
 Pull Up .... 9 times
 Running High Jump............... 4 ft. 4 in.
 220-Yard Run .... 28 seconds

STANDARD EFFICIENCY TEST FOR GIRLS
First Test:
 All Up Indian Club Race.............30 seconds
 Basket-Ball Throwing.....Two goals in 2 minutes
 Balancing.................24 feet in two trials
Second Test:
 All Up Indian Club Race.............28 seconds
 Basket-Ball Throwing....Three goals in 2 minutes
 Balancing Beam, bag on head..24 feet in two trials

A badge was designed by the Association for
each of the three tests for the boys and for each
of the tests for the girls, to be awarded upon cer-
tification by the local playground authorities that
a given test was satisfactorily met, providing the
winner paid for the badge "as a young man or
woman at college elected to Phi Beta Kappa pays

[89]Cf. *The Playground*, Vol. VII, pp. 58-59, and X, pp. 165-
71, for revised test for girls.

for the key awarded." All badges are of bronze
and thus of little intrinsic value to emphasize that
for which they stand.

6. The teaching of swimming and life-saving
and the organization of aquatic competition, in
the place of mere "playing at will" in the water,
is another evidence of a transition from "free"
to "directed play." Periodic instruction given in
swimming pools, excursions to beaches under the
chaperonage of play leaders, and aquatic "meets"
conducted in both indoor and outdoor pools are
among the forms which this type of direction has
taken. The swimming meets are open to both
sexes and all ages. The more common events are:
the 50-, 100-, and 220-yard swims; the 50-yard
breast stroke, and swim on back; and diving. The
individual or team obtaining the greater number
of points is declared the winner.[90]

[90]Among the diving events are the following:

1½ back jack-knife	15 points
Double corkscrew (2 full twists)	15 "
1½ back somersault with front twist	14 "
1½ gainer	14 "
1½ back somersault	13 "
Standing corkscrew	12 "
Hand stand dive with front somersault	12 "
½ gainer with ½ twist	12 "
Standing 1½ somersault	12 "
½ gainer	10 "
Running corkscrew	10 "
Front jack-knife ½ back twist	10 "
Running 1½ somersault	10 "
Back hand stand	8 "
Standing back dive with front twist	8 "
Plain back	7 "
Back jack-knife	7 "
Front hand stand	6 "
Plain front	6 "
Front jack-knife	6 "

7. The supervision of "passive" as well as
"active" play is a sixth phase of the transition
from "free" to "directed" play. After the "sand
garden," and until the "recreation center" stage,
attention was given to vigorous, motor play.
"Outdoor gymnasium" is a term synonymous
with playground throughout the United States,
while both the equipment and the organization of,
activities suggested vigorous rather than quiet,
"active" instead of "passive," play. Administrators of play facilities have prepared many sta-
tistical tables and made glowing comments upon
the energetic uses of their apparatus as they
have heaped criticism upon sedentary amusements.

If young folks can be involved in active rather than
passive recreation, the tide has, in nearly every case, been
turned from vicious pastimes to constructive pleasures.[91]

Thus the needs of children physically handicapped and of youth engaged in physical occupations during the day were overlooked by many
directors of play before the "recreation center"
stage. Beginning then, and developed subsequently, "passive" recreation has been organized
for those physically or socially handicapped. It has
also been observed that sustained "active" play
is physically deleterious even to normal persons.
Especially is the heart of the growing individual
affected by vigorous activity if performed for
long periods at a time. Therefore "marathon

[91]E. B. DeGroot, *Annual Report South Park Commissioners*,
Chicago, 1909, p. 111.

races" have been tabooed from the track meet of the playground, and "girls' rules" have been arranged for basket-ball and other team-games while the "dashes" in which girls are permitted to participate are of shorter distance than those designed for boys. No longer is the whole day devoted to "physical" activities. Periods of "active" and vigorous play are alternated with "passive" and quiescent occupation. Increased attention to the rôle of "passive" play in the life of normal as well as subnormal persons has been given ever since the World War, first suggested by the needs of convalescent and handicapped soldiers and sailors. New York perhaps leads in the organization of "passive" activities on the playground and in the recreation center. Generally the concept of the function of "passive" play involves the following five ends: (1) to promote restful play; (2) to develop concentration; (3) to instill an element of quietude for the weaker child; (4) to provide safe play diversions; (5) to make the individual more than a mere spectator.[92]

The activities involved in the direction of quiet play include: the story hour, story building, story playing; table games, such as checkers, caroms and carom pool; declamatory, debating, dramatic and musical entertainments; bean bag, ring toss, and box-ball games; phonographic concerts; motion pictures; reading room and branch libraries;

[92]Cf. *Twentieth Annual Report Superintendent of Schools,* New York, p. 201.

lectures and forums; construction "work," such
as paper and cardboard folding and cutting, raffia and reed craft, weaving and sewing, book
binding, leather work, printing, photography,
sketching, stenciling, drawing, making herbar-
iums, sloyd, toy making, playing with dolls,
building with blocks, "biogeography"; and modeling and ceramics.

8.   Co-operation between play centers for
other purposes than that of athletic competition
is an eighth feature in the transition from "free"
to "directed play." This aspect of supervision
was analyzed above in the study of the "neighborhood organization "stage of the movement,
the league of neighborhood school centers being
the most complete example. The two common
purposes of co-operation between centers is the
stimulation of interest in given activities in the
less highly organized centers and the promotion
of self-support in all through the collective treatment of money-getting devices.

9.   The formulation of schedules of events, for
the class period in the indoor gymnasium, the
day in both the indoor gymnasium and the outdoor playground, the week in both the indoor and
outdoor gymnasium and the entire play center,
and the annual calendar emphasizing the celebration of holidays and the organization of festivals
and sports belonging to the respective seasons.
The sequence of activities incorporated in the
schedule of a class period in the indoor gymna-

sium involves three types, as shown by Table XX.
The "progressive exercises" comprise twenty-five
per cent of the period for men and thirty-five, for
women; the "play group," thirty-five for men
and forty, for women; while "competitive games"
consume forty per cent for men and twenty-five,
for women.[93]

TABLE XX

THE SEQUENCE OF ACTIVITIES IN THE CLASS PERIOD OF AN
INDOOR GYMNASIUM IN A RECREATION CENTER

Progressive Exercise	Play Group	Competitive Games

1. Free exercises.
2. Light apparatus.
  (a) Dumb-bells.
  (b) Indian clubs.
  (c) Wands.
3. Heavy apparatus:
  (a) Buck.
  (b) Horse.
  (c) Booms.
  (d) Bars:
    (1) Parallel.
    (2) Horizontal.
4. Tumbling.
5. Folk-dancing.
6. Gymnastic
   dancing.
	1. Free play by
	   graded groups.
	2. Games:
	  (a) Singing.
	  (b) Low organi-
	    zation.
	  (c) Home and
	    yard.
	3. Social dancing:
	  (a) Women alone.
	  (b) Men alone.
	4. Children's parties.
	  (a) Doll.
	  (b) Stories.
	  (c) Table.
	5. Socials (Informal
	   good times, for
	   boys and girls
	   together).
		1. Basket-ball.
		2. Volley-ball.
		3. Indoor baseball.
		4. Wrestling.
		5. Indoor track
		   athletics.

During the school vacation, a "daily sequence"
of activities is arranged. It is based upon two
facts: the temperature changes, and the groups
attending the playground. With respect to the
former, the day is divided into four periods:
(a) the early morning hours prior to eleven
o'clock; (b) the mid-day and early afternoon, the

[93]Cf. *Annual Report South Park Commissioners*, 1905, and
the book of instructions to employees, 1917.

time of highest temperature, from eleven until four; (c) the later afternoon, between four and six; and (d) the evening period, from seven until closing time, which is nine-thirty or ten o'clock. The group attending the playground during the first period is predominately that of little children; during the second and third, children and youths who are not employed; and during the last period the working boys and girls, and adults. There is some difference between the events of the men's and the women's gymnasiums, as the Tables XXI and XXII show.   An analysis of these

TABLE XXI

TYPICAL DAILY SEQUENCE IN MEN'S OUTDOOR PLAYGROUND, ATTENDED BY BOYS ABOVE TEN YEARS OF AGE, SHOWING CHARACTERISTIC EVENTS IN EACH PERIOD

8:30 to 11 a. m.	11 to 4 p. m.	4 to 6 p. m.	7 to 10 p. m.
1. Individual instruction on apparatus 2. Games of low organization 3. Stunts 4. Tennis 5. Baseball	1. Apparatus work 2. Badge test training 3. Swimming pool 4. Story telling 5. Lunch days 6. Games	1. Team coaching: a, Track b, Playground ball c, Baseball 2. Apparatus work 3. Games	1. Team coaching: Track 2. Games 3. Social hours 4. Apparatus

charts discloses a progression from vigorous games of both low and high organization in the first period to less strenuous events during the second, with a return to vigorous activities during the third and fourth as the temperature falls and older groups attend the playgrounds.

The "weekly sequence" was arranged in both the outdoor playground and the indoor gymnasium to furnish greater variety to the activities from day to day. In the former, a typical sequence of this kind, involves vigorous activities every day, although the form may vary from team-games to track athletics, while features such as story telling, dramatics, picnics, social hours,

TABLE XXII

TYPICAL DAILY SEQUENCE IN WOMEN'S OUTDOOR PLAYGROUND, ATTENDED ALSO BY BOYS UNDER TEN YEARS OF AGE

8:30 to 11 a. m.	11 to 4 p. m.	4 to 6 p. m.	7 to 10 p. m.
1. Swings and see-saws	1. Swings: a, Rope b, Lawn	1. Badge test training	1. Personal talks on getting ac-quainted
2. Individual instruction on apparatus	2. Story telling	2. Training for teams: Play-ground ball	2. Running games
3. Sand court work	3. Wading pool, boats, etc.	3. Vigorous games	3. Apparatus
4. Tennis	4. Swimming pool	4. Apparatus work	4. Social nights
5. Games for little children	5. Quiet games 6. Park picnics Lunch days		

badge tests, instruction in swimming, sand pile contests, and apparatus work are provided periodically. This does not mean that certain of these events may not occur daily, for the facilities are there and no one is forbidden to use them, but rather that instruction and direction are offered only at stated intervals. The weekly sequence of the indoor gymnasium is characterized by two features: first, the members are classified according to age and formed into seven or eight groups to insure fair competition between them and to enable the instructor to adapt the exercises to the psychic stage and physical ability of each group; and second, the use of a limited

TABLE XXIII

TYPICAL WEEKLY SEQUENCE IN MEN'S AND WOMEN'S OUTDOOR GYMNASIUMS

Men's Gymnasium

	8:30 a.m. to 11 a.m.	11 a.m. to 4 p.m.	4 p.m. to 6 p.m.	7 to 10 p.m.
Monday....	Individual instruction on apparatus	Apparatus work	Games	Social evening
Tuesday....	Games	Badge test work	Track team	Games
Wednesday.	Individual instruction on apparatus	Swimming pool (2 to 4 p.m.)	Track team	Track
Thursday...	Games	Apparatus work	Playground ball	Games
Friday.....	Stunts	Story telling	Apparatus	Track
Saturday...	Tennis	Lunch day	Games	Apparatus
Sunday.....	Baseball	Games	Apparatus	Social hour

Women's Gymnasium

	8:30 a.m. to 11 a.m.	11 a.m. to 4 p.m.	4 p.m. to 6 p.m.	7 to 10 p.m.
Monday....	Games, swings, and see-saws	Story telling and dramatic play	Vigorous games	Personal talks and general play
Tuesday....	Individual instruction and games	Swimming lessons (2 to 4 p.m.)	Badge test training	Running games
Wednesday.	Sand court	Wading pool play	Vigorous games	Instruction on apparatus
Thursday...	Games	Games on grass	Apparatus work	Social evening
Friday.....	Individual instruction	Swimming lessons	Badge test training	Running games
Saturday...	Tennis coaching	Picnic lunches at noon	Team training	Apparatus
Sunday.....	Sand court	Swings and apparatus	Games and apparatus	Games and swings

number of periods by inter-group and inter-playground team-game competition, at which spectators are admitted. Each class or group, furthermore, meets two or three times per week, although members of these groups may also participate in league games held at other periods, as on Wednesday and Saturday evenings. Also, the hours between 5:30 and 7:30 each day are frequently devoted in the men's gymnasium to practice games, while the corresponding periods are sometimes used by the women for the rehearsal of dancing and dramatic numbers on coming programs.[94]

The necessity for a sequence in the gymnasiums, both indoor and outdoor, however, was found to be no greater than that of the recreation center as a whole. When a schoolhouse is being used as an evening recreation center, or a playground or fieldhouse has more than one room and its field of activities includes more events than a single play leader may direct in person, it has been found desirable to arrange the time for the meeting of the gymnasium classes for boys and girls of the same age at the identical hour of the day in order that these groups may thus be permitted to engage in another activity, such as a dramatic club, a mixed chorus, or a dance. This plan is known as the "correlated schedule" of the play center. It is prepared through the co-

[94]Consult Appendices C and D for typical weekly schedules in the indoor men's and women's gymnasiums, South Park Commissioners, Chicago.

operation of the director of the center, the instructors in each gymnasium, the coaches and teachers of special classes, and the leaders of the neighborhood groups. Its function is the social utilization of the leisure of those persons who attend gymnasium classes or other activities twice or three times a week, and who at other times are likely to develop a habit of loafing about the premises when the classes to which they belong are not in session, thus nullifying the moral gains through organized play in which they participate. By such an arrangement as the "correlated schedule" each person frequenting the play center may be brought into contact with supervised play, and thus the efficacy of the playground or recreation center may be greatly increased.[95]

As the "daily schedule" led to the "weekly sequence," so the "correlated schedule" led to the "annual calendar" by which definite objectives were conceived for each month and season of the year.[96] The first feature of this scheme was the division of the year into two periods: the "indoor season" from October to April; and the "outdoor season" from May to September inclusive. During the former, activities are organized in the indoor gymnasiums, the assembly halls, and the clubrooms. Gymnasium classes are registered, clubs for the study of music, dramatics,

[95]Cf. Appendices E and F for typical weekly schedules for entire play center.
[96]Cf. Appendices G and H for annual calendars for a single center in 1915–16, and of the entire South Park system for 1920–21.

and dancing are organized, and social and civic events promoted. With the return of spring, the plan is reversed; indoor activities and organizations are disbanded and outdoor sports are resumed. Certain facilities remain open throughout the year, such as the branch library, the locker and shower rooms, and the clubrooms and assembly hall for special social or civic activities. The second trait of the ''annual calendar'' of play is the emphasis which it gives to the celebration of holidays and the establishment of neighborhood festival customs, repeating given programs year by year until they become social heritages of the community. In time the neighboring population comes to look forward with joy to the possibility of participation in seasonal events and their organization is thus facilitated. Repetition is essential to success in community recreation, for by this means only may social standards be established and community attitudes maintained. Among the activities organized in a well supervised community center are the mid-winter gymnastic exhibition, the spring festival, the Independence Day, and Labor Day, and Christmas celebrations, community days, band concerts, community sings, indoor artist recitals, and lectures.

The incorporation in the structure and the concept of the function of the play movement of attempts to group participants according to sex, age, weight, and as open or closed division, or novice or classified, or amateur or professional;

to classify the supervisors of play according to their functions; to train these supervisors in the technique of directing play; to organize athletic competition between persons, teams within the local playground, and groups representing different playgrounds; to develop co-operation between play centers for the exchange of talent and other functions of mutual benefit; and to regulate activities by the establishment of schedules for the class period, the day, the week, and the year, discloses a transition from "free play" involving miscellaneous activities to "directed play" utilizing correlated schedules.

G. *From a simple to a complex field of activities, involving manual, physical, aesthetic, social, and civic events.* A comparison of the sand gardens with the structure and function of the play movement as conceived in its subsequent stages discloses a transition from a simple to a complex field of activities. In this development, emphasis has been placed successively upon "manual," "physical," "aesthetic," "social," and "civic" events. The result, however, has been a cumulative one, in that each of the five types of activity is incorporated in the present structure and concept of the function of the movement. The meaning of each type and the history of its incorporation in the field of activities is as follows.

At the inception of the "sand garden" stage, the occupation of the groups attending the playgrounds was exclusively "manual," that is, a type

of play in which the distinctive feature was handicraft, such as molding the sand, digging in it with
little shovels, filling little buckets with sand and
emptying them again, cutting and folding paper,
and sewing. The explanation for this restriction
is indicated by the following quotation from the
chairman of the committee then in charge of the
sand gardens of Boston, in which frank acknowl-
edgement is made of an attempt to imitate the
provisions for the play of little children in Berlin, the prototype of the first adjustments in this
country.[97]

There . . . . princeling and peasant dug together in the
sand heaps under the kindly care of policemen.

And ten years later one of the five reasons
given by the committee for supporting the work
of conducting sand gardens was this sentence:

They [children] are taught, in the guise of play, to use
their hands and brains.

Kindergarten games, involving "physical"
and "aesthetic" characteristics, and story-telling
were added about 1893, when kindergartners were
employed to assist in supervising the children, but
even then the greater portion of the time and
attention of the children was given to "manual"
play. The structure of the sand gardens was
suited to the concept of their function: the space
was small, thus limiting the variety of events that
might occur simultaneously; the time of operation
was short, usually one-half day, thus preventing
the succession of a number of occupations; and

[97]Ellen M. Tower, *supra.*

the equipment invited sedentary activities, such as molding, cutting, sewing, since each yard was provided with movable benches, toy brooms, buckets and shovels, and six pairs of scissors. On two days each week, in Boston, sewing and bright worsteds were the chief attraction; on two other days, brilliantly colored soldiers, animals, and other pictures were distributed to be cut out by the children. In the remaining four cities studied in the analysis of the ''sand garden'' stage above, similar situations prevailed; in Providence whittling classes were conducted twice a week. At that time, the promoters of the movement did not have a definite concept of the field of activities. Their idea of the function of the playgrounds was, as stated above,[98] to keep the children off the streets and thus away from certain physical and moral dangers by inducting them into safer places for play, a social situation in which a constructive use of materials and social forces was made for the development of personal and group life.

During the ''model playground'' and ''small park'' stages, ''physical'' activities were emphasized. These activities comprised the various active or motor plays and games; the ''tag'' games, ''team'' games, ''field'' sports, and track events. The ''model playgrounds'' furnished space and apparatus for older boys and girls as well as little children, for the sand garden was

[98]Cf. pp. 53–55.

located in "the children's corner"; the "small parks" for all ages, with ample facilities for field sports and track events. The Charlesbank Outdoor Gymnasium was the prototype of this concept of structure and function, and the recreation centers of the South Parks, Chicago, the most complete embodiment. At that time, the conservation of health through the promotion of "active"rather than "passive" play, that is, vigorous games, gymnastics, and athletics instead of the sedentary occupations of the sand gardens and the commercialized amusements.[99] The efficiency test and "amateur athletics" represent the highest development of this phase of the movement and are closely followed by the indoor gymnasium, the swimming pool, and the camp. But these facilities appealed only to those who were of comparatively rugged physique. Continuity of interest depended upon one's showing in the contest, the winners being regular in attendance while the losers tended to drift into the ranks of the spectators, and a demand for the development of quiet games and other pursuits beyond the limits of the occupations of the sand gardens was perceived. In response, three types of activities were added: "aesthetic," "social," and "civic," in the order named.

The "aesthetic" provisions included such as the story-hour, story-playing, junior dramatics, festivals, and pageantry. These events were

[99]Cf. p. 253 above.

A RURAL SCENE

A SUBURBAN VIEW

A CITY BY THE SEA

"WORLD BUILDING," HAMILTON PARK PLAYGROUND, CHICAGO

usually led by the instructors in the women's
gymnasiums and children's playgrounds, although
in some communities special organizers were
provided. Especially was this true of the festivals and pageants, although many playground instructors composed, and directed with credit,
festival and pageantry programs of a modest
nature.[100]

The period of greatest emphasis upon this
phase of play was between 1912 and 1915, or during the "civic art and welfare" stage. The concept of the function of the play movement at this
point of its evolution was somewhat reversionary,
"individual" rather than "group," namely the

[100]A typical playground pageant was that of Palmer Park,
Chicago South Parks, given at 2:00 P. M., Labor Day, 1913. It
was entitled "A Pageant of Chicago," and comprised the following ten episodes:

I—Naming the River. The Indians seek a western hunting ground by means of an unknown river. It dwindles into
two small branches. They name it Chi Cagou (Alas! It is
nothing). Legendary times.

II—The White Stranger. Father Marquette, 1673.

III—The First Citizen. Jean, the trader, 1779.

IV—Buying Chicago. Americans buy Chi-cagou of Indians, 1796.

V—Fort Dearborn. The massacre of 1812.

Interlude: Lament of the Spirit of the Lake.

VI—A Day in Early Chicago. About the time of 1837.

VII—The Rail Splitter. Chicago's part in the Civil War,
1860–65.

VIII—The Great Fire. Flames attack sleeping city in 1871.

IX—The World's Fair. Chicago presents the nations to
Columbia, 1892.

X—The New City. The months present the dance of the
future. Labor and capital meet; and join hands to free the
city of the future. Soldiers of the past enter and give place
to soldiers of peace. Eugene Field, Chicago's Children's Poet,
appears with his dream children. The future citizens give
the dance of youth. The builders of the past pay tribute
to the new city. Processional.

satisfaction of personal desires through the exercise of the imagination in the dramatic, dancing, and musical arts.

The next addition to the field of activities, chronologically, was "social" events, that is, dances, parties, stunt-nights, table-games. This phase attained greatest popularity about 1914 in the "municipal dances" previously described, but has continued to occupy a place in the schedules of gymnasiums as well as fieldhouse and public school "recreation centers." The concept of the function of the "social" events was quite the opposite of that of the "aesthetic" activities in at least one respect, since it provided concourse with real persons rather than imaginary ones, but it resembled them in seeking to provide a constructive social environment. It utilized the simple expressions of gregariousness in an effort to counteract the commercialized dance halls outside the play centers and the loafing inside them during the periods between gymnasium classes or other activities and at all times by some people who found no other events sufficiently to their liking to cause them to enroll in any organized activities. The group not enrolled, in all communities, greatly outnumbered those registered in the more highly organized associations; and while the conduct of "social" activities was at first but an expedient preliminary to an attempt to induce them to participate in either the "physical" or "aesthetic" activities, in the end, "social" events were incorporated in the regular schedules of the recreation centers because of the particular function which they exercised in opening channels of social intercourse through which group life might flow more freely. A fourth permanent realm was thereby added to the field of activities of the play movement. During the "community service" stage, this phase found expression in "block parties," "street dances," "community days," "stunt-nights," "spelling bees," and free motion pictures presented out-of-doors in public parks.

A fifth addition to the field of activities of the play movement was that of "civic" enterprises, efforts toward the exercise of the rights and duties of citizens in ways that were voluntary and pleasurable. For adults, the most highly organized activities were the "community councils" and the "community forums" developed in connection with fieldhouses and public schools during 1915–18, and "community service" since that date; while for juveniles, there were the boy scouts and campfire girls, "junior republics, cities, and councils," and Red Cross associations.

An analysis of Table XXIV discloses an increase both in the variety of activities, when compared with the initial provisions made for play, and in the number of cities reporting these respective features from year to year. Rearranging them according to types, 7 and 8 are manual; 6, 7, 16, 19, 20, 21, and 22 are physical; 4, 5, 6,

9, 13, 15, and 18 are aesthetic; 5, 12, and 17 are social; while 1, 2, 3, 5, 7, 10, 11, and 14 are civic in nature. Thus the statement that the field of activities of the play movement has evolved from a simple to a complex form is abundantly supported, notwithstanding the fact that the reports are incomplete both with respect to the number

TABLE XXIV

SELECTED LIST OF PARTICULAR ACTIVITIES AND THE NUMBER OF CITIES IN WHOSE PROVISION FOR PLAY THEY WERE INCORPORATED DURING 1911–1916, INCLUSIVE

	Activities	1911	1912	1913	1915	1916
1.	Boy Scouts	55	56	77	98	160
2.	Campfire Girls	....	21	63	85	134
3.	Debating	....	15	30	42	56
4.	Dramatics	37	37	61	93	110
5.	Evening Entertainments	43	53	84	119	131
6.	Folk-dancing	120	132	178	273	229*
7.	Gardening	52	67	79	105	133
8.	Industrial Work ...	100	112	138	191	180*
9.	Instrumental Music..	27	38	51	69	85
10.	Lectures	27	36	67	89	106
11.	Libraries	49	56	71	106	122
12.	Moving Pictures	....	35	48	67	....
13.	Pageants	41	44	52	102	....
14.	Self-Government	44	52	55	65	55*
15.	Singing	78	84	95	150	151
16.	Skating	....	....	55	88	102
17.	Social Dancing	....	42	65	100	108
18.	Story Telling	148	143	196	259	243*
19.	Summer Camps	26	27	65	62	160
20.	Swimming	75	83	138	188	55*
21.	Tramping	....	74	115	164	197
22.	Wading	69	75	91	127	....

*The report under 1916 for folk-dancing, industrial work, self-government, story telling, and swimming are not to be taken, necessarily, as indications of a reduction in the number of cities providing them for that year, since the whole table is compiled from voluntary reports submitted by the recreational authorities of the cities, the number varying from year to year. Often a city in which facilities have been in operation for some time will fail to submit a report, while one in which the work is new seldom does so. While thus the figures for each year are incomplete they are indicative of the tendency.

of activities mentioned and the number of cities reporting.

Table XXV shows the addition of ten new types of activity to a significant number of cities during the year of 1917. While most of these had appeared before and many had long been incorporated in municipal organizations of recreation,

TABLE XXV

ACTIVITIES ADDED DURING 1917, WITH NUMBER OF CITIES REPORTING THE SAME*

Activities	Cities
1. Americanization	30
2. Canning	87
3. Domestic Science	67
4. First Aid	101
5. Hiking	102
6. Junior Red Cross	60
7. Knitting	184
8. Military Drill	100
9. Sewing for War Relief	106
10. War Garden Clubs	119

*The record of this year is significant for two reasons: (a) it confirms the tendency in question; and (b) it occurred during the first year of the participation of the United States in the Great War.

the fact that many cities reported their inauguration for the first time that year indicates their concept of the field of activities as including more than manual events, for physical and civic receive great consideration. Thus 2, 3, 7, 9, and 10 are manual; 4, 5, 8, and 10 are physical; 1 and 6 are civic. The absence of the aesthetic and social is probably due to the fact that war interests dominated developments, and during its early days at least, those activities that seemed to be more directly related to that undertaking were given preference over other events such as music, dramatics, social pleasures, whose values in war were not as readily surmised.

A classification of the activities promoted at the present time by the play movement comprises the following five groups:

Manual activities: bio-geography; book-binding; cardboard work; designing; drawing; kite tournaments; knot-tieing; kodak clubs; leatherwork; mumble the peg; nature study, gardening, caring for pets, and making herbaria; paperwork, cutting and folding; photography; printing; raffia and reed weaving; sand modeling; sloyd; sketching; stenciling; sewing; toy-making; world-building.

Physical activities: athletics, aquatics, badge tests, calisthenics, camping, dancing, excursions, exhibitions, field-days, games, gymnastics, hikes, marching, plays, sports, stunts, tournaments.

Aesthetic activities: concerts by band, chorus, or orchestra; dramatics, both adults' and children's; debating; declamations; essay-writing; festivals; literaries; musical societies; modeling; newspaper-making; opera and operetta; minstrels; pageants; public speaking; recitals; sings; scenario writing; story-building, -playing, -telling, and -writing.

Social activities: amateur nights; banquets; clubs; dances; dinners; game rooms; legerdemain; motion pictures; musical stories; mock-funerals, -trials, -weddings; open road evenings; block, children's, doll, fiction, fad, hobby, juvenile, lawn, and national costume parties; parlor games; parlor magic; parlor track and field meets; "phunites"; pet shows; receptions; shadow-graphs; socials; spelling bees; stunt-nights; tableaux; trained animal acts; vaudeville entertainments; young men's and young women's nights.

Civic activities: Americanization work; barbecues; community councils, -dramas, -forums, -gardens, -music, -kitchens, -organization, -service; Christmas trees; co-operative enterprises, involving banks, loan associations, stores; mass meetings; night schools; lectures; political meetings; safety first surveys; thrift town meetings; welfare exhibits; vigilance committee meetings.

A comparison of the field of activities indicated by the above classification with that of the "sand garden" stage of the movement discloses a transition from simplicity to complexity, homogeneity to heterogeneity, of concept of function.

H. *From the provision of facilities to the definition of standards.* The equipment of sites for play characterized the concept of the function of the movement at the time of its inception. Thus the "sand gardens" during the first two years of their history were nothing more than selected spaces furnished with equipment suitable to the play of little children. These facilities were without supervision, except that volunteered by kindly neighbors, and offered no scheme of organization designed either to direct the play of the children attending the grounds or to correlate their activities with the social organization of the neighborhoods in which they were located. Later playgrounds, also, both of the sand garden and other types within and without the city of Boston, were similarly provided. When supervision was first incorporated, as exemplified by the later "sand gardens" and the "model playgrounds," the concept of the structure and the function of the movement still remained unchanged with respect to the relation which facilities for play were believed to sustain to the social organization of the communities in which they were situated. Likewise during the "small park" and "recreation center" stages, no alteration was made in the theory of the adjustments proposed. This theory has been stated by Thomas[101] to be one of several fallacies that may be pointed out in legislation, education, and reform measures in general; namely, the belief that persons will develop spontaneously, that is, without external influence, "tendencies which enable them to profit in a full and uniform way from given conditions, and that therefore it is sufficient to create favorable or remove unfavorable conditions in order to give birth to or suppress given tendencies." The "sand garden," the "model playground," the "small park," and the "recreation center" were each constructed and operated on that basis.

[101]W. I. Thomas and Florian Znaniecki, *The Polish Peasant in Europe and America*, Vol. I, p. 12.

During those stages of the movement, consequently, efforts looking toward an adjustment to the social situation with respect to play were confined to the provision of facilities, rather than to some scheme that would have included an incorporation of psychological aspects as well, in its structure and concept of function. While presenting children, first, and youths and adults, subsequently, with the opportunity for play—spaces equipped and later supervised, thus constituting "favorable conditions" to wholesome play—the movement failed to take into account the necessity for a correlation of these conditions with the organized life of the community, by which "standard" uses of these facilities and of leisure time in general might be made by all the members of the community. During the "civic art and welfare" stage, however, the beginning was made of the application of this concept to the structure of the movement. Fuller use was made in the "neighborhood organization" stage, and a more extensive utilization of the principle during War Camp Community Service, and subsequently. This feature may be described as an attempt to "define standards" for the use of leisure time by all the members of the community in activities performed both within and without the facilities provided specially for play. It involves the education of the public in the use of spare-time, resulting in the gradual development, through the co-operation of the people, of traditions,

sentiments, opinions regarding play that shall pro-
voke behavior harmonizing with the consensus of
the group concerning community welfare; in short,
"social attitudes," or tendencies to act toward
social values, the social value, in this case, being
the wholesome use of leisure, or play in the sense
defined at the outset of this report. Prior to the
fact of this transition, the movement was virtually a "playground movement" rather than a
"play movement," although there were some
leaders who held slightly different concepts of its
function and structure[102] as there were instances
of its application. But it was "war camp community service," during 1918-19, that completed
the transition from the provision of facilities to
the "definition of standards" for the use of
leisure. In this concept of the function of the
movement, the provision of facilities was still an
integral part of the plan of adjustment, that is,
there was no abatement of campaigns for more
playgrounds, recreation centers, or the like, but
facilities such as these were considered as aids in

[102]Consult: L. H. Gulick, "Play and Democracy," paper
read at first annual meeting of the Playground Association of
America, 1907, and published in *Charities and the Commons*, August 3, 1907; Allan T. Burns, *The Relation of the
Small Parks of Chicago to Juvenile Delinquency*, Russell Sage
Foundation publications; Edward B. DeGroot, in *Annual Report of South Park Commissioners*, Chicago, 1910. These articles, however, did not contain points of view identical with
the concept of the transition as formulated in this investigation, as will be seen below, since they held that the establishment of standards would follow as a result of the operation
of well equipped and supervised facilities rather than that the
definitions of standards should be attempted directly as a conscious objective of the movement.

the larger work of defining and diffusing certain ideas and norms,[103] so to speak, concerning the use which anyone may make of his leisure time.

The transition from the provision of facilities to the "definition of standards" involved a number of changes in the concept of the function of the movement, each one adding an integral part of the present structure. The principal steps included the following:

First the attempts to make adjustments to the social situation with respect to all ages of people as a means of conserving certain types of behavior regarded as beneficial to community welfare, in the place of continued efforts in behalf of children and youths alone. Thus, during the earlier stages of the movement, it was assumed that adult behavior would follow the interests awakened in childhood, if those interests were transformed into social attitudes and habits during the experience of the child on the playground. Toward adult recreation, a *laissez faire* attitude was maintained until the "recreation center" stage, while all attention was focused upon the problem of making some adjustment of the play of children

[103]Thomas, in the work cited above, criticizes the establishment of "norms" at the present time on the ground that such an action is an expression of "common sense" and not "science." Yet while his point is true, as far as ultimate method is concerned, the fact of life is here, now, and its problems must be met somehow, as he also points out, and hence there have sprung up "rules of behavior, by which the group tends to maintain and make more general the corresponding type of action among its members." These rules include our customs, beliefs, legal and educational methods, and institutions.

to the current social situation. A good statement
of this viewpoint is the following:[104]

Democracy must provide not only a seat and instruction
for every child, in school, but also play and good play traditions for every child in a playground. Without the development of these social instincts, without the growing of the
social consciousness—which has its roots in the early activities of the playground—we cannot expect adults to possess
those higher feelings which rest upon the earlier social virtues
developed during childhood. The sandpile for the small child,
the playground for the middle-sized child, the athletic field
for the boy, folk-dancing and social ceremonial life for the
boy and the girl in the teens, wholesome means of social
relationships during these periods, are fundamental conditions without which democracy cannot continue, because upon
them rests the development of that self-control which is
related to an appreciation of the needs of the rest of the
group and of the corporate conscience, which is rendered
necessary by the complex interdependence of modern life.

Here was an expression of the relation of
personal behavior to group influence as far as
juveniles are concerned, but the range of vision
did not include the dependence of adult sentiment
and opinion upon the "social organization" of the
group or community. The adult, as truly as the
child, belongs to the group functionally and spa-
tially, that is, shares in its "consensus" as well as
resides within its territory. And for the normal
action of play, in any community, it is necessary,
therefore, that there be both adequate facilities
and functional organization for both maturity and

[104]Luther H. Gulick, "Play in Democracy," *Charities and
the Commons*, August, 1903.

immaturity to participate in wholesome uses of leisure time.[105] But for some time the play movement seems to have failed to observe that both facilities and organization for adult play did not exist, nor was the behavior of adults all that it should have been during night leisure and holiday vacations. It may be more than a mere coincidence, therefore, that contemporaneously with the stages of the play movement prior to that of "civic art and welfare," commercialized amusements developed and multiplied exceedingly, as sports and other wholesome recreations by adults declined. The concept of the situation that became distressing to the leaders of the movement during its recent stages was based at first, however, upon the desire to make the provisions for children more effective, rather than a consideration of the pleasure of adults, since it was observed that anti-social behavior by adults during their leisure inhibited to some extent the control of juveniles by the community. Thus provision for maturity, which came, first, with the provision of benches for mothers and fathers to sit on while watching their children play in the "model playgrounds," second, with the development of "small parks" in which adults were not forbidden, but not encouraged, to participate in games, skating, etc., and, third, in the construction of "recreation centers" for all ages and operated throughout the year, was made imperceptibly with

[105]Cf. E. S. Bogardus, *Introduction to Sociology*, pp. 130–34.

that for youths and children. Not until the presence of adults had become general at the facilities provided originally for younger persons, did conscious efforts in their behalf become a part of the history of the movement. Since the development from provision for children to that for all ages of people was a transition in itself and has been analyzed above, the object of this reference to it is merely to indicate its influence upon the transition now under consideration, its causal relation to the attempt to "define standards" for the use of leisure by all the members of the community. The two transitions were thus involved, the present one being somewhat of a sequel to that which widened the age-group with which the movement was concerned.

A second step in the development of the transition from provision of facilities to the "definition of standards" was that of municipal and state legislation concerning both the control of existing recreational institutions and activities and the construction of public and community facilities. The facts relative to this phase of the movement were fully analyzed above under the discussion of the "civic art and welfare" stage. Thus, in many communities, where there was no interest on the part of the majority of the people in providing facilities for play, the enactment of state legislation of a mandatory character opened the way for the formation of a new concept by presenting a problem to the community.

A third step in the transition was the revival of festivals.   The first conspicuous example was that held in connection with the first annual meeting of the Playground Association of America, in Chicago, June, 1907.   In this open-air performance, hundreds of children, youths and adults participated, groups from nearly all of the playgrounds and small park recreation centers entered.   Many of the folk-dances were performed by immigrants dressed in the national costume appropriate to the dance.   Subsequently an open-air festival, consisting ·of folk-dancing and gymnastic events, became an annual event in the history of the movement in Chicago, and in other cities and rural districts.   At the third meeting of the association, a committee on festivals reported with gratification increasing signs of the growth of the festival spirit in America in dance festivals, play festivals, and national festivals; in pageant and drama; in procession and commemorative ceremonial.

The committee is impressed, however, by the need of some expert guidance and help in the arrangement and conduct of some of these festivals.   Some of them lack expressiveness because there is no central and co-ordinating idea.   Some are ill adapted to actual conditions. . . . .

The aim of these festivals should be to involve the people in self-amusement and self-expression.   The festival should be the greatest and most characteristic form of democratic art.   It should interpret the ideals of the people to themselves.   It should stimulate the creative energies of the people, and bring forth the latent imagination and poetry which is in them.[106]

[106]*Proceedings of the Playground Association of America*, Vol. III, p. 442.

During the following decade considerable progress was made in the standardization of festivals by the incorporation of dramatic and musical activities as well as dancing, games, and athletics in the plan of organization, and by a unification of the program through the use of a "theme" or story and a loose plot in the place of the former sequence of miscellaneous numbers that characterized the earlier programs. The themes chosen were "group" rather than "personal," and the plot, interrupted action on many incidents rather than connected action in a single situation, the distinction thus between a pageant and a play. The action is, furthermore, both symbolical and realistic. When the latter is followed, the folk-customs—dances, songs, merrymaking—are re-enacted; while in the use of the former either traditional legends or original masques are presented. In every program of this type the common gymnastic activities, such as running, wrestling, "stunts," and "feats of strength or skill," are incorporated. A typical program of a festival of this type is the one below, which was given at Fuller Park, Chicago, in May, 1914; the prelude is symbolical, while the remainder is realistic."

Prelude: The elves and fairies dance to celebrate the coming of Maytime.

I. King Richard surprises Robin Hood in Sherwood Forest. They become reconciled and together attend the May Festivities at Nottingham.

II. The Queen and her ladies join them.

III.   The children play upon the green. "Garden Dance," "Little Mother," "The Little Girl's Dance," "Here We Come Over the Green Grass," "Roman Soldiers."

IV.   Robin Hood's Men compete in archery contests.

V.   The Queen's Ladies dance.

VI.   The boys race and tumble on the green.

VII.   With song and dance the May Pole is brought in. "Today's the First of May," "How Do You Do!"

VIII.   The May Queen is selected and the May Pole wound.

IX.   King Richard then calls for his Jesters.

X.   The Morris Men dance: "The Blue-Eyed Stranger," "Figure of Eight," "Country Gardens."

XI.   They are joined by the Villagers and the Queen's Ladies: "The English Tempest," "Brighton Tempest."

XII.   The young men wrestle and perform feats of strength.

XIII.   Rewards are given the victors by the King.

XIV.   The King and Queen leave escorted by the throng.

The prelude of this festival program was designed for little children; numbers III and VII for pre-adolescent boys and girls; IV and VI for boys in early adolescence; XII and XIII, boys in middle or later adolescence; VIII, adolescent girls; I, IX and X, adult men; II and V, adult women, and XI and XIV, all ages of participants. While programs of this character are often presented entirely by children and adolescents, and frequently by girls alone, they are given at other times by neighborhood groups including all ages of people as in this case.

Thus the "play festival," as these events were popularly known, contributed directly to the "definition of standards" for the use of leisure time.

It was probably the most widely used instrument
and the most potent influence, with the possible
exception of "community service," in bringing
the play movement to its present concept of function, as far as the definition of standards is
involved.

The fourth step, the awarding of victory in
team game contests to the side making the highest
record in sportsmanship, is another phase of the
transition from facilities toward the "definition of
standards." The earlier method of determining
the winner in an athletic contest was by the number of "goals," or "strikes," or "points" made,
the score, while the only effort to suppress "foul
play" was by certain penalizations as defined
in the rules of the game. Under that policy of
supervising athletic competition, groups were frequently quite willing to permit a weaker player
to commit "personal fouls" against a stronger
member of the opposing team; for should the
offender be excluded from the game, as was
rarely done in fact, nevertheless he was regarded
as having been "heroically sacrificed" in the
"melee" which disabled the "star" on the opposite team, and thus his team was in a position to
make the higher score by virtue of the physical
handicap under which the better players of the
opposing side were working, while the moral value
of competitive sport was thereby nullified. The
first recreation system to devise a scheme to pre-
vent such unsportsmanlike behavior, common in

spirited contests such as "championship" games, was the South Park Commissioners, Chicago, in 1914; since then a number of playground systems have followed it. This plan as it was originally formulated involved the rating of all teams on a percentage basis: 35 per cent for sportsmanship; 25 per cent for reliability, and 40 per cent for winning the highest score, the number of points or goals.[107] Thus it is possible for a team making the lower score to win the contest by securing a higher rating in sportsmanship and reliability. Sportsmanship as here used signifies the omission of personal fouls, unnecessary roughness, improper language, and the prompt and courteous acceptance of official decisions. Reliability designates the prompt appearance at the game, correctness in weight and batting order, where used.

A fifth event involved in the transition was that of the supervision of street play. Whereas the play movement attempted, in its earlier stages, to "keep the children off the street," now it seeks to organize and direct the play of children and adults upon certain streets in sections of cities in which the population is congested and other facilities for outdoor activities are lacking. This was an attempt to define the standards of "free play" by providing "copies," or "suggestions," for groups to imitate in their play outside of playgrounds and recreation centers. A play leader was thus sent into certain streets at

[107]Cf. Appendices I and J for a statement of the plan as it was later developed by the South Parks.

regular periods to direct the children or mature members of the block or neighborhood in their use of the street as a playground. Special games and other activities were selected or developed with the nature of the space in mind. The use of streets for purposes such as this was termed "zoning" them, and that portion of a street, between two other intersecting streets so used, was known as a "play zone." It could not be used for other purposes, except by the fire or police departments, during the time in which it was designated as a "play zone." The play movement resorted to this method of directing play as a result of a consciousness that all play did not, could not, and should not take place on a playground or in a recreation center, because facilities such as these were, first, too few, and, second, too limited in resources.

A sixth factor in the transition, namely, the provision of camps outside of the city limits but under municipal control and support, came from a consciousness of the inadaptation of the playground and recreation center to the changing concept of the function of the movement. While in most instances these camps were open during the summer only, in others, as in Los Angeles, the camps have been open during the year, but used only week ends, Saturday and Sunday, during the school year.

A seventh step in the transition is seen in the employment of play leaders throughout the year in some cities in which all-year facilities had not yet been opened. The object of this action was to arouse interest in the wholesome use of leisure time, by the organization of pursuits off the playground, the development of co-operation between philanthropic and public agencies supervising play, and the formation of a public opinion concerning play. In these communities "standards" as well as "facilities" were thus emphasized from the first. A variation of this last method was made by the appointment first of "recreation secretaries" and later of "community secretaries," whose function was the conduct of educational propaganda relative to community organization of leisure. These offices differed in function from that of "superintendent of recreation" or "playgrounds" in that the responsibility of the latter was the administration of a given system of playgrounds and recreation centers maintained either by a playground commission or department of municipal government or by a park or school board.

An eighth feature of the transition from facilities to "standards" was that of "community organization," first undertaken in connection with recreation centers in Chicago and New York during 1914–15, and fully described and analyzed above in the discussion of the "neighborhood organization" stage of the movement. The distinctive features of this scheme of recreation were the "community council," the "public forum,"

the "civic pageant," and the "play festival."
These activities have been either developed or
multiplied by community organization.

But while the play movement did accumulate
considerable information and did also perfect a
technique for "defining standards" for the use
of leisure time prior to 1917, it was during the
Great War that this concept of function was dif-
fused. "Community service," first in war camps
and industrial centers, and in cities generally,
since the signing of the armistice is the instrument now being employed to emphasize this point
of view.[108] During the past three years, more
than ever before, the play movement has been
endeavoring to "define standards" rather than
simply "provide facilities" for play.

I. *From "individual" interests to "group"
and "community" activities.* Further analysis
of the play movement discloses a transition from
provision for the fulfilment of "individual"[109]
wishes and desires to that for the development
first of "group" and later of "community" activities. The "individual" interests involved in
the adjustments made during the earlier stages
of the movement may be described as having consisted of opportunities to fulfil the wish for "new
experience" and for "recognition," both of which
were provided in some measure by the "sand

[108]Abbie Condit, "Recreation," *American Yearbook*, 1920.

[109]Cf. A. W. Small, "Sociology," article in *Encyclopedia
Americana*, edition of 1919, for discussion of the term "individual."

garden,'' the "model playground,'' the "small park,'' the "recreation center,'' and the "civic art and welfare'' stages. In these respective facilities many "new experiences'' were available to the "individual,'' such as molding in sand, listening to stories at the "story-hour,'' wading or swimming in the pool, running a "dash'' or a "mile race,'' doing the many "stunts'' performed upon the apparatus which involved considerable courage as well as skill, "hiking,'' and numerous other activities.[110] Likewise many opportunities to gain "recognition'' also were presented to the "individual,'' if he "won the race,'' or could do the most daring "stunt'' on the apparatus, or jump the farthest or highest, or "pitch'' the best game of ball. There were opportunities to some extent for "response,'' as in the formation of friendships and the association of members of the same "team'' in the inter-playground contests, but conscious effort was not made to fulfil this wish directly during the earlier stages of the movement. Everything organized or suggested was primarily to give "new experience'' or "recognition'' to the "individual'' conceived as a more or less particular, separate, and discrete being. A "common sense'' and "naïve'' assumption that play was a "natural'' expression and

[110]Cf. R. E. Park and H. A. Miller, *Old World Traits Transplanted*, and W. I. Thomas and F. Znaniecki, *The Polish Peasant in Europe and America*, for discussion of "the four wishes," namely, (1) new experience, (2) security, (3) recognition, (4) response.

should be utilized in the education of the "individual" prevailed, and colored the entire scheme of provision proposed by the movement, during its first five stages. It amounted to saying that the child would become a good citizen, that is, a valuable member of society in mature life, if given an opportunity during childhood and youth to exercise his natural responses, without a correlative development of some kind of a "life organization," as Thomas calls it, whereby he might develop a personality that would be a phase of social reality rather than an independent entity.[111]

As a practical measure for the control of "individuals," and thus, the expedition of the efficacy of the playground or recreation center, and apparently without any scientific understanding of the full significance of the action, the individualistic concept of structure and function came to be supplanted by an emphasis upon the social aspect, the group relation of play. The object here was to harmonize personal ideals with social welfare, and thus bring to pass an automatic regulation of the behavior of the persons engaged in playground or recreation center activities. Thus certain activities were organized for the promotion of group rather than personal ends, except as the two ends were conceived as one, as coincident with each other. The "individual" did not participate in the game merely that he might experience the feeling of winning, but rather that

[111]Cf. E. S. Bogardus, *Social Psychology*, pp. 1–4, 81–90.

he might also share with the other members of the team a consciousness of group superiority, which applied not only to his teammates but to his playground or school or neighborhood as well, for all members of these groups aided, by cheering or personal encouragement of some other kind, the effort toward victory.[112]

The concept "group" here designates a small or large number of persons related to each other by accommodation and co-operation and involved frequently in competition with similar bodies of persons. The words "social" and "community" are marginal concepts; the former being general, the latter, territorial. The word "crowd" is a marginal term. In the play movement it describes a class in school, the daily attendance on the playground, or a similar aggregate of persons, including both spectators and actors, as in a holiday celebration. The group is a "primary" association, as defined by Cooley,[113] "a face to face meeting"; but on the playground the group relation is less rigid and dominant, that is, one does not attain status merely "as a member of the group,"[114] as is true of the immigrant groups and primitive societies, but one's status is elevated by the transitory success of the group, the team or class or school. The "play group" does not "maintain the security of the whole community

[112]A "song" which the present writer has often heard at competitive games contains the following phrase, "You do your best, boys; we'll do the rest, boys; fight on to victory."

[113]C. H. Cooley, *Social Organization*, p. 23.

[114]Park and Miller, *op. cit.*, p. 39.

at the sacrifice of the wishes of its individual members,''[115] as is the case with primary groups in the earlier stages of social evolution, except for transitory periods and in limited ways. Yet in so far as the members of the team accommodate themselves to the demands of the captain or coach that they play in certain positions, that they make ''sacrifice hits'' as in baseball, that they play the rôle of fool or villain in the drama, and in like instances, there is a transitory period during which the individual feels himself a person ''to the degree that he is incorporated in an organization.''[116]

The ''community'' is spatial as well as functional. It is removed but a step at most from the ''group,'' and often involved in it; the ''group'' in many instances being a ''community,'' that is, including all persons within a given area in a functional relationship. In the play movement the full development and utilization of the ''community'' concept came subsequently to that of the ''group.'' It did not supplant the group relation but extended it, modified its application so as to involve a more democratic, heterogeneous, ''free'' relation between the members. That is, the ''community'' grants greater ''liberty'' to its members, more variety in life organization, and consequently, a higher degree of personality, as the term applies to the ''neighborhood organization'' and ''community service'' stages of the

[115]Park and Miller, *op. cit.*, p. 38.   [116]*Ibid.*

play movement. The "community," here, then is less dominant and binding than in primitive societies and the elementary stages of civilized social organization. This fact is due, doubtless, to the presence of the "state," the "nation," the "city," and the "public," all of which are marginal terms with respect to the "community," and all tend to weaken the power of the "community" over the "individual" in his quest for the fulfilment of "the four wishes." The "community" activities are less spontaneous than those of the "crowd" or the "group" in the history of the play movement. The development of its function has involved a great amount of rationalizing, of conscious effort, as a result of the disorganizing influences present in the modern social situation, especially in the cities where "secondary organization" frequently prevails.

Quite unconsciously, therefore, play has been treated by the promoters of the movement as a mode of collective behavior. Evidence of this fact is furnished by an analysis of the organization of activities for the development of "group" and "community" attitudes. Relative to this feature there are six devices that have been employed: (1) the "group test" in athletic competition; (2) the awarding of "trophies" to teams rather than to persons; (3) the method of determining "athletic supremacy" for a given playground or school; (4) the development of self-supporting and self-governing clubs; (5) the control of dancing by "group" or "neighbor-hood" associations in place of attempts to "inspect" or "supervise" commercial halls and "public" dances; (6) the organization of communities for the aid that they thus may render the administration of play facilities.

1. The "group test" is a form of competition, either on apparatus or in other exercises, in which the average attainment of one group such as a class in school, or a transitory classification made for the purposes of the contest, is compared with that of another group to determine the victor. Here each contestant competes against a "standard" and a record of the results of each attempt is kept until each member of a given group has taken part in like manner, then the average for the group is figured out and compared with a similar average of another or any number of groups. Thus class may compete against class, or a school or playground against another institution. This plan of competitive athletics permits every member to participate and to count equally in determining the final result. It differs greatly from the older form of athletics wherein each winner gains at the expense of some other or possibly several opponents. If ten boys compete in a foot race, only one may be declared the winner, while in the "group test" the effort of each is satisfactorily rewarded. Taking the same ten boys again, if the same one continues to win in each race, the other members will eventually de-

cline to compete with him, or if second, and third places are given, as is generally done in this type of athletics, then seven of the ten will soon lose interest in the race. The "group test" was designed to induce universal participation for the hygienic and moral benefits that were believed to accrue from it, in the place of the tendency toward professionalization which inevitably results from the traditional method of inviting an indiscriminate number to enter the contest and then announcing only the winner of first, second, and third places in each event.

2. The awarding of trophies to teams rather than to persons is another plan for emphasizing the "group" versus the "individual." Here some inexpensive evidence of having won a place, either first, second, or third, in a competitive event, such as a ribbon of appropriate color, blue for first, red for second, and white for third, is given each successful contestant, while the greater prize, usually a "loving cup," is awarded the team, or rather the playground, park, or school which the winning team represents. The name of the institution to which the team winning the contest belongs and the names of the members of the winning team are usually inscribed upon the cup or other prize that is awarded in this manner. Loyalty to the group and to the community alike is developed in all who can compete in athletics, declamation, or debate, or in any other form of competition in which this method of award is

followed. A social attitude is fostered, a social consciousness engendered, by this form of sport.

3. Another plan for emphasizing the "group" versus the "individual" in competition is that known as "athletic supremacy" for the month and year, by which a count is made of all contestants entered from each play center in an inter-center contest and one point allowed each team for each event in which a contestant from that team participates whether he "places" or not, except that the number of points that any team may win in this manner is definitely limited before-time on the basis of the probable average number entering from each center. This is placing numbers against skill; the mass against the "star" performer.

4. A fourth method of recognition of the "group" is the development of self-supporting clubs, especially among people between seventeen and twenty-five years of age. These organizations were of three types: for young men only, for young women only, and for both sexes. Their objects were either primarily for study or for sociability, but in either case a certain amount of "social" activity, in the sense defined above under transition G, always developed. One of the most frequent forms of this type of occupation was dancing.

5. The control of dancing, however, constitutes a fifth method by which "group" interests assumed ascendency over "individual" activities.

"CINDERELLA." STORY-PLAYING, USING THE DRAMATIC, PANTOMIME, DANCING, CHORAL AND PAGEANTRY ARTS, 135 CHILDREN IN CAST, HAMILTON PARK, CHICAGO.

The principal sources of anti-social behavior in conjunction with commercialized dance halls have undoubtedly been due, as play leaders have come to believe, not to the lack of chaperonage nor of wholesome personal beliefs of many attending them, but to promiscuity of admissions and alcoholic liquors sold or distributed at the dance. The "municipal dances" described above in the discussion of the "civic art and welfare" stage, and similar activities conducted under the auspices of War Camp Community Service, corrected the latter of these two sources of misconduct, but failed to obviate the former. And it is where promiscuity is permitted, especially in our cities, that the normal restraining influence of the "group" breaks down; any one, especially if immature, behaves differently while among strangers from what he does while among neighbors or friends. Also there is no way of supervising a crowd in a dance hall if evil persons are admitted along with others seeking innocent amusement, as pointed out by Halbert after considerable experience in supervising and inspecting dance halls in Kansas City.[117] In some communities, therefore, dancing in public play centers has been restricted to neighborhood associations or smaller groups who reserve the hall and invite guests, each of whom is known and vouched for by some member of the club or crowd conducting the dance. The best example of this method

[117]Cf. discussion above of the "Civic Art and Welfare" stage.

of conducting dancing is probably that offered by the South Park Commissioners, Chicago, who in their sixteen years of experience have never permitted a promiscuous crowd at a fieldhouse dance, although the number of dancing parties averages fifty per week during the winter. In every instance, the assembly hall or other room of the fieldhouse is "reserved" by a club, or a person representing a definite although unorganized group, no admissions are charged at the door or elsewhere, and no one is admitted except with the approval of the person or club reserving the room in which the dance is being held. All groups are required to provide their own chaperones, doormen, and wardrobe attendants, although the director of the fieldhouse is always present in the building and a patrolman, regularly detailed to the park, is within call to aid, if necessary, the group reserving the hall in carrying out its agreement to exclude "loafers," "hangers-on," and the like from admission to the dance. The police never enter the hall for the purpose of chaperoning the dance. Here is a clear example of an attempt to exercise social control by the instrumentality of self-governing groups.

6. An elaboration of the "group" concept of the structure and function of the play movement led to that of "community" organization and service and completed the transition from "individualistic" interests. This phase of the transition came last as a natural consequence of the

fact that the earlier stages of the movement were concerned with adjustments that involved juveniles rather than adults. When the concept of the structure and function of the movement involved provisions for persons of all ages in all wholesome uses of leisure time, as it did during and since the "recreation center" stage, a far more complicated situation faced its administrators. The problem, then, was how to develop self-control and self-support of leisure pursuits in harmony with the public welfare, in order that provision for play in all communities might be adequate to the demands of the changed social situation of modern times. "Community organization" as a form of "community service" represents the solution of this problem proposed by the movement. The history of this solution was presented, above, in the analysis of the last two stages of the movement. It is unnecessary to restate here the facts involved in its development. A further analysis of the concept of "community organization" as a method of administering play is necessary, however, to establish the fact of a transition from "individual" to "community" activities. Three aspects of that theory may be briefly mentioned in this connection:

First, it came to be the consensus of the promoters of the play movement, that a community may and therefore should do for itself many things that external forces alone are unable to do for it. It was pointed out that in the cities in particular, there were many neighborhoods or "little communities" in which large sums of money were spent annually by various social welfare agencies, that continued to yield the usual harvest of poverty, crime, misery, because the population of these districts did not co-operate collectively rather than individually with the agencies at work in their vicinity. Philanthropic and governmental agencies, it was said, were working on the analogy of machine industry,[118] on the assumption that we human beings, that the material we are dealing with through our ministrations, is passive material, like iron ore or cotton thread, which can be taken and put in a machine and hammered or woven and put through specialized processes and turned out at the end a finished product.

But people, it was pointed out, are not things; character is not a product, the result of an external application to their nature while they remain passive in the process, but an achievement and a collective achievement which was previously described by A. W. Small,[119] who defines a person as "a center of conscious impulses which realize themselves in full only in realizing a society." Persons then are phases of social reality; they live in groups and, as shown by Cooley,[120] in these group relations, "everywhere, human nature comes into existence. Man does not have it at birth; he

[118]John Collier, "Community Organization and the Great Decision," reprinted from the *Seward Park Community Center Magazine*, New York, 1919.

[119]A. W. Small, *General Sociology*, p. 476.

[120]C. H. Cooley, *Social Organization*, p. 23.

cannot acquire it except through fellowship; and it decays in isolation.''

Both play groups and neighborhood groups are primary, that is, universal and fundamental, and in primitive societies concentric, the latter being marginal to the former. But in our present stage of social organization this face-to-face group is frequently disorganized, and play among many other types of behavior is treated "individually" and by a machine-like process, in which even families are divided in their recreation. Most of the types of commercialized recreations are of this character. The social situation is lacking, in such instances, in the factor essential to achievement. Play cannot be purchased, neither can it be given away. It can only be created, and it attains its most intense and highly developed form in co-operative, collective, life of the group. A group, a neighborhood, therefore, can do for itself, with respect to play as in certain other activities, what other forces cannot do for it. It must create its own play if its leisure is to yield all it may. "Community organization" was conceived as a device for mobilizing the resources of neighborhoods in adjustment to the changed social situation, in which face-to-face meetings had largely disintegrated, so as to make possible self-selection, support, and government of leisure pursuits in harmony with public welfare.

A second aspect of the theory that underlay "community organization" was the belief on the part of play leaders that communities may be over-organized,[121] that is, may contain territorially more societies than they can support or utilize. Whatever may be the truth of that belief, it is history that the idea was held by many and that it served as a spur to the work of attempting not to add another organization but to correlate those already existing into a more or less unified whole. The "community council" was said to be an organization *of* the community, not an organization *in* the community. It was believed not to add *another* organization but *more* organization. It was designed to be comprehensive and to correlate all useful agencies, strengthening the weaker but essential ones, preventing duplicating ones from forming, and exposing those that exploit to the fresh air of public opinion. It sought to "put first things first, and second things second,"[122] by its allegiance to the good of the whole community. It would be presumptuous, of course, for an "organized community" to set up a claim to such a utopian function as the advocates of the "community movement" described "community organization" to be, but in many communities the movement doubtless did tend to give greater cohesion and unity to neighborhood life, to restore in part the instrument of social contact previous generations had found useful, the "face to face meeting" of the community.

[121]Henry E. Jackson, *A Community Center*, The Macmillan Co., 1918.
[122]*Ibid.*

The third element in the philosophy of the "community organization" movement, one directly related to the support and control of wholesome leisure pursuits, was the concept of the relation of the neighborhood to the perpetuity and efficiency of self-government, especially in municipal administration and national policies. The organized neighborhood was described as "a little democracy,"[123] and was said to be generically and dynamically related to the larger democracy of city, state, and nation. Past failures by the latter were attributed to the absence of the former. "Community organization" was roughly defined as a medium through which responsibility for efficient government in all of its phases could be made real and personal to the members of the community.[124] The leisure period, it was pointed out, was a fertile field for either commercial exploitation and anti-social behavior leading to political and cultural disintegration, or for behavior of quite the opposite kind. The determining factor, it was held, was the character of the "social organization" of the group. It should involve, it was said, the "little democracy," the "face to face" association small enough to permit personal acquaintance and full communication, but large enough to enable every member to visualize

[123]Mrs. Ida Clyde Clark, *The Little Democracy*, D. Appleton & Co., New York, 1918. This volume was prepared as a textbook on Community Organization.

[124]John Collier, "Community Councils, What They Have Done and What Is Their Function," National Conference of Social Work, 1919.

the whole of society.[125] "Community organization" seemed to many to meet these specific requirements. It was a leisure-time activity. Its action would make possible collective play, again, as in the more elementary stages of social evolution, with this difference, however, that in modern times greater variation and freedom of personality would prevail owing to the influence of the state and nation upon local organization.

Thus, in the sequence of stages and transitions in the play movement, "community organization" as a form of "community service" was conceived as a process for the conservation of leisure and the development of play as a mode of collective behavior. "Community organization" may be regarded as *a* scheme of "community service" and *the* scheme of community recreation today. Wherever it is utilized a play center becomes a community center, and play contributes directly to community interests instead of merely satisfying "individual" wishes as characterized the adjustment established during the earlier stages of the play movement.

[125]R. A. Woods, "The Neighborhood in Social Reconstruction," *American Sociological Society Papers and Proceedings*, 1913, pp. 14-28.

V. THE TREND OF THE STAGES AND THE TRANSITIONS IN THE PLAY MOVEMENT

An analysis of a movement is incomplete if its tendencies are not disclosed. As stated in the introduction to this report, movements are transitory, becoming in time either transformed into institutions or disintegrated. In the former case, their plans of adjustment to the changed social situation are adopted by society and made a part of its "more or less connected and harmonious 'system of rules of behavior.'"[1] In the latter case, their schemes are discarded with the passing away of the particular feature in the social situation, or the illusion concerning the same, which incited them. This phase of a movement may be denominated its "trend." It is manifested by the sum of its "stages" and "transitions." It indicates the probable success or failure. It is a test of the efficacy and a criterion of the achievement, at a given time, since it marks the degree of attainment of the object for which the movement was inaugurated. A definition of the "trend" of a movement involves the formulation of a concept of the process as a whole, unifying the facts of its history, and establishing a basis upon which to evaluate it.

A statement of the "trend" of the play movement in the United States may be deduced from

[1] W. I. Thomas and F. Znaniecki, *The Polish Peasant in Europe and America*, Vol. I, pp. 31-33.

the foregoing analysis of its respective "stages" and "transitions"; and, consequently, the defense of the following formulation rests in part upon the accuracy of the classifications and explanations of the data examined in chapters iii and iv above. If these inductions were correct, then the "trend" of the play movement is toward an integration, rather than a dissolution, of an adequate scheme of adjustment to the social situation which it has perfected from time to time as changes in the concept of its function and structure have been made, and incidentally, toward institutionalization.

Any discussion of the "trend" of a movement must, as a matter of course, consider its relation to the possibility of its institutionalization; for every movement tends either toward the probability or improbability of such a termination of its activities, whatever else may be true of its "trend." With respect to the play movement, however, two groups of tendencies seem to characterize its "trend": the one, toward an evolution in the concept of its function correlative with changes in its structure which has been repeatedly indicated in the discussion of the "stages" and "transitions" above and will be clearly disclosed in the paragraphs that follow; and the other, toward the institutionalization of many phases of its changing and growing scheme of adjustments to the modern social situation.

These two aspects of the "trend" of the play movement may, for the sake of convenience and economy of effort, be considered somewhat together in the following analysis, since they involve the same groups of facts with emphasis now on their significance for institutionalization and now for the evolution in structure and concept of function, as parts of a unified whole. Before undertaking an analysis of the "trend" of this movement, however, the characteristics and genesis of institutions in general should be explained for the sake of a mutual understanding between the writer and the reader—since the term institution is carelessly used by some writers— and particular attention given to the process of transformation of a movement into an institution as was asserted in the introduction above to be a frequent occurrence in social evolution. An institution[2] may be defined as a rule of behavior or instrument for accomplishing human purposes that has been rationally established; that is, approved

[2]Among the more careful formulations are the following:
"An institution is simply a definite and established phase of the public mind, not different in its ultimate nature from public opinion, though often seeming, on account of its permanence and the visible customs and symbols in which it is clothed, to have a somewhat distinct and independent existence."—C. H. Cooley, *Social Organization*, p. 313.
"The rules of behavior, and the actions viewed as conforming or not conforming to these rules, constitute with regard to their objective significance a certain number of more or less connected and harmonious systems which can be generally called social institutions."—W. I. Thomas and F. Znaniecki, *The Polish Peasant in Europe and America*, Vol. I, pp. 32–33.
"An institution is a section of corporate human nature plus the machinery and the instrumentalities through which

by the mind of the group and adopted by some kind of public action as a result of the formulation of public opinion and sentiment concerning the issue which it raised at the time of its establishment. An institution differs from a custom essentially by its origin; having arisen in some more or less clearly defined crisis in the life of the group in which a period of disorganization,[3]

that human nature operates."—Robert E. Park, "The City," *American Journal of Sociology*, March, 1915, p. 577.

"An institution is a social relation that is established by adequate and rightful authority."—F. H. Giddings, *Elements of Sociology*, p. 175.

"An institution is a set of activities which a society adopts as its deliberately accepted method of attaining a deliberately approved end."—E. C. Hayes, *Introduction to Sociology*, p. 405.

"First of all, in attempting a classification of the forms of association, we come upon the distinction between the sanctioned and unsanctioned forms. The sanctioned forms are types of relationships between individuals which have been reflected upon by the mass of the group in which they occur, and agreed to. These sanctioned forms are, then, as we have already said, synonymous with human institutions, because social sanction can rise only after self-consciousness has appeared. They are not found in the social groups below man. The tendency is manifest in all advanced stages of social evolution to institutionalize all forms of association. Nevertheless, in even the most advanced groups which we know, there are many unsanctioned forms or groups. These are the spontaneous, unreflected types of relationship between individuals. They especially characterize animal societies and the lower human groups, but in the form of the gang, the mob, factions, amusements, and conflicts, they characterize also the most advanced human groups. It is, of course, frequently very difficult to decide whether any particular form of association belongs to the sanctioned or the unsanctioned class. There might, for example, be some difference of opinion as to whether the saloon and the brothel were institutions in western civilization or not."—C. A. Ellwood, *Sociology in Its Psychological Aspects*.

[3]Cf. Robert A. Park and Ernest W. Burgess, *Introduction to the Science of Sociology*, University of Chicago Press, 1921, p. 55.

such as that caused by disease, war, accelerated mobility, unrest, was followed by a more or less rational plan of adjustment to the changed social situation occasioned by the crisis, that ultimately attained group approval. A custom, on the other hand, is an unsanctioned but powerful force which arose without rational adjustment to a passed social situation. While a custom is in vogue, however, the members of the group must adhere rigidly to its practice, group condemnation falling upon any one who deviates, even a crisis may be provoked whereby the custom is made an institution. The characteristics of an institution, then, are five: (1) group approval based upon a belief in the value of its function in the life of the group; (2) physical accompaniment or embodiment in the form of a personnel, symbols, charters, constitutions, and the like; (3) historical continuity, indicated by traditions, beliefs, sentiments, and even customs in the course of time, which accrue as habit displaces thought in the functioning of the institution; (4) organization for specialization and differentiation of function; (5) relative permanency involving the establishment of a given adjustment as a feature of the social organization of the group, and often a tendency toward self-perpetuation after the passing of the social situation in which it first took form.

The process by which adjustments are formulated is a social movement. It originates during a period of disorganization of social life and

leads the group either forward, or backward, to
a stage of reorganization of association with
respect to the given issue to which it is related.
Movements, thus, are not only transitory, as has
been stated but also indispensable operations in
social evolution. They may be said to have become institutions when their plans of adjustment
to the social situation in which they arose have
been approved and adopted by the deliberate
action of the group so that they become recognized features of the established system of
regulative or operative arrangements in the
organization of society at a given time and
place. Social institutions, then, are created
by positive movements and dissolved by negative ones;[4] the former organizing a proposed adjustment, the latter disorganizing an
established arrangement, as determined by the
consensus of the group involved, whether community, city, state, or nation, or even a group
of nations, as in the case of treaties and international law. In the transformation of a movement into an institution, the arrangement approved and enforced by society may be of a regulative or an operative type. In the former
instance, it is a "mould to which the relations,
attitudes, or behavior of individuals are required
to conform . . . . a channel in which activity
must flow."[5] In the latter case, it is an instrument for accomplishing a given purpose, "when

[4] Cf. p. 2 above.
[5] E. A. Ross, *Principles of Sociology*, 1920, p. 485.

society is intent on obtaining a service rather
than canalizing individual conduct, a special organized personnel working under an authority,
charter, or constitution and provided with continuous support. Whether the support comes
from taxes, gifts, or fees makes no difference.
The essential thing is that the institution is
bound to render what is believed to be a service
of public importance.'"[6] If this discrimination between regulative and operative types of institution is a real one, then the play movement has
given rise primarily to one of the latter type, that
is, to an adjustment to the current social situation
that renders service of public importance by the
sanction and support of the community. Attendance at all facilities established by the play movement is voluntary not compulsory. These
facilities are operated in behalf of the common
welfare according to the belief and desire of the
group, and not for pecuniary profit to some member or coterie of members of the community while
public opinion is indifferent or tolerant, as is the
case with the motion picture, for example, in
most American communities at the present time.
If the question of the policy, the method of control and support, of the motion picture industry
in the United States were to come to the attention of the public so as to make possible the formation of a public opinion concerning its
administration, one that would require that films

[6]Ross, *op. cit.*

be produced and exhibited primarily for social rather than individual ends, for the common welfare instead of pecuniary profit to given persons engaged in it as a business, and under the supervision of some branch of constituted authority, governmental or otherwise—as the elementary and high schools, the majority of our religious societies, the Y.M.C.A. and Y.W.C.A., the Boy Scouts and Campfire Girls, not to include the court, the police, the fire, the street cleaning, garbage and sewage disposal departments, boards of health, and many more—then the motion picture would be institutionalized as the "playground" and similar phases of the play movement have recently come to be.

Until recently the play of children was in no wise a community concern, but a private and domestic concern. Now, however, the provision for play has been institutionalized by the establishment of the public supervised playground, equipped with all needful apparatus, where children frolic under the expert direction of trained adult play leaders.[7]

The transformation of the play movement into an institution, however, has not been as simple nor as complete as the above statement may imply. While it is true that facilities for the play of children are almost universally approved and provided by either public or community means in connection with parks and schoolyards in the respective cities and rural districts throughout the country, there are phases of the concept of the

[7]Ross, *op. cit.*

function and structure that have not yet been
sanctioned by group or public action, although
other adjustments than that of the "children's
playground" have been adopted through public
approval.

An analysis of the "stages" and the "transitions" in the play movement from the standpoint
of its tendencies discloses five types of development in its structure and in the concept of its
function which constitute its "trend." The
first, is that of *group sanction,* by the approval
and adoption of certain adjustments worked out
by the movement. This tendency has not reached
the extent of its probable development, but significant progress has been made since the "model
playground" stage when the question of "municipal" support and control was first agitated, and
also since the "small park" stage when its application on a fairly large scale was first made.
During the "recreation center" and "civic art
and welfare" stages the concept of public responsibility for the construction and administration of suitable and sufficient recreation facilities
for all ages of persons was clearly presented to
the public mind. The issue, as the problem was
then formulated, was whether or not the people
through their government should support and control adequate and suitable facilities for the recreation of young people and adults as well as for the
play of children. That public approval was par-
tially and incompletely given to the proposition

is attested by the policy followed during those stages and the succeeding ones. Thus, during the "civic art and welfare" stage, although commercialized amusements were "inspected" and required to conform to specified regulations concerning hygienic and moral conditions, they were nevertheless permitted to be operated primarily for individual pecuniary profit rather than for social welfare; they were not institutionalized. During the "neighborhood organization" stage, likewise, the principal factor emphasized was that of community control and support, that is, institutionalization of given opportunities for leisure-time occupations.   Still the commercialized amusements remained outside the plan of adjustment.   In so far as "self-support" and "self-control," as those terms were defined and used above,[8] have since been attained, the movement may be said to have become an institution. Since, however, this method of administration has not as yet been applied to more than a very small percentage of the leisure-time functions of any community—in New York City, for example, only five per cent of the recreational activities are administered in this manner—the play movement as a whole can not be regarded, at present, as an institution; it retains in certain respects the features of a movement.   And the daily activities of the Playground and Recreation Association of America, and Community Service, Incorporated,

[8] Cf. chapter iv, transition E.

each with field secretaries and monthly publications carrying on propaganda for public administration of leisure-time pursuits of the people,
indicate the present incomplete social sanction as
they both suggest and indicate the probable con-
summation of that fact at some future date.   The
whole field of commercialized amusements, however, has scarcely been affected by the movement.
The theatre, the motion-picture house, the commercial dance hall and skating rink, the shooting
gallery, the private club, the summer and winter
resorts, and many more, may be said to lie outside the sphere of its influence at present, and
this notwithstanding the many efforts made to
"define standards" of leisure-time activities.
Group sanction of the adjustments proposed by
the movement is, then, partial and incomplete,
but gradually extending its field of approval and
adoption.   The concept has been formulated, but
its social significance has not gotten the attention
of the public mind.   The channel of influence in
that direction, at present, is "community service."

A second type of development, indicative of
the nature of the "trend" of the play movement,
is that of the *physical accompaniments* which
have been produced, and in which its concept of
function and structure have been embodied or by
which they are now symbolized.   These features
are both regulative and operative, although for
the most part of the latter type.   Among the
former are the "sand garden," the "playground"

in parks and schoolyards, the "athletic field," the "outdoor- and indoor-gymnasium," the "small park," the "swimming pool," the "bathing beach," the "fieldhouse," the "community center," the "branch library," the "public forum," and the "community council." Among the latter are "recreational legislation," "amateur athletics" with its implements such as balls, bats, gloves, bases, spiked shoes, costumes, nets, jumping standards, hurdles, horses, bucks, beams, play-fields, goal-posts, pennants, yells, processions and serpentines and the like, "efficiency tests," with their respective gold, silver, and bronze badges, buttons, or pins, the "schedules for the day and week," the nine thousand "play-leaders," the "group test," the "play festival," "street play," "block parties," "community sings," "self-supporting and self-governing clubs," and "community organization." Each of these respective adjustments has been either created or developed by the play movement; and each one has since been approved and established by community opinion and constituted authority, either governmental or otherwise. They give evidence of both an evolution in structure and concept of function and of progress toward institutionalization. They may be regarded, in fact, as being institutions themselves, although from another concept of the movement they may be more accurately described as phases of the development of an institutionalization of play.

A third type of development distinguishing
the "trend" of the play movement, is that of
increasing *historical continuity* as shown in the
accumulation of beliefs, traditions, sentiments,
and to some extent customs, by which the public
gains a better idea of its function in the life of
the community. These characteristics disclose,
also, certain developments in structure and
changes in the concept of function, as well as incidents in the development of an institutionalization of play. They add the force of sentiment
to the plan of adjustment evolved by the movement, and thus hasten the development of institutionalization. Among the facts involved are
those analyzed above in the study of: (1) transition F, from "free play" and miscellaneous
events to "directed play" and "correlated schedules," such as the classification of patrons and
play leaders, the organization of amateur athletic competition in track, field, and aquatic
sports, the "efficiency tests," and the organization of "passive" as well as "active play";
(2) transition H, that is, from the provision of
facilities to the definition of standards, especially
"recreational legislation," "play festivals," the
rewarding of "sportsmanship," "street play,"
and annual provision of facilities; and (3) transition I, that from individual interests to community activities, involving the "group test,"
the awarding of trophies to the "institution"
instead of giving prizes to the individuals

composing a track, field, tennis, baseball, or gymnastic team, the "neighborhood dance," and "community organization" for the control and support of recreational facilities. Some of the common phrases formulated to express the sentiments of the movement are "fair play," and "good loser," in athletic competition; "take turns," in the use of the gymnastic apparatus; and "each for all and all for each," in the self-governing and self-supporting associations. Among the customs that have arisen are: "the return game"; the "home team acting as hostess to the visiting team," especially in girls' competition; the "yells" by the winning group for the losing team after the contest, and the association of "formal activities" with the indoor gymnasium and of "informal events" with the outdoor gymnasium.

A fourth aspect of the "trend" is that of *increasing organization,* involving specialization and differentiation in function. This trait was disclosed above by the study, in chapter iv, of transitions A, B, C, E, F, and G, respectively. Transition A showed an increase in organization with respect to the age groups involved; B, with respect to the length of time during the year in which the facilities were operated, thus increasing the organization of the schedule and the personnel in order to meet the differences in play due to the respective seasons; C, concerning the place, whether indoors or outdoors, and consequently

the types of activities; E, the method of control
and support, whether philanthropic, public, or
community, the last method being much more
complicated and difficult of execution, although
permitting a more diversified and complete provision than either of the former; F, was confined almost exclusively to the evidence of increasing organization, since the facts which it
contained related to the classification of both
patrons and leaders of the play center, the organization of athletic competition, "efficiency tests,"
and the posting of "schedules" or sequences of
events for the class period, the day, the week, and
the year; and G, from a simple to a complex field
of activities, involving greater variety and thus
specialization and differentiation, since all attending the play center would not, of course, participate in all of the activities taking place at the
same time, such a fact would be a physical impos-
sibility as well as a psychological undesirability
on their part.   Yet by the presence of a complex
field under specialized leadership and grouping,
the interest of a greater number of persons is
obtained and their participation in play activities
made more regular and of greater social value.
This is the function of organization in the play
center and in the community.   Under "community service" this principle is being extended to
activities outside of the center in connection with
efforts toward a definition of standards for the
use of leisure time, as shown in transition H.

A fifth aspect of the "trend" of the play movement is also one indicative of growth in structure and change in idea of function as well as progress toward institutionalization, namely, the *relative permanency* of the adjustments executed. The play movement is now thirty-six years old; the Playground and Recreation Association is now in its fifteenth year. It is of interest, therefore, in closing the present analysis of its "trend," to determine to what extent the original adjustments are now being advocated and whether or not they dominate the current idea of function so as to impair the efficacy of the movement; that is, whether the original pattern by which they were organized has prevented the development of others, correlative with them, as experience accumulated. This is what is meant by "relative permanency" of the adjustments proposed. Some of the original ones still survive, but, as has been disclosed above, they have not prevented the development of others. The concept of the structure and function of the movement has been relatively permanent and not inflexible, changeless, throughout its history. In fact, some of the later structures are receiving greater attention than the earlier ones. Thus, among the early adjustments that still survive, are: the "sand garden" and the "playground," which date from the original stage of the movement and have since become institutions; and the idea of leadership of play, of schedules of events, and of public support, which date from the second stage of its history, and are also institutions. While these original or early features are still utilized, it seems that they have interfered in no way with the development of others, some of which have been established, and whose nature has been described above under the head of physical accompaniment. Their repetition is therefore unnecessary here. But the fact that they are retained and have appeared successively is the point to be noted in this connection. That fact discloses an evolution in structure and concept of function as well as a degree of institutionalization of play. As to the future, it is not within the limits of this study to predict, but, if it resembles the past, it will involve a continuation of the process described above for at least an indefinite period of time, that is, new structures and ideas of function will appear in the effort to make a more perfect adjustment. There is nothing that indicates even a remote possibility, however, of the discontinuance of such features of the movement as provision: (1) for all ages of people; (2) throughout the year; (3) by both indoor and outdoor activities; (4) in all communities, whether urban or rural, whether populated by the poor or the rich; (5) with directed, as well as free, play involving correlated schedules and the classification of both patrons and leaders; (6) by community support and control as well as subsidy from the public treasury and philanthropy; (7) including opportunities for all manner of wholesome use of leisure time, such as manual, physical, aesthetic, social, and civic interests; (8) emphasizing standards of sportsmanship and behavior believed to be conducive to the public welfare by all persons, whether in the play center or elsewhere; (9) with increasing insistence upon group rather than individual purposes, thus magnifying co-operation and correlation rather than competition and displacement of individuals through conflict. These facts are clearly defined in the minds of those promoting the movement and have been sanctioned, also, by most communities in one degree or another. The tendency and the history is toward their extension rather than their restriction.

The "trend" of the play movement, therefore, is unquestionably toward an elaboration of structure with correlative changes in concept of function, involving institutionalization, with much already made a fact. The full development of public opinion on all the phases of the concept of the structure and function of the movement, however, has not yet been reached. Among the adjustments that have rarely or never received group approval today are: the supervision of passive play, the conduct of community playground camps, the substitution of "neighborhood dances" for the commercialized dance hall and academy, the awarding of victory in athletic competition to sportsmanship rather than for the

higher score, the conduct of inter-playground declamation contests, street-play under trained leadership, inter-community center devices for raising
money to support self-maintenance of leisure-time
activities, community presses and thoroughly
democratic public forums for the discussion of
local, national, and international questions of
public policy, and the whole field of commercialized amusements which are now maintained for
private profit while the community is indifferent
as it was formerly toward the problems of child
play, and the many other adjustments discussed
in the preceding pages.

While it is true, as Ellwood has pointed out,
that there are many relationships between the
members of an advanced society that are not and
may never become institutionalized, and while he
would doubtless include many types of play
among such relationships, yet, as he also said, it
is the tendency of all advanced societies to extend
institutionalization. The probable limits of an
elaboration in structure and concept of function
and of the institutionalization of play have not
been reached in the present age of more or less
disorganization, characterized, on the one hand,
by social isolation, unrest, crowd phenomena, dis-
eases of degeneration, alien immigration, and the
breaking down of the neighborhood or local community relation between members of the ·same
vicinity, and, on the other hand, by the growth
of the democratic spirit and of co-operation in

industry. Shall play escape the influences of the expanding collectivism? Will not a future generation discern, what is believed by the leaders of the current play movement, the inconsistency of the present attitude of the public mind toward the problem of play whereby millions are being expended in the maintenance of public facilities, for the use of leisure, that are socially productive as far as they succeed in attracting the pleasure seeking groups, that in our largest city, and the one most generous in public support of recreational opportunities, meet only five per cent of the need, while unscrupulous persons commercialize the play of the people for private gain, exploiting a legitimate desire of the public and debasing the social sense, as was forcibly stated above in a quotation from J. R. Richards in the discussion of the "neighborhood organization" stage, but which may well deserve a repetition here:

Commercial recreation has signally failed to meet the demands of the people during the leisure period. Public (i. e., socially institutionalized) recreation consciously aiming at the things agreed, as best in our social organism, we feel, must take its place.

Commercial recreation is charged with: debasing the tastes of the people; offering passive (i. e., spectatorship) recreation only; anti-social tendencies in breaking up the family groups seeking pleasure; consorting with vice; levying a terrible tax—perhaps over a hundred and fifty million a year in Chicago; never attempting developmental or educational programs.

Shall the public, rather than given individuals, enter the field of "commercialized" play by owning and operating all recreational agencies as it now does most of the bathing beaches by requiring a small fee for their utilization,[9] or by some other less collectivistic plan, perhaps one similar to the United States railroad administration, or the United States telegraph control, and the like during the Great War? The financial difficulties are perhaps the least doubtful ones, since, as Zueblin[10] has figured it out, the cities of the United States of over one hundred thousand population expended, during the year 1912, $110,000,000 for public education, while five years earlier, the private street railways of those same vicinities netted a profit of $138,000,000; the inference being, of course, that if the cities had owned the street car systems operating within their borders and, as Zueblin ironically remarked, had operated them no less efficiently, they could have reduced their school tax by the considerable amount of $28,000,000, or 25.4 per cent, or could have applied that significant sum to the cost of providing wholesome opportunities for the social use of leisure. It is not the public supervision of the play of the school children, comprising only 20 per cent of the population,

[9]The first year the Clarendon Beach of Chicago was open, the operating expenses amounted to $40,000, while the number of adult patrons was 400,000; thus at 10 cents each the beach was self-supporting.

[10]Charles Zueblin, *American Municipal Progress*, 1916, p. 32.

that is the most significant fact in the scheme of
socialized recreation, important and necessary as
that may be, but it is rather the control of the
remaining 80 per cent of the population during
the sixty-four hours per week in which even the
laboring element is at leisure.   (Figured on the
basis of an eight-hour day six days per week and
without deducting for the national holidays, the
stormy days, nor the periods of unemployment
and convalescence.)   As Jane Addams[11] has said,
the city utilizes the labor of these people during
the day and wrings from them their meager earn-
ings when night comes, for the problem of play
in America, as MacKaye[12] has pointed out, is
essentially the problem of "the night leisure."

It is toward the formulation of adjustments
that shall ensure the social utilization of all leisure through the organization of opportunities
for participation in behavior that is both personally developmental and socially constructive, the
upbuilding of personality, that the play movement seems to be tending.   In play now, as never
before, may the majority of our population find
opportunities for "new experiences" and "recognition"; work is too specialized and monotonous
to afford the fulfilment of those "wishes" except
for a very few.

[11]Jane Addams, *The Spirit of Youth and the City Streets,*
1909, p. 8.
[12]Percy MacKaye, *The Civic Theatre in Its Relation to the
Redemption of Leisure,* 1912, p. 35.

VI. CONCLUSION

The facts involved in the history of the play movement in the United States have now been analyzed. It has been found that there has been an evolution both in its structure and in its concept of function in adjustment to the modern social situation. The original scheme of adjustment has not served as the pattern of action throughout its history. Both the idea and its physical and social embodiments have changed from time to time as experience altered what was believed ought to be done in order to effect a more acceptable adjustment to the current social situation with respect to play.

The analysis of events reported above has shown that the play movement originated with the "sand gardens" in Boston in 1885, since that event, while not the first conscious provision for play in the United States, was the first of the connected series which is known as "the play movement," also sometimes referred to as "the playground movement," or "the playground and recreation movement." This fact was established by the evidence related to the influence of these "sand gardens" upon the development of provision for play, first, for little children and progressively later for youths and adults, in the City of Boston; and, second, the leadership of Boston during the early stages of the movement.

It was shown that there is a great difference between the structure and the concept of the function of the movement during the first decade and that at the present time. The "sand gardens" were provided for little children, were operated only during a short summer vacation period, were unsupervised and maintained by philanthropic support, were equipped with outdoor facilities and located in the most congested sections of the city, and permitted only manual play based on an individualistic point of view; but, today, the play movement endeavors to make provision for all ages of people, throughout the year; in both indoor and outdoor activities, in rural and suburban communities as well as in the crowded urban districts, by the use of directed play, as well as unorganized activities, involving correlated schedules, trained play leaders, and the classification of patrons; by including opportunities for all kinds of wholesome uses of leisure time, such as physical, aesthetic, social, and civic, in addition to the manual play of the first sand gardens; by emphasizing standards of sportsmanship believed to be conducive to the public welfare and to be followed by all persons during their leisure time, whether within or without the specially provided play centers; and, with a community rather than an individualistic purpose in view.

The details of the origin of the movement were presented in chapter ii above, those of the structure and concept of function that prevailed during the first stage, were given in division A of chapter iii, while the facts relative to the changes that have taken place in the concept of function were told in the respective transitions A to I, in chapter iv, and those that had reference to the development of structure were related in the discussion of the last six stages, chapter iii. The tendencies were disclosed in chapter v, and ,summarized at the close of that portion of the report.

The difference between the structure and idea of function which characterized the movement at the time of its inception, and that which distinguishes it at present, has come about by an orderly and progressive development, a growth from simplicity to complexity in the scheme of adjustment—an evolution. This evolution was characterized, in the first place, by seven more or less clearly defined periods of emphasis upon certain features in the concept of its function which were correlative with the incorporation of particular changes in structure. These periods constituted the sand garden, model playground, small park, recreation center, neighborhood organization, civic art and welfare, and community service stages. The evolution of the movement was distinguished, in the second place, by nine changes in its policy and activities that were fundamental to its stages, but not coterminous with them, and that were designated above as transitions. These transitions were: from provision

for little children to that for all ages of people;
from facilities operated during the summer only
to those maintained throughout the year; from
outdoor equipment and activities only to both
outdoor and indoor facilities and events; from
congested urban districts to both urban and rural
communities; from philanthropic to community
support and control; from free play and miscellaneous events to directed play with organized
activities and correlated schedules; from a simple to a complex field of activities including manual, physical, aesthetic, social, and civic projects;
from the provision of facilities to the definition
of standards for the use of leisure time; and
from individualistic interests to community activities. In the third place, the development of the
play movement, as analyzed above, disclosed a
definite trend toward an integration rather than
a dissolution of its scheme of adjustment, which,
incidentally, tends toward institutionalization.
This trend comprises: the public sanctioning of
many plans of adjustment proposed by the movement; the creation of certain physical accompaniments, which have come to embody certain aspects
of its structure and function; the development of
historical continuity shown in the gradual accumulation of beliefs, tradition, sentiments, and, to
a limited extent, customs; the increase in organization involving specialization and differentiation
in function with a greater complexity of the
field of activities; and the fact of relative per-

manency, by which certain features of the original pattern of adjustment are still retained but do
not dominate the concept of function sufficiently
to preclude the addition of others as experience
indicates, from time to time, their expediency.

Thus there has been an evolution in the structure and the concept of the function of the play
movement in the United States as the result of
numerous attempts to bring about an adjustment
to the modern social situation with respect to play.
This evolution has involved a series of conscious
attempts designed to bring about the social utilization of all leisure through the provision of
opportunities for participation by all ages of
people in behavior that is both personally developmental and socially constructive. The probable
summit of achievement in the development of a
technique for the control of leisure has not been
attained by the movement; it will most likely
continue to develop for many years to come; but
this fact does not dim the truth of the statement
that there has already been an evolution in that
direction. Many instances of an institutionalization of play have been cited above, and some
application of science has been made in the formulations of its plans of adjustment. And, if
the present writer were attempting to state what
ought to be, instead of what is and how it came
about, he would advise an extension of the present scheme until science gives us more light upon
the nature and function of play.

APPENDIX A

The sources consulted in arranging the account here given of the origin of the play movement include the following:

Annals of the American Academy of Political and Social Science, March, 1910; relating to developments in Chicago and Philadelphia.

Annual Reports, Boston Park Commissioners, especially 1888.

Annual Report, Brooklyn Park Commissioners, especially 1897.

Annual Reports, Brooklyn Society for Parks and Playgrounds, Brooklyn.

Annual Reports, Children's Playground Association of Baltimore, Baltimore.

Annual Report, Department of Parks, New York City, 1902, pp. 35-45.

Annual Reports, Massachusetts Emergency and Hygiene Association, Boston, for 1885-1901.

Annual Reports, New York Society for Parks and Playgrounds, New York City.

Annual Reports of Pittsburgh Playground Association, Pittsburgh, especially for 1908, which contains chronology of events in that city.

Annual Reports of the Philadelphia City Open Park Association, for later events in Philadelphia.

Annual Reports, Provident Free Kindergarten Association, Providence, especially 1894-97.

Annual Reports, Union for Practical Progress, Providence, R. I., for beginnings in Providence.

Annual Report, United States Bureau of Education, 1903, containing an article on playground developments in the United States.

Annual Reports, South Park Commissioners, Chicago.

American, Sadie, "The Movement for Small Playgrounds," *American Journal of Sociology*, September, 1898, pp. 159-76.

Betts, Lillian N., "Tenement House Life and Recreation," *Municipal Affairs*, March, 1899, pp. 164-5.

Curtis, H. S., *The Play Movement and Its Significance*, The Macmillan Co., 1917.

Hull-House Papers, Chicago, 1895.

Lee, Joseph, *Constructive and Preventive Philanthropy*, The Macmillan Co., 1902. Chapter xvi, "Public Recreation."

League of Social Service, "Recreation Plus Education," *Municipal Affairs*, September, 1898, pp. 433–38. Origin of vacation schools in New York City.

Mero, E. B., *American Playgrounds*. Baker & Taylor Co., 1908, New York. Valuable because it contains extracts from an unpublished thesis by H. H. Buxton, prepared while a student at the Y. M. C. A. Training School, Springfield, Mass.

O'Brien, E. C., "Recreation Piers," *Municipal Affairs*, September, 1897, pp. 509–14.

Playground, The, "A Brief History of the Playground Movement in America." April, and May, 1915. A statement of facts gathered by the association, no author, dates quite inaccurate.

Proceedings of the Playground Association of America, Vol. III, for outline of early history of movement.

"Public Playgrounds for Children," *Nineteenth Century Magazine*, 1893, pp. 267–71.

Riis, Jacob A., *A Ten Years' War*, Houghton, Mifflin & Co., 1900. Refers to developments in New York City.

Riis, Jacob A., "Small Parks and Public Playgrounds," *Harper's Weekly*, September 11, 1897.

Robinson, Charles Mulford, "Improvement of City Life," *Atlantic Monthly*, April, 1899, pp. 533–36. Relates early developments in general.

Tolman, William H., "Vacation Schools in New York," *Review of Reviews*, August, 1897.

Tsanoff, Stoyan Vasil, "Children's Playgrounds," *Municipal Affairs*, 1898, p. 578.

"Vacation Schools," editorial, *Charities*, September 6, 1902. Origin of vacation schools with classification in four groups, playground, workshop, experimental laboratory, and annex to public school.

Wharton, G. W. "Municipal Playgrounds," *Gardens and Forests*, December 16, 1898.

Wharton, G. W., "Playgrounds for City Schools," *Harpers*, LXVIII.

Zueblin, Charles, *American Municipal Progress*, The Macmillan Co., 1916, chapter xvi, "Public Recreation."

Zueblin, Charles, "Municipal Playgrounds in Chicago," *American Journal of Sociology*, September, 1898, pp. 145–58.

APPENDIX B

CLASSIFICATION, REGISTRATION, AND ELIGIBILITY OF ATHLETES IN THE SOUTH PARK RECREATION SYSTEM, CHICAGO.[1]

These classifications are to serve in all South Park Sports, such as track athletics, basket-ball, swimming, wrestling, baseball or any other sport that may be adopted from time to time for interpark contests and tournaments. These classifications pertain only to the sport in which the man is involved as a competitor. He may be a closed division track man, but an open division wrestler or basket-ball player.

CLOSED DIVISION

A closed division man is one who has not, since the opening of the park he represents, competed "unattached" or for any club other than the South Park. This means that a man who has competed on a high-school team, college team, Y. M. C. A. team, athletic club team, Bible-class team, or any other team, or as an individual in "open competition," is not eligible to compete in closed division sports.

Competing in school (high school or college) as a member of a class team against another class team or teams, in the same school would not make a man ineligible for closed division competition.

Competing within one separate and distinct institution of any character will affect a man's eligibility as defined in the above paragraph on "competing in school," etc.

OPEN DIVISION

An open division man is one who may have competed for a high school, college, Y. M. C. A., athletic club, or dif-

---

[1] *Annual Report of South Park Commissioners*, 1910, pp. 43 f.

APPENDIX   335

ferent clubs, or "unattached," but who at the time of competition in South Park meets is not registered "unattached" or for any other club than the South Park. This means that any man registered "unattached" or for a club of any kind, except for South Park, is ineligible. To be eligible, the man must either not be registered in other clubs, or be registered for South Park. A man may not resign his registration in any organization and thus become eligible to compete in open division sports.

NOVICE (CLOSED DIVISION)
A novice is one who has not won a first, second, or third place in any event in a South Park meet or in open competition.

CLASSIFIED (CLOSED DIVISION)
A classified man is one who has won a first, second, or third place in a South Park closed division meet, South Park open division meet, or in open competition.

NOVICE (OPEN DIVISION)
A novice is one who has not won a first, second, or third place in open competition or in a meet of two or more clubs or institutions of the same or different character.

CLASSIFIED (OPEN DIVISION)
A classified man is one who has won a first, second, or third place in open competition or in a meet open to two or more clubs or institutions of the same or different character.

RELAY RACES
Relay races in South Park meets will not be taken into consideration when classifying men "novice" or "unclassified." Relay races in "open competition" will be regarded as other events are regarded for purposes of classification.

AMATEUR
Only those who observe the best amateur standards in sport will be allowed to compete in interpark contests and tournaments. An amateur is a person who has: (1) never

competed for a money prize; (2) never competed under a false name; (3) never knowingly competed with a professional for a prize; (4) never knowingly competed with a professional where gate money was charged; (5) never pursued, worked at, or assisted in, any branches of athletics, gymnastics, or aquatics as a teacher or instructor, for a salary paid directly or indirectly for such service.

REGISTRATION

No one may compete in any interpark contest unless registered with the park he represents at least thirty days prior to day of competition.

For further information concerning classifications and registration see the instructor.

Membership on one of the teams, classification, and right to compete as a representative in any park is secured by filling out and forwarding to the administrative office the following form:

(Front)
SOUTH PARK COMMISSIONERS
DEPARTMENT OF FIELDHOUSES AND PLAYGROUNDS

APPLICATION FOR ATHLETIC REGISTRATION

Date....................

Name ....
(Print your name.)

Address ....

Park........................ Division $\begin{cases} \text{Open}.......... \\ \text{Closed}.......... \end{cases}$

Are you under suspension by any athletic governing body?....

What athletic organizations have you represented at any time?

....

What organization did you last represent?...................

When?.................... What event?...................

I hereby give my word of honor that I have not violated, nor will I violate, any of the amateur clauses set forth on the reverse side of this form. I also agree to abide by the spirit as well as the letter of amateur sport as set forth from time to time in the rules and regulations issued by the South Park authorities.

In attaching my signature below, I certify that I have read and that I understand the terms of my registration, as set forth on either side of this form.

Signed...

As soon as the athlete has been classified he is given the following membership card:

(Front)
SOUTH PARK COMMISSIONERS
DEPARTMENT OF FIELDHOUSES AND PLAYGROUNDS

ATHLETIC MEMBERSHIP CARD

This Certifies that..

of.....................is registered as....................
(Park)
Division athlete, and is entitled to compete in any sport promoted by the above park on and after.......................

....

Number.............   Expires...................

This card will be recalled if any of the rules governing athletic competition in the South Park system are violated by the person holding the same.

The rules printed on the reverse side of this card must be strictly observed.

(Back)
1. This card is not transferable. 2. Must be shown when requested. 3. Is valid only as long as bearer is a member of and represents park named on other side. 4. No individual may hold a registration card for more than one park. 5. Is not valid unless signed by athlete whose name is on opposite side.

Sign here..

In order to insure fair play in all of the dual and
interpark contests, the names of athletes who compose the
teams are forwarded from park to park or to the main
administrative office on the following form:

SOUTH PARK COMMISSIONERS
DEPARTMENT OF FIELDHOUSES AND PLAYGROUNDS

CERTIFICATE OF ELIGIBILITY

Park...................... Date.................19....

To...

This is to certify that the contestants named below are bona

fide members of................................(Park)
and are registered in the Department of Fieldhouses and Playgrounds as amateurs and are in every way qualified to repre-

sent this park in the..

at............................ Date...............19....

Instructor must sign on the line below the last contestant's
name.

....
....
....
....
....
....
....
....
....
....
....
....

APPENDIX C

WEEKLY SCHEDULE INDOOR ACTIVITIES: MEN'S GYMNASIUM, HAMILTON PARK, CHICAGO, 1915-16.

Classes	Monday	Tuesday	Wednesday*	Thursday	Friday	Saturday*	Sunday
Business Men	8:30-9:30	......	......	8:30-9:30	......	......	......
Young Men	......	7:30-9:30	......	......	7:30-9:30	......	......
Employed Boys	7:30-8:30	......	......	7:30-8:30	......	......	......
High School Students	4:30-5:30	......	......	4:30-5:30	......	......	......
Boys' "A" 13-15 Yrs	......	4:30-5:30	......	......	4:30-5:30	......	......
Boys' "B" 11-15 Yrs	......	......	3:30-4:30	......	......	3:30-4:15 1:30-2:30 85-lb. team practice	......
Boys' "C" 9-10 Yrs	3:30-4:30	......	......	3:30-4:30	......	2:30-3:30 Tm. organ.	......
Boys' "D" 7-8 Yrs	......	3:30-4:30	......	......	3:30-4:30	......	......
Specials	Wrestling 8:30-9:30	......	4:30-5:30 Matchd. Gms. 85 and 95 lb.	......	......	4:15-30 H.P. Gym. Team and Leaders	1:30-3:30 Boys und. 15
Basket-ball 5:30-6:30	95 closed 95 grammar	Willow A.C. Eng. Bapt.	Hamilt'n105	Champ. A.C. Nor.Pk.Pres.	Eng. M. E. Ing'sideM.E.	Salem Evangel.	3:30-4:30 15 to 18
6:30-7:30	AuburnM.E. Heavy wt.	Hamilt'n 115 Hamilt'n 125	Hamilt'n135	WkfordM.E. Aub. Pk. 135	Hamilton Heavy wts.	Chand. M.E. Eng. Bapt.	Mtchd. Gms. 4:30-6:00

*Inter-park and intra-mural competitive games, Wednesday and Saturday, 7:30-9:30.

APPENDIX D

WEEKLY SCHEDULE INDOOR ACTIVITIES: WOMEN'S GYMNASIUM, HAMILTON PARK, CHICAGO, 1915–16.

Classes	Monday	Tuesday	Wednesday	Thursday	Friday	Saturday	Sunday
"A" Advanced Women	....	7:30–8:30	....	....	7:30–8:30	....	....
"B" Advanced Women	....	8:30–9:45	....	....	8:30–9:45	....	....
"C" Advanced Women	8:30–9:30	....	....	8:30–9:30	....	....	....
1st Year Women	7:30–8:30	....	....	7:30–8:30	....	....	....
Advanced Girls	....	....	7:30–9:30 Class 7:30 Games 8:30	....	....	7:30–9:30 Class 7:30 Games 8:30	....
Girls, 13–15 Years	4:30–5:45	....	....	4:30–5:45	....	....	....
Girls, 11–12 Years	....	4:30–5:45	....	....	4:30–5:45	....	....
Girls, 9–10 Years	3:30–4:30	....	....	3:30–4:30	....	....	....
Girls, 7–8 Years	....	3:30–4:30	....	....	3:30–4:30	....	....
Boys & Girls, 4–6 Years	....	....	3:30–4:30	....	....	Plays & Gms. 1:30–3:00	....
Special Activities	Colonial Class 8:30–9:30	....	Rehearsals and Games 4:30–5:45	....	....	Crafts 2:00–4:00 Mtchd. Gms. 4:30–5:30	Directed Plays & Gms. 1:30–6:00

WEEKLY SCHEDULE OF ACTIVITIES OF SLAUSON PLAYGROUND CLUBHOUSE*

Day	Time	Sex	Division	Age	Organization	No. Members	Purpose
Monday....	2:30	Boys	Junior	8–10	Slauson Indians	Var.	Meet on playground for instruction in games and plays of simpler sort. Usually for rehearsals and committee meets.
	7:30	Boys	Intermediate or Senior	......	Any Club	10 to 40	
Tuesday....	2:30	Boys	Junior	8–10	Slauson Indians	......	*See Monday.*
	5:30	Boys	Junior	10–15	Little Brothers	40	For gymnastic work and instruction in simpler form of team games.
	8:00	Men	Senior	......	Slauson Playground District Improvement Association	38	Men's Club, organized for mutual and neighborhood benefit.
Wednesday.	2:30	Boys	......	......	Slauson Indians	......	Gymnastics and Dramatics.
	4:30	Girls	Intermediate	10–14	Epsilon Kappa	35	Gymnastics and Dramatics.
	6:30	Girls	Intermediate	14–16	Alajas	45	Literary Study and Dramatics.
	7:30	Young Women	Senior	16 up	Delta Lamda Kappa	38	
Thursday..	2:30	Boys	......	......	Slauson Indians	......	Social Training.
	7:30	Young Men	Senior	18 up	Big Brothers	24	
Friday.....	2:30	Girls	Junior	8–10	Slauson Indians	......	Scrap Books and Raffia.
	4:30	Boys	Junior	10–15	Little Workers	20	*See Tuesday.*
	5:30	Boys	Intermediate	15–18	Little Brothers	40	Debating, Athletics, Social.
	7:30				Modios	32	
Saturday...	2:00	Boys	......	......	Slauson Indians	......	
	8:00		For families	......	Lecture and entertainment course	......	

*From Annual Report, Playground Department, Los Angeles, 1915.

APPENDIX F

The following table of fieldhouse activities that are open to the public during the indoor season expresses the scheme of administration in operation during 1915-16. It was arranged by the present writer while director of Hamilton Park and was published without his knowledge in *The Playground*, June, 1916.

REGULAR AFTERNOON ACTIVITIES

Monday—

Gymnasium: Girls, 9-10 years, 3:30; 13 and over, 4:30.

Gymnasium: Boys, 9-10 years, 3:30; high school boys, 4:30.

Table Games: Boys and girls, 4:00-5:00.

Tuesday—

Gymnasium: Girls, 7-8 years, 3:30; 11-12 years, 4:30.

Gymnasium: Boys, 7-9 years, 3:30; 12-13 years, 4:30.

Children's Chorus: Boys and girls, 3:30-4:30.

Kindergarten: Boys and girls, 4:00-5:00.

Minerva Women's Club: First and third Tuesdays, 2:00.

Gymnasium: Women's class, 2:00-3:00.

Civic League, 32nd Ward: First Tuesday, 2:00-4:00.

Wednesday—

Gymnasium: Children, under 7 years, 3:30; **girls' team,** game practice and rehearsals, 4:30-6:00.

Gymnasium: Boys, 10-12 years, 3:30; **matched practice** games, 4:30-5:00.

Table Games: Boys and girls, 4:00-5:30.

Dramatics: Junior, Sections A and B, 4:00-5:00.

Thursday—

Gymnasium: Girls, 9-10 years, 3:30; 13 years and over, 4:30.

Gymnasium: Boys, 9-10 years, 3:30; high school boys, 4:30.

Story Hour: Children, under 10 years, 4:00; over 10, 4:30.

Friday—

Gymnasium: Girls, 7-8 years, 3:30; 11-12 years, 4:30.

Gymnasium: Boys, 7-9 years, 3:30; 10-12 years, 4:30.

*The above list of activities is not complete. It does not include the regular meetings of private clubs, classes, dances, parties, receptions, concerts, recitals, etc., that are held daily in the fieldhouse. The following facilities should also be added: the Library, a branch of the Chicago Public Library, open on week days from 1:00-9:00 P. M. and on Sundays from 1:00-6:00; the Shower Baths, open daily from 12:00-9:30 P. M.

Children's Chorus: Boys and girls, 4:30–5:30.
Gymnasium: Girls, plays and games, 1:30–3:00; class, 3:00–4:00.
Gymnasium: Boys, 85 lb., team practice, 1:30–2:30; team organization, 2:30–3:30; Hamilton Park Gym. Team, 4:15–5:30.

Saturday—
Grammar School Social Dancing Class, 2:00–3:00.
Doll Club, children, 2:00–3:00.
Table Games, 3:00–5:00.
Interpretive Dancing, 2:00–3:00.

Sunday—
Gymnasium: Girls, directed plays and games, 1:30–6:00.
Gymnasium: Boys, under 15, 1:30–3:30; over 15, 3:30–4:30; matched games, 4:30–6:00.
Pleasant Hour: October–December and March–April, 3:30.
Civic Music Concerts: January and February at 3:30.

REGULAR EVENING ACTIVITIES

Monday—
Colonial Class: Folk-dances, alternate Mondays, 8:30–10:30.
Community Dancing Class: Sec. A, alternate Mondays, 8:30–10:30.
Civic Music Chorus: 8:15–10:30.
Boy Scouts' Drill: 7:30–8:30.
Gymnasium: Women beginning, 7:30; advanced, 8:30–9:30.
Gymnasium: Employed boys, 7:30; business men, 8:30–10:00; wrestling, 8:00–10:00.

Tuesday—
Hamilton Park Neighborhood Council: Second Tuesday, 8:00–10:00.
Gresham Treble Clef Club: First and third Tuesdays, 8:00–10:00.
Gymnasium: Women's advanced, 7:30–8:30, 8:30–9:15.
Gymnasium: Young men's class, 7:30–9:30.
Ladies' Modern Social Dancing Class (private): 8:00–9:00.

Wednesday—
Adults' Social Dancing Class (private): 7:30–9:30.
Gymnasium: Advanced girls, 7:30–9:30.
Gymnasium: Men's matched games, 7:30–10:00.

Thursday—

Ladies' Modern Dancing Class: 7:30–8:30.

Community Dancing Class, Sec. B: Alternate Thursdays, 8:30.

Gymnasium: Women beginning, 7:30; advanced, 8:30–9:30.

High School Modern Social Dancing Class: Alternate Thursdays, 8:30–9:30.

Friday—

Boy Scout Drill: 7:30–9:30.

Parent-Teachers' Association: 2nd Friday, 8:00–10:00.

Gymnasium: Advanced Women, 7:30–8:30; 8:30–9:30.

Gymnasium: Young Men's Class, 7:30–8:30.

Young Peoples' Dramatic Club: 8:00–10:00.

Saturday—

Special Adults' Modern Social Dancing Class: 7:30–8:30.

Gymnasium: Men's, Matched Games, 7:30–10:00.

Gymnasium: Women's, Advanced Girls, 7:30–9:30.

APPENDIX G

PALMER PARK YEARLY CALENDAR,* 1915

Data concerning activities of the groups which the park is promoting and with which the park is co-operating.

INDOOR SEASON, OCTOBER TO END OF MAY

October—

1. Gymnasium: Formal opening and registration for classes.
2. Choral Society: Beginning of rehearsals for winter season.
3. Soccer Football: Teams playing every Saturday.
4. Rugby Football: Games Saturday and Sunday.

November—

1. Plays: Palmer Players.
2. Civics Club: Initiation of new members (from the 8th grade).
3. Soccer Football League: Championship games.
4. Rugby Football: Continues until Thanksgiving.

*This calendar does not include all uses of the recreation center facilities but only those established by the administration or organized by neighborhood organizations for community purposes; thus numerous dances, parties, club meetings, rehearsals, etc., are omitted.

December—
1. Concerts: Choral Society.
2. Plays: Palmer Players; Christmas plays by Children's Dramatics.
3. Christmas Parties: United Charities for poor children; Girls' Gymnasium classes.

January—
1. Pleasant Hour Series: Beginning second Sunday in January and continuing every Sunday until May.
2. Skating: Three acres of ice is provided during freezing weather.
3. Recitals: Local teachers and conservatories.
4. Celebration: Annual "Burns" celebration by Scottish Club.

February—
1. Pleasant Hours Series: Sundays at 3:30.
2. Plays: Palmer Players.
3. Basket-ball: Match games and tournaments, Wednesdays and Saturday evenings.
4. Volley-ball: Tournaments for girls held Saturday evenings and afternoons.
5. Recitals: Given by local teachers and conservatories.
6. Lincoln's Birthday: Celebration by Veterans and Daughters of Veterans.

March—
1. Pleasant Hours Series: Sundays at 3:30.
2. Concerts: Palmer Park Musical Society.
3. Exhibit: Chicago Tuberculosis Institute during first two weeks. Programs every afternoon and evening. Lectures, entertainments, plays, recitals, moving pictures, etc.
4. Artists' Fete: Annual banquet and dance of members and friends of Art Club.
5. Plays: Junior Dramatic Club, and Palmer Players.

April—
1. Pleasant Hour Series: Sundays at 3:30.
2. Exhibition: Annual gymnastic exhibition by girls' and boys' gymnasium classes.
3. Plays: Palmer Players, and Children's Dramatic Club.
4. Annual Exhibit of Art Classes.

May—

1. Concerts: Palmer Park Musical Society.
2. Plays: Palmer Players.
3. Gymnasium: Closing of indoor work and opening of outdoor gymnasiums.
4. Baseball: Inter-grammar school league; other match games played Saturdays and Sundays.
5. Recitals: Graduations of conservatories and teachers of music.
6. Memorial Service: Regular service on Memorial Day by G. A. R.

OUTDOOR SEASON, JUNE TO END OF SEPTEMBER

June—

1. Swimming: Pool opened (suit and towel furnished). Hours, 10:00 a. m. to 10:00 p. m. Girls' days, Tuesday and Friday. Boys' days, Monday, Wednesday forenoon, Thursday, Saturday, Sunday afternoon.
2. Play Festival: Afternoon program furnished by grade schools, Park, and Turners. Evening by Park, high schools and Turners.
3. Cricket: Cricket team starts regular practice.
4. Tennis: Tournaments.
5. Baseball: Match games Saturdays and Sundays.

July—

1. July Fourth: Water circus in swiming pool.
2. Concerts: Community chorus of 500 gives annual outdoor concert. Band concerts every two weeks.
3. Activities: Daily, swimming, tennis, baseball, and outdoor gymnasiums.

August—

1. Concerts: Band concerts every other week.
2. Activities: Daily, swimming, baseball, tennis and outdoor gymnasium.
3. Meets: Track meets and athletic tests in outdoor gymnasiums.

September—

1. Pageant: Program supplied on Labor Day in Play Field.
2. Activities: Regular outdoor work continued.

APPENDIX H

YEARLY SCHEDULE OF PROMOTED COMPETITIVE AND RECREATIONAL ACTIVITIES, NOT INCLUDING CLUB AND LIMITED GROUP PROGRAMS, MAY 25, 1921

SOUTH PARK COMMISSIONERS, CHICAGO

[COURTESY OF SOUTH PARK COMMISSIONERS]

Month	Events Required of All Park Centers		Events Suggested and Optional Promoted Locally
	Promoted Through the Department Office*	Promoted by Local Park Staff	
JANUARY	Basket-ball: 85, 95, 105, 115, 125, 145 pound Divisions. Women's Volley-ball: "A" and "B," Limited and Un-limited. Public Schools Athletic League: Grammar Schools Basket-ball.	Winter Carnival: Snow Sports. Sled Races. Snowball Target Shooting. Skating Events. Out-of-Doors Day.	New Year's Celebration. Fathers'-and-Sons' Day. Mothers'-and-Daughters' Day. Pleasant Sunday Afternoons. Lecture Courses. Movies. Thrift Week. Amateur Night. Forum. Community Nights. Model Iceboat Races. American Legion Competition.
FEBRUARY	Basket-ball, *cont.* Volley-ball, *cont.* Business Men's Volley-ball. A. A. F. Tournaments. P. S. A. L.: Basket-ball, *cont.*	Valentine Parties Valentine Making. Holiday Observance: Lincoln's Birthday, Washington's Birthday.	Gymnasium Stunt Night. Soap Bubble Party. Social Games Evening. Pleasant Sunday Afternoons. Community Night. Movies. Forum. Burlesque Track Meet. American Legion Competition Lecture Courses.

*Events in this column, except those marked with an asterisk, are inter-park competition.

MARCH	Wrestling Tournament. Girls' Volley-ball, *cont.* Basket-ball, *cont.* Business Men's Volley-ball, *cont.* P. S. A. L.: Basket-ball, *cont.* A. A. F. Tournaments. A. A. U. Tournaments. Indoor Pentathlon.	Gymnasium Exhibitions. Wrestling Preliminaries. Marbles Tournament.	Table-tennis Tournament. Indoor Quoits Tournament. Sewing and Fancy Work Exhibit. St. Patrick's Day Program. Pleasant Sunday Afternoons. Social Games Evening. Community Nights. Table Games Tournaments. Odl-timers' Day. Community Concerts. Community Dramatics. Children's Concerts.
APRIL	Indoor Track Meet. Roller Skate Tournament. Skipmobile Tournament. Boys' Volley-ball Tournament. Seniors' Volley-ball Tournament. Bus. Men's Volley-ball, *cont.* Girls' Volley-ball, *cont.* Basket-ball, *cont.* A. A. F. Tournaments.	Gymnasium Exhibitions, *cont.* Indoor Track Preliminaries. Roller Skate Preliminaries. Skipmobile Preliminaries. Doll Day (Competitive): Carriage Parade, Dressmaking Exhibit, Doll-house Exhibit, Paper Doll Exhibit, Doll-baby Show, Doll-house Furnishings, Doll Drama, etc.	Folk-dance Contests. Roller Skate Hockey. Minstrel Show. Clean-up Week. City Beautiful Week. Home Gardens Week. Children's Concerts. Community Dramatics. Community Concerts. Art Clubs Exhibit. Mock Trial. Bird Day Program. Arbor Day Program. Child Hygiene Institute. Home Recreation Institute. Carroms Tournament.

MAY	Baseball Tournament: Grammar Schools, Public and Parochial. Kite Tournament.	Preliminary Kite Tournament. Annual Exhibitions, *cont.*	Community Orchestra Concerts. Mothers' Day Programs. Top Spinning Tournament. May Day Celebration. Boys' Week Programs. Children's Chorus Festival. Safety-First Day. Community Hike. Memorial Day Celebration.
JUNE	Baseball Tournament, *cont.* City Play Festival.* South Park Play Festival.* Summer Instructors Institute.* Volunteer Leaders Institute.*	Community Play Festivals. Jackstones Tournament. Mumble-the-peg Tournament.	Music Festival. Flag Day Celebration. Band Concerts. Croquet Tournament. Community Sings. Community Pageants. Outdoor Community Nights. Community Chorus Festival. Twilight Athletic Leagues. Summer Foods Institute. Summer Camps Institute. Community Baby Show.
JULY	Playground Baseball: 85, 95, 105, 115, 125, 145 pound Divisions. Horseshoe Tournament. Bicycle Road Race. Badge Tests.	Playground Ball Preliminaries. Horseshoe Preliminaries. Bicycle Preliminaries. Pet Show. Aquatic Stunt Day.	Sane Fourth Celebration. Naturalization Day. Outdoor Community Dance. Quoits Tournament. Outdoor Community Nights. Twilight Leagues. American Legion Field Day. Community Motor Trip. Band Concerts. Life Saving Institute. Community Sings.

AUGUST	Badge Tests, *cont.* Tennis Tournament. Sailboat Regatta. Aquatics Day. Outdoor Track, 105 pound and Unlimited. Playground Baseball, *cont.* Point Track and Field Meet.	Sand Court Contests. Modeling, Story Dramatizing, etc. Sailboat Preliminaries. Aquatics Preliminaries. Tennis Preliminaries. Point Meet Preliminaries.	Doll Dressmaking Exhibit. Outdoor Community Dance. Twilight Leagues. Home Gardens Contests. Outdoor Community Nights. Outdoor Drama. Band Concerts. Community Sings. Progressive Luncheon Picnic. Learn-to-swim Week.
SEPTEMBER	Playgrounds Department Picnic.* Girls' Field Day. Summer Sports Finals. Bonfire and Basket Lunch.* Lantern Parade. Checker Tournament. Grammar School Soccer. South Park Soccer.	Checker Preliminaries. Athletic Stunt Night. Junior Exhibition: Handicrafts Exhibit, Kites, Wind Mills, Gliders, Beads, Laces, Embroidery, Doll Houses, Furniture, Dressmaking, Paper Flowers, Sand Table, Lanterns, Basketry, etc. Better Health Week: Hygiene, Dietetics, Exercise, etc.	Community Amateur Circus. Home-Grown Flower Show. Labor Day Celebration. Community Hike. Community Picnic. Community Pageants. Collections Exhibit. Handicraft Contests: Sand Engines, Motor Toys, Wind Mills, Bird Houses, etc. Bowling Tournaments. Canning and Preserving Institute. Indian Day Celebration. Cross-Country Run. Vocational Guidance Institute. Rope-Skipping Contests.

October	Soccer, *cont.* Pushmobile Tournament. Tricycle Races. P. S. A. L.: Grammar School Soccer, Boys' Grammar School Volley-ball, Girls'.	Pushmobile Preliminaries. Halloween Parade: Novel, Amusing, and Artistic Costumes.	Community Bicycle Trip. Roosevelt Anniversary. Home Gardens Contests. Home Arts Exhibit. Community Nights. Hoop Rolling Tournament. Pleasant Sunday Afternoons. Nutrition & Dietetics Courses. Forum. Movies. Home Nursing Course. Columbus Day Celebration. Citizenship Week.
November	Soccer, *cont.* P. S. A. L.: Girls' Volley-ball, *cont.* Boys' Soccer, *cont.*	"Come and See" Day. Armistice Day Celebration.	Home Decoration Institute. Model Glider Tournament. Model Airplane Tournament. Story-telling Contests. Amateurs' Nights. Pleasant Sunday Afternoons. Community Nights. Home Nursing Course. Nutrition & Dietetics Courses. Forum. Movies. Thanksgiving Day Celebration. Lecture Courses.
December	P. S. A. L.: Girls' Volley-ball, *cont.* Boys' Soccer, *cont.*	Christmas Celebration. Community Tree. Community Caroling, etc.	Winter Foods Institute. Declamation Contests. Debating Contests. Loan Art Exhibit. Pleasant Sunday Afternoons. Community Nights. Movies. Forum. Lectures.

APPENDIX I

SOUTH PARK MERIT SYSTEM OF SCORING

BASKET-BALL LEAGUE, 1920-21.

The Grammar School League consists of Chicago Public Grammar School and Parochial Schools in the South Park district. Each scheduled game will be scored on a Sportsmanship basis, as follows:

Sportsmanship ....60 points
Reliability 10   "
Winning 30   "

SPORTSMANSHIP

Sportsmanship to include: (1) fouls and infractions of the rules, charged to a team; (2) prompt acceptance of the official's decisions; (3) language and conduct of players during the contest; (4) conduct of spectators and partisans of a team during the game; (5) conduct of team and followers, to and from game.

RELIABILITY

Reliability to include: (1) promptly appearing for play at scheduled hour and date; (2) faithfully carrying out all rules as to eligibility; (3) captain's having line-up ready for scorers (this rule is to punish trickery of any kind).

WINNING

The team that wins will be credited with 30 points.

SPORTSMANSHIP MARKINGS

Sportsmanship, in all games, will be marked as indicated below:

Personal Fouls.

For each personal foul made by a player, 2 points will be deducted from the sportsmanship mark of his team, except where the foul is of a flagrant nature; then the penalty will be from 3 to 20 points, as decided by the referee.

Player Expelled from Game.

If a player is expelled from the game for unnecessary roughness, 25 points will be deducted from the mark of the team to which the player belongs.

Spectators and Partisans at Game.

The spectators and partisans of a team, guilty of bad sportsmanship, though in no way chargeable to their team, will cause their team to lose 40 points.

Conduct of Players and Followers, to and from Game.

Unsportsmanlike conduct of a team and its followers, to or from a game, will cause that team to lose from 20 to 60 points, as decided by the Administration Office, or Board of Control.

Captain Addressing Official.

A request on the part of a captain of a team for explanation of a rule, will not be charged against his team, if such request is to get information as to the meaning of a rule, and not to question the official's judgment. Such request, however, must be made in a courteous manner.

Language and Conduct of Players.

Lanuage and conduct of players refers to such things as swearing, losing temper, calling names, and other acts of rowdyism.

Both Teams Receive Sportsmanship Mark.

Both teams will receive a mark for sportsmanship and reliability. Should both teams exhibit good sportsmanship, and meet all rules as to reliability, both will receive credit for same.

CHAMPIONSHIP, HOW AWARDED

The championship will be awarded the team that has the greatest number of points after all scheduled games have been played, all games being scored on the point basis.

APPENDIX J

SOUTH PARK MERIT SYSTEM OF SCORING

BASE-BALL LEAGUE, 1920-1921.

The Grammar Schools League consists of Chicago Public Grammar Schools and Parochial Schools in the South Park district. Each scheduled game will be scored on the Merit System, as follows:

Sportsmanship ....50 points
Reliability ....20 "
Winning ....30 "

SPORTSMANSHIP

Sportsmanship to include: (1) fouls and infractions of the rules, charged to a team; (2) prompt acceptance of the official's decisions; (3) language and conduct of players during the contest; (4) conduct of spectators and partisans of a team during the game; (5) conduct of team and followers, to and from game.

RELIABILITY

Reliability to include: (1) prompt appearing for play at scheduled hour and date. This does not mean that a team will be penalized for postponing a game on account of bad weather, in accordance with the rules of the league; (2) faithfully carrying out all rules as to eligibility, before the game is called; (3) captain's having batting order ready for scorer before the game is called.

WINNING

The team that wins will be credited with 30 points.

SPORTSMANSHIP MARKINGS

Conduct and Language of Players.

Sportsmanship will be marked on the conduct and language of the players during the game, special attention being paid to blocking or attempting to bock a runner who is trying to make a base and the prompt acceptance of the official's decision at all times. For each block or attempt to block, a team shall be charged from 3 to 20 points, as decided by the umpire.

Failure to accept the umpire's decision promptly shall cause a team to lose from 5 to 50 points, as decided by the umpire.

Language and conduct of players refers to such things as swearing, losing temper, calling names, and other acts of rowdyism.

Spectators and Followers of a Team.

Spectators and followers of a team, guilty of bad sportsmanship, though in no way chargeable to their team, will cause their team to lose from 10 to 40 points from the sportsmanship mark of the team.

Conduct of Players and Followers to and from Game.

Unsportsmanlike conduct of a team and its followers, to or from a game, will cause that team to lose from 20 to 50 points, as decided by the Board of Control.

Captain Addressing Official.

A request on the part of a captain of a team for explanation of a rule, will not be charged against his team, if such request is to get information as to the meaning of a rule, and not to question the official's judgment. Such request, however, must be made in a courteous manner.

Both Teams Receive a Sportmanship Mark.

Should both teams exhibit good sportsmanship, both will receive credit for same.

CHAMPIONSHIP, HOW AWARDED

The championship will be awarded the team that has the greatest number of points after all scheduled games have been played, all games being scored on the point basis.

A SELECTED BIBLIOGRAPHY[1]

I. INTRODUCTION

A. Containing Bibliographies

Angell, Emmett D., *Play, Comprising Games for the Kindergarten, Playground, Schoolroom, and College.* Little, 1910.

Bancroft, Jessie D., *Games for the Playground, Home, School, and Gymnasium.* Macmillan, 1909.

Barnes, H. E., "Social and Reform Movements," *Encyclopedia Americana,* 1919.

"Book Reviews" and "Bibliographies," in *The Playground,* Vols. I–XVI.

"Community Service in Periodical Literature," War Camp Community Service, 1920. A bibliography of thirty-eight pages.

Edwards, Richard Henry, *Popular Amusements,* Association Press, 1915. Annotated bibliographies at close of chapters.

Hanmer, Lee F. and Knight, Howard R., *Sources of Information on Play and Recreation,* Russell Sage Foundation, 1915. Thirty-six pages, classified according to subjects.

Mero, Evert B., *American Playgrounds,* The Baker & Taylor Co., 1908.

Zueblin, Charles, *American Municipal Progress,* Macmillan, 1916.

B. The Concept of a Movement[2]

Park, R. E. and Burgess, E. W., *Introduction to the Science of Sociology,* University of Chicago Press, 1921, pp. 54–55, and chap. xii.

Thomas, Edward, *Industry, Emotion and Unrest,* Harcourt, Brace and Howe, 1920, pp. 252 ff.

Zimand, Savel, *Modern Social Movements,* New York Bureau of Municipal Research, 1921.

---

[1]This bibliography is not intended to be a comprehensive one, neither does it include all the sources consulted in the preparation of the report above. It is a selected list of the more accessible of the important references, suitable for collateral reading.

[2]The references here are chosen because of their summaries and bibliographies. They are suggestive only. The best way in which to formulate a concept of a movement is by studying particular movements; many are indicated in the references given here.

C. *Definition of the Term "Play"*

Appleton, M. Estelle, *A Comparative Study of The Play of Adult Savages and Civilized Children,* University of Chicago Press, 1910. Exposition of social and biological aspects of play.

Baldwin, J. Mark, *Social and Ethical Interpretations in Mental Development,* Macmillan, 1902. Social and educational aspects of child play.

Dewey, John, "Play," *Encyclopedia of Education.* Ed. by Paul Monroe, 1914. A psychological explanation of play.

Gillin, John L., "The Sociology of Play," *American Journal of Sociology,* 1914, pp. 826–33. Emphasizes group aspect of play.

Groos, Karl, *The Play of Man,* Appleton, 1901. Exposition of the practice theory of play.

Hall, G. Stanley, *Adolescence,* Vol. II, pp. 206–36. Statement of the recapitulation theory of play. Interesting analogy but has become a moot question in science today.

McDougall, William, *Social Psychology,* 1908, pp. 107–15, and 345–47. Reviews theories of Schiller, Spencer, Bradley and Groos. Suggests interesting revision of Groos' theory.

Patrick, G. T. W., *The Psychology of Relaxation,* Houghton Mifflin Co., 1916, pp. 47 ff. Explanation of nature of play from the "genetic" standpoint. Requires correction.

Patton, Simon, N., *Product and Climax,* Huebsch, 1909. Discussion of the relation of play to work.

Spencer, Herbert, *Principles of Psychology,* Appleton, 1896, pp. 628 ff. Conceives play to be the expression of surplus energy.

D. *The Scope of the Play Movement*

Addams, Jane, *The Spirit of Youth and the City Streets,* Macmillan, 1909.

Aronovici, Carol, "Organized Leisure as a Factor in Conservation," *American Journal of Sociology,* Vol. XXIV, pp. 373 ff.

Collier, John, "Leisure Time, the Last Problem of Conservation," *The Playground,* Vol. VI, pp. 93–106.

Curtis, Henry S., *The Play Movement and Its Significance,* Macmillan, 1917.

Davis, M. M., *The Exploitation of Pleasure,* Russell Sage Foundation, 1910.

Edwards, R. H., "Public Recreation," *Bulletin, Extension Division, University of Wisconsin.*

Gulick, Luther H., "Play and Democracy," *Charities and the Commons*, Aug. 3, 1907. Reprinted in *A Philosophy of Play*, 1920.

Johnson, George E., "Education Through Recreation," Russell Sage Foundation, 1916. Portion of Cleveland, O., survey.

Lee, Joseph, "American Play Traditions and Our Relations to Them," *The Playground*, 1913, pp. 148-59.

Lee, Joseph, "Restoring Their Play Inheritance to Our City Children," *The Craftsman*, Vol. XXV, pp. 545-55.

Mero, E. B., *American Playgrounds*, Baker and Taylor Co., 1909, pp. 68-119.

Perry, C. A., *Community Center Activities*, Russell Sage Foundation, 1916.

Richards, John R., "Chicago's Recreation Problem in Relation to a City-Wide Plan of Administration," *The American City*, December, 1915.

Report of the Recreational Inquiry Committee of the State of California, September 28, 1914.

Scott, Temple, *Use of Leisure*, Huebsch, 1913.

II. THE ORIGIN OF THE PLAY MOVEMENT

For bibliography cf. Appendix A., pp. 332-34 above.

III. THE STAGES OF THE PLAY MOVEMENT

A. *The Sand Garden Stage, 1885-95*

Annual Reports of Massachusetts Emergency and Hygiene Association, 1885-1895.

Annual Report Metropolitan Park Commissioners of Boston, 1893, pp. 67-81.

Lee, Joseph, *Constructive and Preventive Philanthropy*, Macmillan, 1902. Cf. chapter on "Playgrounds for Small Children."

McGough, Frances J., "The Sand Pile, Its Use and Care," *The Playground*, 1915, pp. 160-64.

B. *The Model Playground Stage, 1895-1900*

Annual Report of Massachusetts Civic League, 1901.

Lee, Joseph, *Constructive and Preventive Philanthropy*, Macmillan, 1902, pp. 127, 164-67, 172, 175 ff.

Tsanoff, Stoyan Vasil, "Children's Playgrounds," *Municipal Affairs*, 1898, pp. 578 ff.

Zueblin, Charles, *American Municipal Progress*, Macmillan, 1916, pp. 298-300.

C. *The Small Park Stage, 1900-5*

De Groot, Edward B., "Recreation Facilities in Public Parks," *The American City,* Vol. X, pp. 9–15.

Leland, A., and L., *Playground Technique and Play Craft,* Doubleday Page & Co., 1913, pp. 54–59.

Riis, Jacob, *A Ten Years' War,* Houghton Mifflin, 1900. Story of first small parks in New York City.

Robinson, Charles Mulford, "Landscape Gardening for Playgrounds," *Proceedings of the Playground Association of America,* 1908.

Robinson, Charles Mulford, *Improvement of Towns and Cities,* Putnam, 1901.

D. *The Recreation Center Stage, 1905-12*

Annual Reports of Bath Department of Boston, since 1904.

Annual Reports of the Board of Recreation, Philadelphia, since 1913.

Annual Reports of Pittsburgh Playground Association, since 1912.

Annual Reports of South Park Commissioners, Chicago, since 1905.

Annual Reports of West Chicago Park Commissioners, since 1908.

Foreman, Henry G., "Chicago's New Park Service," *Century Magazine,* February, 1903, pp. 610–20.

Perry, Clarence A., *The Wider Use o,' the School Plant,* Russell Sage Foundation, 1910.

Raycroft, Joseph E., "Construction and Administration of Swimming Pools," *The Playground,* Vol. VII, pp. 417–33.

"Rochester Social and Civic Centers," *Report of the Civic League,* Rochester, N. Y., 1909.

Stoddart, Bessie D., "Recreative Centers of Los Angeles," *The Annals,* March, 1910, pp. 427 ff.

Taylor, Graham Romeyn, "Recent Development in Chicago's Parks," *The Annals,* March, 1910.

Ward, E. J., *The Social Center,* Appleton, 1913.

E. *The Civic Art and Welfare Stage, 1912-14*

Annual Reports of the Board of Public Welfare, Kansas City, Mo., since 1911.

Davol, Ralph, *Handbook of American Pageantry,* Davol Pub. Co., 1914.

Dykema, Peter W., "The Spread of the Community Music Idea," *The Annals*, 1916, pp. 218–23.

Dykema, Peter W., "Community Music and Drama," *University of Wisconsin Extension Division Bulletin*, Gen. Series No. 638, 1917.

Farwell, A., "Community Music and Drama," *The Craftsman*, Vol. XXVI, pp. 418–22.

Gordon, Edgar B., "Community Music and Drama," *University of Wisconsin, Bulletin*, 1916.

Hanmer, L. F., and Bruner, A. H., *Recreation Legislation*, Russell Sage Foundation, Pamphlet No. 106, 1913.

MacKaye, Percy W., *The Civic Theatre in Its Relation to the Redemption of Leisure*, M. Kennerley, 1912.

Taintor, J. F., "Rural Pageant, Ripon, Wisconsin," *The Playground*, Vol. VII, pp. 240–56.

F.   *The Neighborhood Organization Stage, 1915–18*

Carver, T. N., "The Organization of a Rural Community," U. S. Department of Agriculture, *Yearbook*, for 1914, pp. 89–138.

Collier, John, "Community Organization and the Great Decision," *Seward Park Community Center Magazine*, New York, July, 1919.

Gibney, E. C., *Twentieth Annual Report of Superintendent of Schools, New York City*, 1918, pp. 1–104.

Hannifan, L. J., *The Community Center*, Silver Burdett Co., 1920.

Hanmer, Lee F., "Organizing the Neighborhood for Recreation," *National Conference of Social Work*, 1915, pp. 70–77.

Morgan, E. L., "Mobilizing the Rural Community," *Massachusetts Agriculture College Bulletin*, No. 23, 1918.

Nason, W. C. and Thompson, C. W., "Rural Community Buildings in the U. S.," *U. S. Department of Agriculture, Bulletin* No. 825.

National Conference of Social Work, 1915–18.   Cf. footnote 89, p. 147 above.

Rainwater, C. E., *Community Organization*, Southern California Sociological Society, 1920.

Woods, R. A., "The Neighborhood in Social Reconstruction," *Proceedings and Papers of the American Sociological Society*, 1913.

G. *The Community Service Stage, since 1918*

Colter, John R., "The Town That Found Itself," *Community Service, Incorporated, Bulletin*, No. 7, 1919.

"Community Service," *Community Service, Incorporated, Bulletin*, No. 2.

Condit, Abbie, "Recreation," *The American Yearbook*, 1920.

Draper, George, *Community Recreation*, Internat. Com. Y. M. C. A., 1918.

Edwards, W. F., "Community Service, a Positive Force in Reconstruction," *Community Service, Incorporated, Bulletin*, No. 1.

"War Camp Community Service, Its First Year," *The Playground*, Vol. XII, pp. 273 ff.

IV. THE TRANSITIONS IN THE PLAY MOVEMENT

A. *Provision for All Ages of People.*

"Adult Recreation," *The Playground*, Vol. XIII, pp. 414–24.

Burchenal, Elizabeth, "Folk Dancing as Social Recreation for Adults," *The Playground*, Vol. XIV, pp. 404–16.

Follett, Mary P., "Aims of Adult Recreation," *The Playground*, Vol. VII, pp. 261–68.

Johnson, George E., *Education by Plays and Games*, Ginn and Co., 1906.

Johnson, George E., "Games Which Young Men and Young Women Can Play Together," *The Playground*, Vol. X, pp. 396–97.

Perry, C. A., *Community Center Activities*, Russell Sage Foundation, 1916.

Report of the Recreational Inquiry Committee of the State of California, Sept. 28, 1914.

Report of Committee at Recreation Conference, 1916, "Education Through Plays and Games," *The Playground*, Vol. X, pp. 445–55.

Ross, E. A., "Adult Recreation as a Social Problem," *The Playground*, Vol. XII, pp. 376–85.

B. *Provision Throughout the Year*

"A Catalogue of Play Equipment," *The Playground*, Vol. XIII, pp. 538–47.

Annual Report Pittsburgh Playground Association, 1908.

Annual Report, New York City School Board, 1899, pp. 28–32.

Condit, Abbie, "What Constitutes a Year Around Recreation System," *The Playground*, Vol. XI, pp. 198–201.

"What One Community Has Done to Develop a Year Around Recreation System," *The Playground*, Vol. XI, pp. 196–98.

C. *Outdoor and Indoor Equipment*

Annual Reports Board of Recreation of Philadelphia, 1913–15.

Annual Reports, South Park Commissioners, Chicago, 1904–5, 1912, 1915.

DeGroot, Edward B., "A Practical Talk on Playground Equipment," *The Playground*, Vol. VI, pp. 145–60.

"Layout and Equipment of Playgrounds," *Playground and Recreation Association of America*, 1921, p. 60.

Leland, A. and L., *Playground Technique and Play Craft*, Doubleday Page & Co., 1913.

Mero, E. B., *American Playgrounds*, The Baker & Taylor Co., 1909.

Nason, W. C. and Thompson, C. W., "Rural Community Buildings in the United States," *U. S. Department of Agriculture, Bulletin*, No. 825.

"Report of the Committee on Recreation Buildings," Recreation Conference, 1916, *The Playground*, Vol. XI, pp. 33–41.

D. *In Urban and Rural Communities*

Lee, Joseph, "Play as an Antidote to Civilization," *The Playground*, Vol. VI, pp. 110–26.

MacKay, Constance D., "Imaginative Recreation in Rural Districts," *The Playground*, Vol. XIV, pp. 30–37, 83–96, 151–57, 229–35, 307–18, 373–86, 417–28, 559–72.

"Report of the Committee on Rural Recreation," Recreation Conference, 1916, *The Playground*, Vol. XI, pp. 152–60.

Tate, W. K., "Rural Recreation," *National Conference of Social Work*, 1915, pp. 65–70.

"Rural and Small Community Recreation," *Community Service, Incorporated*, 1921, p. 152.

E. *Philanthropic and Community Administration*

Addams, Jane, "Recreation as a Public Function in Urban Communities," *American Journal of Sociology*, March, 1912, pp. 615–19.

Baker, Newton D., "Why Recreation Centers Should Be Supported by Public Taxation," *The Playground*, Vol. VI, pp. 183 ff.

Barrows, Edward M., "The Meaning of Self-Support," *The Community Center Magazine*, Feb. 3, 1917.

Braucher, Howard S., "Why I Believe That Community and Neighborhood Centers, Schools and Parks Should Be Under Government Direction and Support," *The Playground*, Vol. X, pp. 83–96.

"Community Recreation," *Playground and Recreation Association of America*, 1919.

Gulick, Luther H., "Freedom Through Self-Support," *The Community Center Magazine*, Feb. 3, 1917.

Mallery, Otto T., "Which Municipal Body Can Best Conduct Public Recreation," *The Playground*, Vol. VI, pp. 86 ff.

Richards, John R., "The Aim and Scope of the Recreation Movement," *The Playground*, Vol. X, pp. 377–81.

F. Free and Directed Play

Angell, Emmett D., *Play, Comprising Games for the Kindergarten, Playground, Schoolroom, and College*, Little, 1910.

Bancroft, Jessie H., *Games for the Playground, Home, School, and Gymnasium*, Macmillan, 1909.

Bowen, W. P., *The Teaching of Play*, F. A. Bassette Co., 1913.

Dickie, George E., "Aids in the Practical Conduct of Playgrounds," *The Playground*, Vol. IX, pp. 46–51, 153–59.

Gibney, E. C., *Twentieth Annual Report of Superintendent of Schools, New York City*, 1918, pp. 174–237.

Gulick, L. H., "The Doctrine of Hands Off in Play," *Proceedings of Playground Association of America*, 1909.

Hanmer, L. F., "Athletic Badge Tests for Girls," *The Playground*, 1916, pp. 165–71.

Holeman, Genevieve Turner, "What We Did on a Summer Playground in Chicago," *The Playground*, Vol. XIV, pp. 157–63, 245–50, 298–305.

Johnson, George E., "Why Teach a Child to Play?" *Proceedings of Playground Association*, Vol. III.

Report of Committee on Games, Recreation Conference, 1916, *The Playground*, Vol. X, pp. 445–55.

G. Simple and Complex Fields of Activities

Bates, E. W. and Orr, *Pageants and Pageantry*, Ginn & Co., 1912.

Braucher, Mrs. H. S., "Making Children's Dramatics Worth While," *The Playground*, Vol. IX, pp. 116–20.

Bryant, Sara Cone, *How to Tell Stories to Children*," Houghton Mifflin, 1906.

Chesley, A. M., *Social Activities*, Association Press, 1910.

Corsan, George H., *At Home in the Water*, Association Press, 1914.

Ferris, Helen, *Producing Amateur Entertainments*, E. P. Dutton, 1921.

Geister, Edna, *Ice Breakers*, Women's Press, 1918.

Gulick, L. H., *The Healthful Art of Dancing*, Doubleday Page & Co., 1910.

Hall, A. Neely, *The Boy Craftsman*, Shepardson, 1905.

Hart, W. R., "Corn Clubs," *The Playground*, Vol. VI, pp. 285 ff.

Langdon, William C., *Celebrating the Fourth of July by Means of Pageantry*, Russell Sage Foundation, 1902.

Mackay, Constance D., *How to Produce Children's Plays*, Holy, 1915.

Mero, E. B., *American Playgrounds*, The Baker & Taylor Co., 1909.

Parsons, Henry G., *Children's Gardens for Pleasure, Health, and Education*, Sturgis, 1910.

H. *Facilities and Definition of Standards*

Collier, John, "Leisure Time, the Last Problem of Conservation," *The Playground*, Vol. VI, pp. 93–110.

Lee, Joseph, "What Are the Best Games for Boys in Crowded Cities?" *The Playground*, Vol. VI, pp. 373–75.

"Recreation for Industrial Communities," *The Playground*, Vol. XIV, pp. 278–82, 356–67, 429–46, 475–80, 554–59, 616–21.

Rumbold, Charlotte, "Games for Girls in Large Cities," *The Playground*, Vol. VI, pp. 375–77.

Ryan, Orson, "The Kind of School Athletics That Are Really Worth While," *The Playground*, Vol. IX, pp. 164–67.

Storrow, Mrs. James J., "Folk Dancing as a Means of Family Recreation in the Home," *The Playground*, Vol. VI, pp. 159 ff.

"Street Play," *The Playground*, Vol. IX, pp. 168–71.

I. *Individual and Group Activities*

Braucher, H. S., "What a Neighborhood Play Center Ought to Be," *The Playground*, Vol. IX, pp. 338–40.

Efficiency Tests for Boys, Playground Association of America, Pamphlet, 1913.

Gillin, John L., "Socialized Recreation," chapter in *Poverty and Dependency*, Century, 1921.

Jerome, Mrs. Amalie Hofer, "The Playground as a Social Center," *The Annals*, March, 1910.

Lee, Joseph, "The Community, Home of Lost Talents," *The Playground*, Vol. XIII, pp. 171–76.

McDowell, Mary E., "Recreation a Fundamental Element of Democracy," *The Playground*, Vol. VII, pp. 189 ff.

Mero, E. B., "The Holiday as a Builder of Citizenship," *The Playground*, Vol. VIII, pp. 101 ff.

Stern, Renee B., "Neighborhood Entertainments," Sturgis & Walton, 1910.

"The Recreation Center as a Neighborhood Institution," *The Playground*, Vol. VII, pp. 188 ff.

Von Borosini, Victor, "Our Recreation Facilities and the Immigrant," *The Annals*, March, 1910, pp. 141–51.

V. THE TREND OF THE PLAY MOVEMENT

Condit, Abbie, "Comrades in Play," *The Playground*, Vol. XIII, pp. 463–75, 522–33, 586–600. Reprinted as a pamphlet.

Devine, Edward T., "How Fundamental Is the Play Movement?" *The Playground*, Vol. VIII, pp. 422–24.

Johnson, G. E., "The Renaissance of Play," *The Playground*, Vol. VI, pp. 85–98.

Mackay, Constance D., "The Need for Imaginative Recreation in the Reconstruction Period," *The Playground*, Vol. XII, pp. 494–505.

Richards, John R., "The Aim and Scope of the Recreation Movement," *The Playground*, Vol. X, pp. 377–81.

"Three Years' Work of the Playground and Recreation Association of America, December 1, 1916, to November 30, 1919," *The Playground*, Vol. XIV, pp. 11–28.

"Recreation Surveys," *Sources of Information on Play and Recreation*, Russell Sage Foundation, 1915, pp. 30–31. A bibliography.

Stewart, Herbert L., "The Ethics of Luxury and Leisure," *American Journal of Sociology*, Vol. XXIV, pp. 241 ff.

"Yearbooks of the Playground and Recreation Association of America," *Proceedings of Association*, Vols. I–III, and *The Playground*, Vols. IV–XV.

INDEX

367

ters, 95; organization, 94; recreation centers, 96, 100; religious prohibitions, 100; restrictions, 101; swimming pools, 98

Sportsmanship, 284

Stages of the play movement: definition of, 45; civic art, 118; community service, 178; model playground, 55; neighborhood organization, 135; recreation center, 91; sand garden, 45; small park, 70

Starr Garden, 110, 219

Stoddart, Bessie D., 106

Street play, 285

Strong, Mayor of New York, 54, 201, 230

Sunday baseball, 100

Supervisor of play for counties, 223

Support and control, 99

Swimming, events, 252; pools, 98; South Parks, 99

Team games, 249

Tenement House Commission, 61, 74

Thomas, W. I., 274, 290

Torpedo sand, 97

Tower, Miss Ellen M., 33, 37

Town Meeting, 140, 144, 145

Training play leaders, 247, 248, 249

Transitions in the play movement: children to all ages, 192; facilities to standards, 273; free and directed play, 239; individual and group interests, 288; outdoor and indoor activities, 209; philanthropic and community

support, 226; simple and complex fields, 263; summer and annual provision, 200; urban and rural communities, 218

Trend of the play movement: definition of, 305; group sanction, 313; historical continuity, 317; increasing organization, 318; physical accompaniments, 315; relative permanency, 320

Triangle Park, 79

Tsanoff, S. V., 59

Ulster County play picnic, 222

Union for Practical Progress, 40

University of Chicago Settlement, 57

Violet Street Playground, 108

Virginia, fairs, 222

Voting in recreation center, 109

W.C.C.S., extent of, 180; organization of, 179

Ward, E. J., 113, 138, 143

Washington, D. C., training school, 249

Washington Park meadow, 17

West Chicago Park Commissioners, 102, 103

West Virginia, 224

Wider use of school plant, 91, 233

Wilcox, D. F., 142

Wilson, Woodrow, 142

Woods, R. A., 143, 226

Zakrsewska, Dr. Marie E., 22

Zoning, for play, 286

Zueblin, Charles, 325